The impact  ical
con

Manchester University Press

The impact of feminism on political concepts and debates

Edited by Georgina Blakeley and Valerie Bryson

Manchester University Press

Manchester and New York

distributed exclusively in the USA by Palgrave

Published by Manchester University Press
Oxford Road, Manchester M13 9NR, UK
and Room 400, 175 Fifth Avenue, New York, NY 10010, USA
www.manchesteruniversitypress.co.uk

Distributed exclusively in the USA by
Palgrave, 175 Fifth Avenue, New York,
NY 10010, USA

Distributed exclusively in Canada by
UBC Press, University of British Columbia, 2029 West Mall,
Vancouver, BC, Canada V6T 1Z2

British Library Cataloguing-in-Publication Data
A catalogue record for this book is available from the British Library

Library of Congress Cataloging-in-Publication Data applied for

ISBN   978 0 7190 7511 7 *hardback*

ISBN   978 0 7190 7512 4 *paperback*

First published 2007

16 15 14 13 12 11 10 09 08 07   10 9 8 7 6 5 4 3 2 1

Typeset in Sabon 10/12 pt
by IML Typographers Ltd, Birkenhead, Merseyside
Printed and bound in Great Britain
by Antony Rowe Ltd, Chippenham, Wiltshire

Contents

List of contributors

Georgina Blakeley is Lecturer in Politics at the Open University. She is the author of *Building Local Democracy in Barcelona* (Edwin Mellen Press, 2004). She has published and presented papers on democracy and civil society in Spain as well as on aspects of Spanish politics more generally. With Valerie Bryson, she is the editor of *Contemporary Political Concepts: A Critical Introduction* (Pluto, 2002) and *Marx and Other Four-Letter Words* (Pluto, 2005).

Laura Brace is Senior Lecturer in Political Theory at the University of Leicester. Her publications include *The Politics of Property: Labour, Freedom and Belonging* (Edinburgh University Press, 2004), and articles on Wollstonecraft, Hegel and Rousseau.

Valerie Bryson is Professor of Politics at the University of Huddersfield. She has published widely on feminist and gender issues, and is currently completing a book on *Gender and the Politics of Time* for the Policy Press. Her publications include *Feminist Debates: Issues of Theory and Political Practice* (Macmillan Palgrave, 1999) and *Feminist Political Theory* (second edition, Macmillan Palgrave, 2003); with Georgina Blakeley she is editor of *Contemporary Political Concepts: A Critical Introduction* (Pluto, 2002) and *Marx and Other Four-Letter Words* (Pluto, 2005).

Sarah Childs is a Senior Lecturer in the Department of Politics at the University of Bristol. With an academic background in both Political Science and Women's Studies she has published widely on sex, gender and politics. Her publications include *New Labour's Women MPs* (Routledge, 2004) and *Women in British Politics* (Routledge, forthcoming 2007). She was also lead author of the Hansard Society *Women at the Top* Report (2006), which examined the representation of women in the UK parliament following the 2005 general election (www.hansardsociety.org.uk).

John Craig is currently a Senior Lecturer in Politics at the University of Huddersfield. He has also taught at the University of Leeds and with the

Open University. His research interests include development strategy, privatisation and public sector reform and he has published articles on these topics in journals including the *Annals of Public and Cooperative Economy, Journal of Modern African Studies* and *Review of African Political Economy*.

Mercy Ette teaches Media and Journalism at the University of Huddersfield. She grew up in Nigeria where she worked as a journalist for six years. She holds an MA in Journalism Studies from University College of Wales, Cardiff, and a PhD in Communications Studies from the University of Leeds. She was the founding editor of *NewsAfrica* magazine, a London-based news magazine with special interest in Africa and its Diaspora. She has published in *The Harvard International Journal of Press/Politics*.

John Hoffman is Emeritus Professor of Political Theory at the University of Leicester. His recent publications include *Beyond the State* (Blackwell, 1995); *Sovereignty* (University of Minnesota Press, 1998); *Gender and Sovereignty* (Palgrave Macmillan, 2001); and *Citizenship Beyond the State* (Sage, 2004). His most recent publication (with Paul Graham of Glasgow University) is *An Introduction to Political Theory* (Pearson, 2006) and he is currently working on a critique of the political theorist, John Gray.

Ruth Lister is Professor of Social Policy at Loughborough University. She was formerly Director of the Child Poverty Action Group and a member of the Commission of Social Justice. Her recent publications include *Citizenship: Feminist Perspectives* (second edition, Palgrave Macmillan, 2003) and *Poverty* (Polity, 2004).

Raia Prokhovnik is a Reader in Politics at the Open University. Her publications include 'Public and Private Citizenship: From Gender Invisibility to Feminist Inclusiveness', *Feminist Review* 60 (1998); *Rational Woman: A Feminist Critique of Dichotomy* (second edition, Manchester University Press, 2002); *Spinoza and Republicanism* (Palgrave Macmillan, 2004); 'Hobbes's Artifice as Social Construction', *Hobbes Studies* 18 (2005); and *Sovereignties: History, Theory and Practice* (Palgrave Macmillan, forthcoming 2007).

Kalpana Wilson is a Research Associate in Development Studies at the School of Oriental and African Studies, University of London. She also teaches development studies at Birkbeck, focusing on gender and development, 'race', war and conflict. She has a background in political economy and has researched and published work on agrarian transformation in Bihar, India, examining women's experiences in rural labour movements, and the implications of neo-liberal discourses of development in this context.

Acknowledgements

This volume arose from a conference at Huddersfield University in November 2004: 'Just something for the girls? The impact of feminism on political concepts and debates'. The editors would like to thank all those who took part for making this such a stimulating and enjoyable occasion and for generating the cross-fertilisation of ideas that inform this book. Particular thanks to the PSA Women and Politics Group for supporting the conference and also to Politics students and colleagues at the University of Huddersfield for their continuing enthusiasm for critical and scholarly debate.

1

Introduction

Georgina Blakeley and Valerie Bryson

Until quite recently, Western political theory almost completely ignored women and gender issues; this neglect was largely unremarked, and there were few feminist (or indeed female) academics in the discipline. A critical first step for feminist political theorists was therefore to expose this exclusion and neglect; here the work of Susan Okin (1980) and Diana Coole (1988) was particularly important. Today, much appears to have changed. Overt discrimination is largely a thing of the past; virtually all political theorists would argue that their concepts apply to all people, regardless of gender, and feminist theory is well established as a sub-discipline.

However, as feminist writers (including Okin and Coole) have also found, extending the concepts and assumptions of political theory to women is not straightforward. Indeed, many have argued that traditional concepts did not simply exclude women but were premised on this exclusion. For example, the liberal argument for a clear distinction between the public and private spheres not only presupposed both a superior public sphere of rational discourse, justice and impartiality and the existence of an inferior private sphere to which the 'messiness' of passion, emotion and partial concerns could be relegated, but also identified women with the latter. From this perspective, allowing women to enter the public sphere could never be straightforward: not only do 'private' needs still have to be met, but women's close identification with 'the world of nature, emotion, desires and private life' (Arneil 1999:7) also means that their very presence in the public sphere both disrupts its boundaries and threatens its foundations.

Many feminists have therefore argued that traditional political concepts may have to be radically reformulated or even replaced if women are to be included on an equal basis, and they have produced an increasingly sophisticated body of thought that attempts to do this. A significant number of academics (male as well as female) are aware that this work has important implications for their specialist area, and would like to incorporate it into their teaching and research. Often, however, they lack an accessible way into feminist analyses and debates. At the same time, many academics (again both male and female) who incorporate feminist analysis into their own work find it difficult to keep up to date with related developments in other specialist areas. The time is therefore ripe for an overview and assessment of the impact of feminism on political concepts and debates. To this end, a conference was held at the University of Huddersfield and the resulting cross-fertilisation of ideas gave rise to this volume.

This volume

The aim of this volume is to examine a range of concepts in the light of feminist critiques, to consider whether they may need to be reconstituted in the light of these critiques and to assess the impact of feminist debates on mainstream thought. Any volume which focuses on a number of key concepts faces the difficult task of deciding which concepts to include and which to omit. This volume is no exception, and we do not claim to provide a definitive list. Rather, we have sought to provide a balance between 'classic' political concepts and those that are being currently developed by feminist theorists, and to reflect the interconnections between the various sub-fields of Politics as a discipline. We have also selected concepts which the chapter authors believe can not only be revised to 'include' women, but can also be reconstructed so as to transform, for both men and women, our ways of thinking and acting. To use John Hoffman's terminology, all the concepts can be viewed as 'momentum' concepts: that is, they are 'progressive' and have 'transformatory potential', and they do not imply a final, static goal or moment of realisation (see Hoffman's chapter below).

Rationality, social contract and *sovereignty* were obvious choices as the starting point for much Western political thought since the Enlightenment. *Citizenship, representation, democracy and democratisation* and *development* were chosen not just for their centrality to political theorising and analysis but also for their centrality to the practice of politics today. Although *agency, empowerment* and *time* have not been so central to Western political thought, their development by feminists shows their potential to act as key concepts without which our understanding of political processes, possibilities and change will remain impoverished; they also have interesting and sometimes unexpected links with earlier concepts.

In addition, many of the chapters inevitably engage with the concept of politics itself and with the public/private dichotomy. Some chapters also discuss issues around the state, power, care, difference and equality and the ways in which different aspects of inequality intersect. These themes knit this volume together, but there is certainly no 'party line' to which all contributors adhere. In engaging with these recurrent themes, to which this introduction now turns, the contributors start from a range of different ontological and epistemological foundations. All, however, are interested in the development of concepts that can help us understand the 'real world' in order to contribute to progressive social and political change.

Themes

All the chapters engage in some way with feminist critiques of the dualistic thinking that underpins conventional and narrow understandings of the political, particularly in liberal thought. In applying critiques of 'A/not-A' modes of thought to particular concepts, the chapters highlight both the sterile cul-de-sacs into which binary, either/or thinking leads political analysis and the gendered and hierarchical nature of its dichotomies, with the dominant, superior category in each pairing associated with men and the subordinate, inferior category with women. The public/private dichotomy, which is constitutive of liberal thought and practice, is of key significance to many chapters; other, less frequently cited dichotomies such as reason/ emotion, clock-time/natural-time, autonomy/commitment are also disrupted in this volume.

Exposing the falsity and gendered nature of 'A/not-A' thinking is the easy part; moving beyond such binary thinking is more difficult. And yet, if we remain trapped within such a binary framework, the feminist argument for a broad understanding of politics which does not privilege activity in any particular sphere is much more difficult to make. Barbara Arneil summarises the importance of not simply reconciling the dichotomies but of attempting to transcend them:

> When one combines the gendered nature of these dualities with the understanding that politics cannot exist without a private and natural world against which it is constructed, then the task cannot simply be to move women from the worlds in which they exist – that is, the private and natural spheres – into the world of politics. Rather, it will be necessary to rethink the nature of 'politics'. (1999:7)

Taken together, the chapters in this volume contribute to this task of 'rethinking' our understanding of politics, and most are concerned to move away from a static, gendered and oppositional framework, towards an approach which sees the dynamic, relational and interactive nature of apparently dichotomous pairings. This means that most contributors have adopted what Judith Squires (1999) has identified as the third, most radical approach to gender. This, she says, is not just about revising theory to 'include' women (the first approach to gender), nor is it about 'reversing' previous assumptions (the second approach). Rather, the third approach, which Squires describes as 'displacement' (or postmodern or post-structuralist feminism), consists of attempting to transcend the binary ways of thinking that both the earlier approaches confirm (1999:3). Although no contributor explicitly identifies themselves as postmodern or post-structuralist, this strategy of 'displacement' is clear in a number of chapters.

Many feminists have identified the ascendancy of neo-liberalism as another obstacle in the way of the broader understanding of politics which they advocate. A number of chapters identify this theme and criticise one of the key effects of neo-liberalism, which is its reduction of the sphere of politics. This depoliticising effect has particular consequences for women, who often remain marginalised in narrow, conventional understandings of politics. By shrinking the political sphere, neo-liberalism has the effect of making it harder for certain issues, viewed as problematic from a feminist viewpoint, to be considered as worthy of attention. Moreover, by operating on the basis of a narrow definition of politics, neo-liberalism tends to view problems as individual ones to be solved by individual endeavour rather than structural problems to be solved by collective action or state policies. Without wishing to portray the state as unproblematic from a feminist viewpoint, many chapters in this volume attest to the fact that the shrinking of the state as part of neo-liberal reforms tends to hurt women far more than it does men.

The relational approach, which, as discussed above, many contributors attempt to use to transcend binary thinking, can also be seen in the emphasis on thinking about concepts in a way that recognises their historical and cultural specificity whenever and however they are used. The chapters therefore criticise the abstraction of much liberal thought and argue for the need to contextualise concepts. For example, individuals are not the abstract, disembodied beings of much traditional political thought; on the contrary, all individuals must be analysed as a product of a complex and diverse set of social relationships. Context is particularly important for attempts to understand another key theme of this volume: the ways in which gender interacts with other systems of power.

Here, some chapters attempt to contextualise gender in relation to other structural inequalities such as class and 'race'. A dominant theme, in particular, is the need to move away from conceptualising these as separate, alternative systems of oppression and towards an understanding which emphasises the complex and contingent ways in which structural inequalities relate and interconnect with each other. The interconnection between gender, 'race', class and disability points to another dilemma with which feminists have long been trying to grapple, namely the need to acknowledge the diversity of women without losing sight of the empowering notion that women need to act collectively as a group if their voices are to be heard and their needs recognised.

All of the contributors are aware of the tension which arises when thinking about women and the variety of experiences that divide as well as unite them. As feminists we want to talk about women as a collective because this is needed both to identify and contest the oppression, discrimination and exploitation which women continue to experience as women. As twenty-first century feminists, however, we also want to avoid essentialism and false universalism and to recognise both the ways in which women may be divided from each other by their different experiences and identities and the extent to which they may share experiences and perspectives with some men. This tension is particularly stark once we attempt to deal not just with concepts in theory but with how concepts are realised in practice. Once we move from theorising about representation, citizenship, agency and democratisation, for example, to realising these in practice, the trap of essentialism becomes ever present. There are, however, no easy answers to these problems. All the contributors acknowledge this tension but none of them claims to have entirely resolved it.

The chapters

The first three chapters, on *rationality, social contract* and *sovereignty,* seem at first sight to start on unpromising terrain, as they all tackle concepts which are imbued with the abstract and dualistic approach of the liberal tradition. Raia Prokhovnik's chapter on *rationality* tackles a key Enlightenment concept which has proved resistant to feminist contributions. She criticises the A/not-A construction in which reason is pitted against emotion, with the former being the dominant and superior category of the pair irrevocably associated with the world of men while emotion is relegated to the private, inferior world of women. Prokhovnik rejects such a static way of thinking and posits instead a broader, dynamic and interactive understanding of rationality which acknowledges the variety of ways in which emotion and reason are intertwined. She argues that 'Emotion is not an added extra, but in a number of ways is a necessary feature of all reasoning'. This extended view of rationality, however, has not, according to Prokhovnik, been taken on board by mainstream writers.

Laura Brace tackles another key foundational concept of the liberal political tradition, the *social contract.* She exposes the false universalism of the notions of freedom and individuality which underpin traditional social contract theory and notes the failure of mainstream theorists to tackle seriously the key question of exactly who counts as a rational individual. For Brace, unless traditional, mainstream social contract theorists move from analysing individuals in a formal and abstract way to analysing individuals in a contextualised manner, the social contract will remain the preserve of white, bourgeois men. In particular, Brace highlights the importance of placing gender in context so we can see its interactions with other systems of power based on class and 'race'.

The chapter by John Hoffman exposes the concept of *sovereignty* to a feminist reconstruction in spite of his acknowledgement that feminists have long been hostile to such a task. In fact, Hoffman agrees with this hostility as long as sovereignty remains linked to the state, which he sees as inherently patriarchal. He argues that in order to reconstruct sovereignty it is necessary to sever the link between the state and sovereignty and, by so doing, to distinguish between states, which use force to tackle conflicts of interest, and governments, which use constraint. By decoupling the state from sovereignty and locating it within individual men and women, conceived not in an abstract formal way but as concrete individuals who are located within a web of social relationships, Hoffman argues that we can move to thinking about sovereignty as self-government.

The next three chapters tackle concepts which are central not just to political theorising but to the way in which women and men engage in political activity. All three chapters deal with concepts – *citizenship*, *representation* and *democracy* – which in their traditional formulation were based on the exclusion of women. Moreover, such exclusion was not some historical aberration which could easily be corrected; these concepts reflect the gendered nature of the public/private dichotomy and the abstract individual which underpin them.

Ruth Lister's chapter on *citizenship* begins by exposing the 'male template' on which traditional citizenship models have been based and the extent to which citizenship theory and practice have depended on the public/private dichotomy, and the narrow definition of politics upon which they rely, so that women were effectively relegated to the private, 'non-political' sphere of activity. Much of the feminist critique has thus concentrated on rearticulating the relationship between the public and private spheres, with much attention paid to the gendered nature of the rights and responsibilities which underpin many discussions of citizenship. Lister's chapter focuses on two key dilemmas to which the feminist regendering of citizenship has led: 'whether a women-friendly model should be ostensibly gender-neutral or explicitly gender-differentiated; and the status of the private sphere in relation to citizenship'. While there are no easy answers to either of these dilemmas and discussions among feminists continue on these issues, feminism has refashioned citizenship so that it is much more sensitive to difference and diversity. In this way, Lister is quite optimistic about the extent to which feminism has been able to influence mainstream debates on citizenship.

Sarah Childs' chapter on *representation* begins with a discussion of the seminal work of Hannah Pitkin and her four-part typology of representation which has structured both mainstream and feminist debates since its publication in 1967. Childs shows how engagement with Pitkin's typology has led to feminists reclaiming the importance of descriptive representation, which claims that our political institutions should attempt in some way to reflect our societies. In particular, feminists have been keen to explore the relationship between descriptive (standing for) and substantive (acting for) representation. This is because, according to Childs, descriptive and substantive representation are two sides of the same coin: while women remain numerically under-represented in our political institutions, their concerns will also remain under-represented. The relationship between descriptive and substantive representation, however, has raised a number of dilemmas for feminists. First, the causal relationship between representatives' characteristics and their actions is far from straightforward. Second, as discussed above, there is a tension between expecting women to act for women and recognising the multiple differences among them. While there are certainly no easy answers to such debates, Childs argues that it is useful to explore the relationship between descriptive and substantive representation in practice by asking how the substantive representation occurs, even though the causal relationship between the presence of women and acting in women's interests (however defined) is 'probably impossible' to prove in practice. Finally, Childs concludes that gender and politics scholars 'are not just speaking to the converted'. Women's work on representation has had an impact on the wider discipline even though the discipline still remains hesitant in embracing gender research.

Georgina Blakeley's chapter focuses on *democratisation*, grounding this in an initial discussion of democratic theory. In so doing, she uses feminist critiques of democratic theory to undertake a feminist analysis of democratisation. She argues that the voluntarist and positivist nature of much of the democratisation literature derives from the narrow definition of democracy which underpins it. This narrow definition of democracy, based on elite agency within the political–institutional sphere, means that key issues which impact on women's political activism are marginalised or simply ignored. A number of these key issues are explored using a case study of the pacted transition to democracy in Chile in order to explore what a feminist analysis of democratisation would entail. In conclusion, Blakeley claims that while there continues to be a gulf between the literature on democratic theory and that on democratisation, feminist insights into the former will remain marginalised from the latter. Thus, although feminism's contribution to democratic theory has been incorporated into mainstream literature, at least to some extent, much of the work on feminism and democratisation remains marginalised by most non-feminist writers.

The next three chapters move our focus towards a sub-discipline of the field of politics, namely that of development studies. The chapter by John Craig tackles the concept of *development* itself. Craig reviews the main feminist approaches, labelled 'Women in Development', 'Women and Development' and 'Gender and Development'. Craig assesses the impact of these three feminist contributions on the field of development studies from the 1970s onwards. He argues that while such approaches have had considerable impact on the mainstream of development theory and practice, this impact remains patchy. He illustrates the unevenness of feminism's impact through a case study of privatisation which, despite its status as a key element in orthodox development practice for almost two decades, remains largely isolated from feminist perspectives. Craig concludes that this is not only a result of the patchy influence of feminism on the discipline but it is also a result of the narrowing of the discipline itself under the 'depoliticising' effects of the neo-liberal agenda.

The effects of neo-liberalism are also a key theme in Kalpana Wilson's chapter on *agency*. This chapter begins with a critique of the origins of the notion of 'agency', not just as a key philosophical ideal of the Enlightenment but also as a historically specific construction, part of the dominant ideology of early European capitalism and imperialism. Wilson then examines how Black and Third World feminists have tried to rescue the idea of women's agency by countering 'racialised' liberal feminist perceptions of 'other' women. Using a case study of dalit women agricultural labourers in Bihar in eastern India, Wilson attempts to counter the trend within some feminist writings and within the dominant development discourse towards emphasising individual agency in the context of strategies for survival. Instead, she stresses the importance of women's agency exercised collectively in movements which are often explicitly political and independent of development initiatives from above and which aim at transformation. Wilson concludes that far from being seen as a concern for women only, the notion of women's agency has been appropriated by mainstream institutions such as the World Bank. However, far from being used in a feminist way, it has been used to effectively marginalise feminist analysis of patriarchal power and ideology. In particular, Wilson argues that the notion of agency has been appropriated by non-feminist writers and policy makers to legitimise and pursue specifically neo-liberal policies. She argues that feminists need to reclaim it.

Mercy Ette's chapter focuses on the concept of *empowerment*, particularly in the context of development discourse. The chapter challenges the top-down, individualistic and static conceptualisations of empowerment in mainstream literature and argues, drawing on feminist arguments, for a more bottom-up, collective, dynamic and contextualised view. In particular, she challenges the idea that power is something that can be given to the powerless by the powerful, and that women can be empowered without wider structural change. Ette illustrates these points in relation to empowerment strategies in Nigeria. She finds that where these empowerment strategies have been influenced by a traditional understanding of the concept which stresses the notion of power as something to be allocated through the provision of resources, they are much less effective than when empowerment strategies are influenced by a feminist perspective which stresses the multi-dimensional, collective and contextualised aspects of the concept. She finds that such a feminist perspective has had an impact on mainstream practices, including those of the World Bank.

In the final chapter, Valerie Bryson argues that although *time* is not conventionally seen as a political concept, most mainstream writers make a number of assumptions about its nature: most also ignore its significance as a scarce political resource. She argues that this means that it is a 'latent' concept of political theory, and that its neglect by mainstream theorists both reflects and sustains male privileges. In contrast, feminists are increasingly seeing time as central to the analysis of structural inequalities. In particular, some feminists are challenging the hegemony of commodified clock-time and asserting the needs of the very different 'time culture' associated with care. Many also argue that inequalities in the public sphere stem from inequalities in time use within the home, setting up a vicious circle through which women's temporal needs are denied political voice. Bryson finds that feminist work on time represents an important contribution to political analysis which has had some limited impact on mainstream political theory and practice.

Mainstream reactions to feminist critiques

The starting-point of this volume is the belief that the work done by feminists has profound and complex implications, not only for women but for the understanding of political processes and ideas. One of the key questions of this volume, therefore, was the extent to which feminist contributions have become part of 'normal' debates, or whether these remain unreflectively 'malestream',[1] with feminist contributions treated as an optional extra.

A number of writers have identified the phases through which feminist perspectives may progress. These are summarised by the sociologist, Nicki Charles:

> The first is the pre-feminist era when women were almost totally neglected as objects of study; the second is marked by the emergence of a critique of this neglect; in the third stage research is undertaken on women in order to 'add them on' to existing studies; and the fourth consists of the full theoretical integration of gender into the discipline. (Charles 1993:2)

Although Charles admits that this is an oversimplification of both the process and the chronology, it can act as a useful benchmark against which to measure progress. While in the past women were routinely excluded from all disciplines, most have now reached at least the second stage, with many progressing to the third stage. For example, Krista Cowman and Louise Jackson have noted that 'It is now virtually impossible to undertake a history degree without encountering material on women's history' (2003:3), while Abbott and Wallace have argued that 'It is now the case that in Britain and the USA few courses in sociology could be designed without at least some recognition of feminist perspectives' (1997:2).

As the chapters in this volume show, the work of a significant number of mainstream political theorists is now clearly informed by recent feminist thought. However, some continue to ignore it, and it is still perfectly possible to do a politics degree without any discussion of the under-representation of women in positions of political power, without knowing that J. S. Mill wrote anything on women, and without questioning the exclusion of privately exercised power from political consideration. Sarah Childs and Mona Krook's recent assessment of 'Gender and Politics: The State of the Art' (2006) confirms this marginalisation and reports that women in the profession have been advised by senior academics 'that they would have a better chance of getting better jobs if they worked on something other than women and politics' (2006:19–20) while mainstream research still 'does not fully engage with feminist analyses' (2006:20). Nevertheless, on the positive side, they argue that gender and politics scholars are increasingly visible in the profession, that gender and politics has emerged as a '"coherent sub-field"' (citing Mackay 2004) and that this work has moved beyond the 'add women' approach to question the gendered nature of the discipline's traditional methods, assumptions and concepts.

The chapters in this volume provide some patchy support for this conclusion, and some chapters are more optimistic than others about the extent to which feminism has altered the terms of debate for good. Nevertheless, most of the chapters agree that feminist contributions have been listened to at least to some extent.

The influence of feminism has been least on the 'classic' political concepts discussed in the first three chapters. The remaining chapters find that many mainstream writers now at least 'add women in' to discussions on citizenship, democracy, development, and so on. Some also engage with the kind of radical reformulation suggested by feminist theory. Others, however, simply lament women's historical exclusion as some kind of anomaly. By failing to consider fully enough, or not at all in some cases, what adding women in might actually mean, such writing, while explicitly including women, continues to implicitly exclude them. There is also a danger that mainstream writers will take an instrumentalist approach to gender, incorporating potentially radical ideas into existing discourses and literatures as a means of achieving other ends. This is particularly clear in the chapters on agency, development and empowerment, which also show that key development institutions such as the World Bank have re-appropriated and transformed feminism's contributions, marginalising feminist analysis and removing its empowering or radical edge.

Conclusion

This volume demonstrates convincingly that if feminist analysis is taken seriously, conventional patterns of thought and practice are significantly disrupted. This means that we cannot simply add feminist analysis to conventional accounts.

Feminists still struggle to get mainstream writers to fully accept this and to change their own theory and practice in the light of feminist critiques. That this should be a difficult struggle is unsurprising given that knowledge and the production of knowledge are so bound up with patriarchal power that men have got a lot to lose by giving up the traditional political concepts which underpin their power and privilege and assume the 'normality' of their worldview. At the same time, however, men are no more a uniform group than are women. Not only are many disadvantaged by their class or ethnicity in unequal, racist societies, but many feel restricted by current gender roles and many support feminist goals because they believe in the possibility of a more just society in which we can all realise our human potential. The support of such men, evident at the conference from which this volume arose, is vital. It is our hope that the following chapters will play a role in encouraging all political theory students and academics to see that good, effective theory – that is, theory that can help us not only to interpret our world but also to change it for the better – requires serious engagement with feminist ideas. As such, these ideas help lay the foundations for more genuinely inclusive political thought.

Note

1 The term 'malestream' is used by some feminists (including some contributors to this volume) to refer to work that unreflectively assumes that men's experiences and perceptions are 'normal', and that women's can therefore be ignored, or marginalised as 'different'.

Bibliography

Abbott, P. and Wallace, C. (1997) *An Introduction to Sociology: Feminist Perspectives* (London: Routledge).

Arneil, B. (1999) *Politics and Feminism: An Introduction* (Oxford: Blackwell).

Charles, N. (1993) *Gender Divisions and Social Change* (Hemel Hempstead: Harvester Wheatsheaf).

Childs, S. and Krook, M. L. (2006) 'Gender and Politics: The State of the Art', *Politics* 26:1, 18–28.

Coole, D. (1988) *Women in Political Theory: From Ancient Misogyny to Contemporary Feminism* (first edition) (London: Harvester Wheatsheaf).

Cowman, K. and Jackson, L. (2003) 'Time', in M. Eagleton (ed.), *A Concise Companion to Feminist Theory* (Oxford: Blackwell Publishing), 32–52.

Okin, S. (1980) *Women in Western Political Thought* (London: Virago).

Squires, J. (1999) *Gender in Political Theory* (Cambridge: Polity Press).

2

Rationality

Raia Prokhovnik

Introduction

This chapter outlines the feminist contribution to an important part of the reconceptualisation of rationality. First of all the chapter describes the feminist critique of the mainstream conception of rationality. Feminists have dubbed some mainstream philosophical concepts like rationality 'malestream', to emphasise the way this supposedly gender-neutral domain is covertly inflected and structured by values and ideals associated with masculinity. For instance, rationality has been closely and positively associated with the notion of transcendence, and a crucial part of the meaning of this valued idea of transcendence has been the overcoming of negatively regarded attributes such as passivity, immanence, particularity and bodily rhythms, all traditionally associated with femininity. The term malestream is also used, at a political level, to underline the difficulties faced by feminist philosophers in seeking to introduce a wider perspective and agenda into the mainstream discourse.

The argument of the chapter then focuses on rethinking rationality in the context of the process and practice of theorising and what counts as philosophical knowledge, by challenging the malestream denial of a constructive link between reason and emotion, and by analysing the relation between them. The chapter examines the range of meanings of the terms 'reason' and 'emotion' and demonstrates the wide and traditionally unacknowledged scope of the connections between them. In the body of the chapter I show, on the basis of the feminist critique and perspective, three of the key ways in which emotions play an important role in the operation of the idea of rationality in knowledge and theorising. Such arguments are, however, still marginalised in malestream theory.

The malestream concept and the feminist critique

Feminists have demonstrated both the historical contingency and conceptual inadequacy arising from the narrowness of our inherited view of reason. They have clearly documented through historical recovery that the dominant understanding of reason and rationality has, in terms of social power relations, contained a strong gender coding that systematically excluded women. They have also shown that a narrow philosophical rationalism that rests on the association of reason solely with the mind and the mind solely with the male person (Lloyd 1993) is one of the dead ends following from Cartesian dualism (Grosz 1994:7) that claimed the independence of mind from body. What feminists have attacked is the rationalist myth that disembodied and disembedded reason is a higher faculty, separate and necessarily distinct from perception, reflection and deliberation upon felt experience. The effect of both social practices around rationality, and ideas and discourses around reason, has been to discriminate against women, and to naturalise their subordination. Feminists also argue that, in terms of the politics involved, the concept of reason and rationality has been one of the key ways in which, in our intellectual tradition and social practices, humanity has been defined against a range of 'others'. Women, other races and places, the working class, those with disabilities, animals, children, the mentally ill and prisoners have all been classed as less than rational.

It follows that we cannot talk about the politics of reason without noting the A/not-A construction in which reason has been the dominant category of the pair, defined not only against but also by demoting and belittling a series of other categories. In this way the not-A term of irrationality, yoked to the A term of reason, has been associated with a series of other categories. All emotion is, according to this logic, unruly emotion, all body and bodily affect is uncontrollable, all nature is disordered, and all women lack the capacity for reason. It is a feature of this A/not-A construction framing ideas and social practices in our inheritance that while individual exceptions to this logic may be made, the general framework has been taken to hold true. In addition, the A/not-A construction has powerfully been thought to provide a means of differentiating between knowledge and mere opinion or custom. 'How we think (the way we organise our concepts, pattern our reasoning, validate our inferences) and what we think (the principles we take as self-evident, the basic truths we take as given, the ideas we reject as backward and superstitious)', as Nye (2004:vii) puts it, have been framed by a secular, abstract, and universalised notion of reason. Reason is thereby closely associated with mind, transcendence, knowledge and truth, and on this basis has traditionally excluded women, body, desire and emotion as legitimate producers of knowledge and significant truth. Moreover, the meaning of rationality has been taken as given and unproblematic, both through its abstract character and by its role as the dominant term in a powerful A/not-A construction.

Having outlined the feminist critique, in what follows I am going to say less about reason and rationality than about one category in particular that has been excluded from its purview in the very bastion of reason, in knowledge and theorising – the role of emotions. My argument is that, on the basis of feminist research, the mainstream acceptance of a broader understanding of rationality is overdue. The wide political consensus developed over the last fifty years in particular, for the acceptance of more egalitarian social principles in political, social and cultural life, has outstripped and is now disjunctive with the persistence of A/not-A thinking and social values around reason and rationality. Mainstream philosophy and the resilience of class hierarchies in the UK continue to ensure that A/not-A ideas and social practices still have a powerful impact alongside more enlightened ones. The kind of reassessment of rationality put forward here has not been accepted into mainstream philosophy and continues to be marginalised.

The most convincing feminist re-evaluations of reason have argued, not for the abandonment of a 'male' reason in favour of 'female' empathy, nor for the renunciation of a fraudulent rational subject in favour of *jouissance*,[1] and not for the blurring of the distinction between reason and emotion. The most persuasive feminist contributions argue for an extended view of rationality that can incorporate an acknowledgment of the relationship between, and interactivity of, reason and emotion, of the ways emotion is intertwined and implicated and invested in reason.

Emotion is not an added extra, but in a number of ways is a necessary feature of all reasoning. Body theorists such as Grosz (1994) and Butler (1993), along with some postpositivists, have demonstrated that mind, and so reason, is embodied and situated, so that a full understanding of reason must contain a contextual element. These writers have also crucially succeeded in delineating this view without reducing the understanding of embodiedness to a species of materialism. Feminist and other theorists (Young 1987; Nussbaum 1990, 1995a, 1995b; Mansbridge 1993) have also made a strong case for the role of emotion in practical reasoning, political reasoning, public reasoning and reasoning in conflict situations.

My argument is a different one. It goes to the heart of the mainstream received notion of reason, and seeks to show that in theorising, reason and emotion need not be ranked nor mutually exclusive, but instead are deeply implicated in each other's constitution. This means acknowledging the role of emotion in theory work as well as the role of rationality in emotion work. Theory or knowledge (putting to one side for a moment the effect of power relations on knowledge-building) can be taken to mean the outcome of theorising that involves (conditional) closure. Theory or knowledge is something which accounts for many but not necessarily all observations and reflections, and which is expressed in a reasoned manner, that is, in a way that can be discussed and justified. Underlying this extended view of rationality is a belief in the importance of, and our ability to transform, the dichotomous structure of our inherited thinking and social interactions. It involves making distinctions but also seeking out illuminating relations and enriching connections between categories, without loss of rigour or truth, rather than being predisposed to proceed by defining on the basis of hierarchy and polarisation.

Rationality and emotion reassessed

The meaning of rationality

The meanings of both terms, reason and emotion, are multiple and contested. Reason can refer to a set of abstract categories formalised in logic such as non-contradiction, consistency and comprehensiveness. It can mean deductive argument, demonstration using universal principles, which is objective and independent of the need for empirical verification. The epistemological project has been seen as solely the domain of reason. Reason can refer to the Cartesian cogito, the rational subject with consciousness and self-consciousness. The use of reason can be seen as providing the means to freedom and equality through mind over body, to act as an autonomous, independent agent and so exercise choice. Instrumental rationality refers to the capacity to calculate, reckon and examine consequences, leading to making choices. In psychology reason refers to cognitive powers such as apprehension, observation, awareness and perception. These meanings of reason differ in part because they represent answers to different questions.

But the meaning of both reason and emotion also derives from specific historical and cultural associations and dichotomies. We cannot talk about reason without talking about the history of its use. Thus, in the Western tradition reason is regarded as inherently secular, the highest source of moral value. It is defined in science in terms of objective reason distinguished from subjective emotion. Reason has referred to the capacity for rational argument as a distinctively human potential, contrasted with the instinct of beasts. Reason was influentially distinguished by Augustine from body and the passions since the Fall. Reason is also contrasted with the realm of custom, tradition, belief and opinion. Being rational (using reason) has been opposed to the irrational, the particular, the subjective, the parochial, the perspectival, as well as to emotion, inclination and desire. Such meanings resonate with Descartes' conception of reason as specifically the faculty of mind, rather than body. In many of these meanings, as Phelan notes, 'the claims of reason are established by marking out what is beyond the pale' (Phelan 2001:79).

In a broad sense, whenever we try to make sense of something (infer, deliberate, discern and respond to reasons) we are attempting to be rational. And whenever explanation 'fits the facts', we have a rational explanation. In this chapter, reason, in the context of theory and knowledge, refers to (and acknowledges its cultural specificity in doing so) sustained rational reflection on conceptual relations and connections. Reason here is taken to mean rational argument, rather than referring to a substantive normative conception. It is systematic reflection in theorising, whose aim is understanding, expressed in arguments that can be publicly defended with intelligible reasons. It is rational argument, recognised as such by others. It is contextual and grounded rather than abstract and universal. This does not imply a vicious relativism because reason operates within inter-subjective social practices and conventions that are not arbitrary but subject to critical reflection. Reason here is recognised as socially constructed in this sense, alongside the idea of reason as a capacity, the role of logical rules such as non-contradiction, and the necessity of actually providing a reasoned argument. In this way reason and its rules are not arbitrary.

Moreover, reason as the cognitive rational faculty is distinguished here from the practical reason or reasonableness appropriate to political deliberation and debate. Reasonableness, compromise, consensus and pragmatism are not appropriate to the use of reason in intellectual work, which is about pursuing rational arguments openly to their (conditional) conclusions. The current work is also, more broadly, distinct from consideration of the interplay of reason and emotion in moral psychology and ethical theory (see for instance Cooper 1999). In sum, the concept of reason in theorising can be broadened to acknowledge its contextual and embodied character, thereby overcoming the mind/body dichotomy that had been mapped on to it with the outcome that the concept of reason relied on women's exclusion.

The meaning of emotion

Turning to the meaning of emotion, this term has been associated culturally and intellectually with a variety of discrepant (often negative) conceptions including unreason, irrationality, anti-rationality (as in fascism), hysteria, intuition, passions, nature, experience, imagination, spontaneity and lack of control. The aspect of emotion that deserves to be highlighted in a very positive sense is the recognition (identified, for instance, in psychology) that emotion is associated with motion and movement, stirring and agitation. This normatively neutral view is an extremely important feature of how emotion functions in the context of theorising, for reason and rationality on their own are inert unless propelled by emotion. As well as this feature of emotion, the kinds of emotions that are highlighted in the use of reason include having a commitment to openness; a sympathy with intellectual problems; fairmindedness, honesty and integrity; having a passionate commitment to a topic or to resolving dilemmas; some forms of love, hate, connectedness, anger and compassion; intellectual interest and excitement; caring for a subject and having a concern for it; and trust.

In general terms emotions play a crucial role in knowledge because the production of knowledge, the discussion of ideas, and the recognition of a piece of theorising as knowledge, all involve social activities expressed in particular social practices which are interpersonal and require 'emotional engagement' (Stocker 1996:175). As Turner demonstrates convincingly, 'the most fundamental dimensions of face-to-face interaction involve the activation of emotions ... for mobilising energy and attention, for attunement, for sanctioning, for moral coding, for valuing/exchange, and for decision-making' (Turner 1996:24). In other words, 'emotions have an intrinsic as well as an instrumental value ... life without any emotion would be life without any meaning' (Jaggar 1989:139).

It is also important to distinguish between emotion and affect. 'Affective', strictly speaking, refers to two phenomena that focus on the body: the affective consequences on the body of cognitive or emotional activity, and the way empirical sense data impinge on the body. Affects are 'panglike ... inner sensations' (Stocker 1996:55). It is because of the biologisation of emotion, and because of the implementation of the mind/body dualism, that emotion has been reduced to, and then is only recognised in terms of, mute bodily sensations and states. It is important to emphasise that, within a non-dichotomous mind–body relation, emotion is located in the mind (part of the body), and not in the senses or affects felt in or on the body. Harré (1986:3) notes that contemporary theorists are beginning to agree on this cognitivist theory of emotion, to recognise that emotions are part of the mind, feelings in the mind, in contrast with feelings in the body more generally. The cognitivist theory adopted here in order to avoid the biologisation of emotion through its reduction to affects, recognises how emotions straddle and transcend the conventional mind/body boundary. De Sousa also confirms that emotions are part of mind and not body more generally. 'Emotions are mental phenomena', he says (De Sousa 1987:77), although of all the elements of what 'we call the "mind"', emotions are 'the most deeply embodied' (De Sousa 1987:47).

Emotion *and* reason

There are many ways in which emotions play a role *in* knowledge, ways in which emotion enables the use of reason, and three major methods are examined here. In order to make these connections I draw here upon work which comes from an explicitly feminist background (such as by Moulton, Little, Grimshaw and Nye) as well as upon mainstream work in related disciplines (for instance by Stocker, De Sousa, Nozick and Hobbes) which can be used to support the feminist case I want to make. The three methods concern, first, salience, or normative as well as instrumental senses in which emotions supply value to cognitions; second, the manner in which emotions accompany intellectual concentration; and third, the way emotion and reason are interconnected in language.

Salience

The literal meaning of salience is the quality of leaping or springing up, jutting out, of prominence among a number of objects, standing out from the rest, of conspicuousness. In terms of the way in which the emotions play a role in knowledge and theorising, there are two meanings of salience that are pertinent. Together they highlight the double work of value in emotions. Salience refers first to the way the emotions identify which observations, perceptions and reflections are significant, noteworthy, apt, appropriate or fitting, that is, have explanatory value. Stocker notes that in 'many areas of knowledge and activity, such as the study and practice of history or philosophy... clearly, a good feel for the relevant particulars is needed if one is to be good in these areas' (Stocker 1996:192). Salience refers, second, to the manner in which the emotions pick out some cognitions as having normative value. Thus when, for example Moulton (1989:8) argues that '[t]heory changes occur because one theory is more *satisfying* than the other, because the questions it answers are considered more *important*', she is referring not just to empirical criteria in terms of evidence, or power relations that invest meaning with the status of knowledge, but to the role of salience in generating normative considerations as the basis for making judgments.

De Sousa's work provides a sound argument for valuing the role of emotion in theorising through the dynamic of salience. He depicts how, '[d]espite a common prejudice, reason and emotion are not natural antagonists. On the contrary ... when the calculi of reason have become sufficiently sophisticated, they would be powerless in their own terms, except for the contribution of emotion' (De Sousa 1987:xv). For emotions, he goes on, help to control the 'crucial factor of *salience* among what would otherwise be an unmanageable plethora of objects of attention, interpretations, and strategies of inference and conduct' (De Sousa 1987:xv–xvi).

As De Sousa argues, as well as controlling the salience of features of perception and reasoning, emotions also circumscribe our practical and cognitive options, play a role that could be played neither by belief or desire, and tip the balance between different motivational structures. All of this confirms the irreducibility of the axiological (valuing) level to either the narrowly cognitive or strategic levels. And while patterns of salience are subjective in De Sousa's sense, they are subjective without being viciously projective (De Sousa 1987:172). For emotions act as frames for both perception and belief (De Sousa 1987:257).

The first way in which emotions are important in theorising, then, concerns the way emotions work to give *normative* value to cognitions, and to identify *instrumentally* which cognitions are valuable. Emotions enable us to select and sift present as well as past perceptions for a particular end, for instance in research and thinking. Nozick recognises the importance of the way emotional capacity constitutes one portion of our value-creating powers, in the sense that emotion as well as ethics is a source of value which reason on its own requires (Nozick 1989:95). He views emotions as 'analog representations of values' (Nozick 1989:93), and indeed argues that '[e]motions are to value as beliefs are to fact' (Nozick 1989:92). Putnam also recognises the value which emotions carry when he notes that '[a]ny word that stands for something people in a culture *value* (or disvalue) will tend to acquire emotive force' (Putnam 1981:209).

Both cognitive and strategic reason are on their own insufficient and deficient. Logic, De Sousa contends, 'leaves gaps. So as long as we presuppose some basic or preexisting desires, the directive power of "motivation" belongs to what controls attention, salience, and inference strategies preferred' (De Sousa 1987:197). The 'gaps' are filled by the roles of emotion, and for this reason 'emotions are often described as guiding the processes of reasoning – or distorting them, depending on the describer's assessment of their appropriateness' (De Sousa 1987:197).

Driving intellectual attention

The second way in which emotions play a role in knowledge is closely related to the role of salience, but here focuses upon the manner in which emotions attend and drive intellectual concentration and attention. Both in identifying salience and in accompanying and motoring reason, emotion crucially provides the cogency of theorising, argument and knowledge. The point here is that reason, on its own, is thin and abstract and emotion, on its own, is dynamic: emotion shows the way to get from A to B, gives direction, selects and stimulates. In this way reason and emotion are quite interdependent. As Stocker demonstrates, there 'is as much movement, as much controlled, directed, purposive, goal-directed movement, and as much desire, force, vigour, energy, drive, urge, and urgency in intellectual action as in physical action' (Stocker 1980:328).

This function of emotion in knowledge holds true, notwithstanding the fact that we can also be carried away, overcome and buffeted by emotions. Emotions *can* be disruptive and get in the way of rational knowledge; they can be agitations that prevent one from being able to concentrate on the train of logical reasoning. Emotions can also distort rational judgment, misinterpret rational perceptions, override rational cognitions, and be based on wrong beliefs. As De Sousa notes, emotions have 'their peculiar way of interfering, and being susceptible to interference, at every level of thought and activity' (De Sousa 1987:48).

Despite these possibilities, the importance of the rational role of emotions as accompaniment to trains of reasoning holds true. It also holds true despite the fact that we can have false beliefs that are rational and true beliefs that are irrational. Even here, however, as Little points out, the 'view that obtuseness is caused *only* by the obscuring effect of emotion ... operates on the faulty picture that seeing is passive' (Little 1995:121). The view in which emotion again gets 'cast in the familiar role of contamination ... clouding what would otherwise be clear' (Little 1995:121) also overlooks other reasons for lack of clarity.

Emotions can also be self-absorbed, subjective in the sense of purely self-engrossing. It is from this possibility that there developed 'the old view that we are in bondage to our emotions, a bondage we can escape both in action and in the pursuit of truth' (Baier 1985:123). However, emotions need not be self-absorbed; when they look outward, and are directed to a purpose, they can also serve reasoning. The idea that emotions are *always* self-absorbed rests upon a false dichotomisation of the subjective/objective distinction, and on what Stocker calls a 'false truism ... that emotions put us in a bad epistemological position for evaluation' (Stocker 1996:122), resulting from the 'idealisation of rationality' (Stocker 1996:91–2). Thus, notwithstanding the possibilities of self-deception and self-absorption, emotion plays an important part in the richness of experience, thought and the moral life. Moreover, emotion does not have to be equated with spontaneity, as assumed by Mansbridge (1993:358), for emotions can be long-term stable accompaniments to thinking.

A strong emotional accompaniment is necessary for theorising, in order to sustain the development of the comprehensive implications and consequences of a piece of argument. Without a sustaining emotional force, the development of rational implications does not occur. For instance, 'intellectual interest and excitement ... are important emotional "aspects" of the intellect' (Stocker 1996:103). A line of argument, in itself, is inactive, and does not get developed without emotional agency. Thus emotions enable us to motivate our projects and endeavours. While one is engaged in theorising (exploring concepts in a spirit of openness, in the sense of not knowing the outcome in advance), one constantly monitors, supervises and reflects upon that thinking. Thinking entails not just rational judgment (such as 'does it follow?', 'is it consistent?'), but also emotional responses (favourable and unfavourable, comfortable and uncomfortable, positive and negative). These emotional judgments are made by sweeping the range of the memory and selecting material from it that is relevant for the thinking in hand.

The social contract theorist Hobbes (1651 [1946]) understood the force of the emotions, in both their positive and negative guises. Negatively, emotions can be expressed in a rhetoric that whips up a rabble or multitude and leads to the breakdown of order and the overturn of legitimate authority. Positively, emotions drive all endeavours and purposes. They also operate uniquely in each individual, even though their general character-istics are universal. Emotions also have a third guise in Hobbes, in making us restless, since there is no final good to arrive at. There is a positive dimension of this aspect, in driving us to seek greater understanding and less conditional philosophical meaning. The secondary literature on Hobbes overwhelmingly highlights Hobbes's castigation of the force of negative emotions in politics and the public realm, but for the most part overlooks the positive features of his view of emotion (but see Skinner 1996 for a rectification of this view).

The medium of language

The third way in which emotions play an important role in theorising concerns the expression of trains of thinking in language. Language is never simply a neutral instrument for naming. All language is saturated with value (triggering personal and intellectual resonances, social norms, intellectual values and power relations) so that we respond to language with both reason and emotion. It carries an emotional force, as well as being rhetorical in the sense that its meaning depends upon the use to which it is put and the context in which it is used, which is always particular. Language is also metaphorical, generating proliferating chains of association. As Grimshaw (1996) discusses, rules attempt to reduce and control this proliferation, but the use of language can involve rule-breaking as well as being rule-governed. Metaphors are not invented by fiat; they catch cultural meanings. And a particular command of language is shared by speakers at a specific time. For all these reasons language is always open to interpretation. Philosophical theories are not exempt from these features, for they are always expressed in language, and therefore they generate responses that cannot be controlled. Thus it is also through the way in which language operates that all reason has an emotional charge which is inescapable. As Nye notes, '[t]hinking necessarily uses concepts with roots in the past. Always in language, thinking is a reshaping, never an original creation. This is especially true of a text-based tradition such as philosophy' (Nye 2004:ix).

Aronovitch makes a convincing case for the rationality of analogical reasoning and the important role of metaphor as 'fundamental to reasoning and justification in law, morality and politics' (Aronovitch 1997:83). On the importance of the contributory role of metaphor and analogy to reason (specifically with respect to political reasoning), Aronovitch notes that the 'presence of images, not to mention more discursively presented analogies, far from being an indication of unreason is rather a manifestation of the form that reasoning typically and rightly takes in politics' (Aronovitch 1997:86–7). A strong argument can also be made that analogical reasoning and metaphor are just as important in theoretical argument (see Prokhovnik 1991: chapters 1 and 2), to help express the density and distinctiveness of a philosophical train of thought.

The idea that all thinking has an emotional charge that sustains it and provides it with coherence is also picked up in attending to the rhetoric of a text. Emotions not only enable us to respond in action (here the action of using language), propelling reason. They also enable us to express the reason and the emotion in the non-neutral vehicle of language. The role of emotions in language is well expressed in Nussbaum's *Love's Knowledge*. One of Nussbaum's major themes in that work is the preoccupation with the way in which, 'with respect to any text carefully written and fully imagined, an organic connection [exists] between its form and its content' (Nussbaum 1990:4).

Conclusion

The dominant view of reason and rationality in mainstream philosophy continues to deny the role played by the emotions, continues to marginalise feminist contributions, and continues to have a strong negative impact on social values and practices around gender differences. For these reasons, the resilience of a narrow understanding of rationality is deeply political. I have outlined three of the ways that emotions play an important part in the processes of thinking and theorising, in order to conceptualise an extended form of rationality that operates on a non-dichotomous basis. The A/not-A construction of the reason/emotion pairing, and of the mind/body dualism that underpins it, are reconceived in relational and interactive terms that recognise and overcome this source of gender inequality. The complex contextual framework (provided by embodiedness, specific cultural norms informing the definition of reason such as secularity, and expression in language) in which reason and emotion interact can now be acknowledged. The element of social construction (for instance in choosing relational rather than A/not-A theorising, in accepting an extended definition of rationality and a cognitivist theory of emotion) of both reason and emotion – and their interplay – can be recognised as a factor in the work of forming conceptual relations, and constraining the extent to which the definition of rationality can be taken as a 'given'. The meaning of rationality is transformed by these shifts, having shown that both claims for its 'givenness' (its abstract character, and being the dominant term in an A/not-A construction) can be critiqued through the concept of emotion.

In *Volatile Bodies*, Grosz shows how 'the body, as much as the psyche or the subject, can be regarded as a cultural and historical product' (Grosz 1994:187), and hypothesises an alternative to the conception of the body born of male Western theory and practice, dominated by biology, a 'mechanics of solids'. Her alternative takes into account now the fluids, leakiness and uncontrollability of both men's and women's bodies – dimensions previously expunged from the realm of truth and knowledge, regarded as defiling and of women's domain. If Grosz presents us with an alternative conception of bodies, what about the mind? Instead of the ideal 'naturally' rational, calculating, clean, abstract, ordered mind, I put forward a representation of the interdependence of reason and emotions – fluid, powerfully integrative and inclusive of aspects previously identified only with woman and irrationality.

Key writers and further reading

Feminist writers such as Lloyd (1993) and Grosz (1994) have played a central role in explicating the terms of the debate with regard to the dichotomies governing dominant understandings of categories such as reason/emotion, mind/body and man/woman. Their work has been vital to the development of a broader understanding and reassessment of rationality. Stocker (1996), Harré (1986) and De Sousa (1987) have fruitfully explored the embodied character of the emotions and the links between emotion and rationality. While their work is not explicitly feminist in purpose, it has contributed powerfully to the argument highlighting the connections between reason and emotion.

Note

1 *'Jouissance'*, translated as feminine sexual pleasure, is a term used by the French postmodern psychoanalyst theorist, Jacques Lacan. Its significance is that it represents, for Lacan, women's inevitable exclusion from the realm of knowledge and meaning provided by the phallocentric Freudian Oedipal Symbolic Order. *'Jouissance'* is also a term of rebellion associated with French feminist writers like Luce Irigaray and Hélène Cixous, precisely to challenge the hegemony of 'the language and knowledge of the fathers' and to assert another source of knowledge and knowing. Irigaray reconceptualises female desire through a notion of women's sexuality that recognises the plurality of their sexual organs rather than by seeing woman through a mirror defined by man. Men's mirrors reflect only themselves. Women must claim a language of their own rather than looking for a gender-neutral language, she argues. Also working within the tradition of psychoanalytic theory, and based on a difference between their genital and libidinal economies, Cixous contrasts the linearity of masculine writing, *literatur*, concerned with labelling and categorising, with the free-flowing and unconstrained character of feminine writing, or *l'écriture feminine*. While the ideas of these writers are innovative and valuable, one of the problems with feminist claims centring on *jouissance* is that they only valorise the otherwise subordinated 'other' of women's experience, and leave the overall dichotomy between man and woman in place.

Bibliography

Aronovitch, H. (1997) 'The Political Importance of Analogical Argument', *Political Studies* 45:1, 78–92.

Baier, A. (1985) 'Actions, Passions, and Reasons', in A. Baier, *Postures of the Mind: Essays on Mind and Morals* (London: Methuen), 15–32.

Butler, J. (1993) *Bodies That Matter* (New York: Routledge).

Cooper, J. (1999) *Reason and Emotion: Essays on Ancient Moral Psychology and Ethical Theory* (Princeton: Princeton University Press).

De Sousa, R. (1987) *The Rationality of Emotion* (Cambridge, Mass.: MIT Press).

Grimshaw, J. (1996) 'Philosophy and the Feminist Imagination', paper presented to Society of Women in Philosophy Conference, 'Women and Philosophy', Canterbury, December.

Grosz, E. A. (1994) *Volatile Bodies: Towards a Corporeal Feminism* (Bloomington: Indiana University Press).

Harré, R. (1986) 'An Outline of the Social Constructionist Viewpoint', in R. Harré (ed.), *The Social Construction of Emotions* (Oxford: Blackwell), 1–14.

Hobbes, T. (1651) [1946] *Leviathan*, ed. M. Oakeshott (Oxford: Blackwell).

Jaggar, A. (1989) 'Love and Knowledge: Emotion and Feminist Epistemology', in A. Garry and M. Pearsall (eds), *Women, Knowledge and Reality: Explorations in Feminist Philosophy* (New York: Routledge), 129–56.

Kennedy, E. and Mendus, S. (eds) (1987) *Women in Western Political Philosophy: Kant to Nietzsche* (Brighton: Wheatsheaf Books).

Little, M. O. (1995) 'Seeing and Caring: The Role of Affect in Feminist Moral Epistemology', *Hypatia* 10:3, 117–37.

Lloyd, G. (1993) *The Man of Reason: 'Male' and 'Female' in Western Philosophy*, 2nd edn, (Minneapolis: University of Minnesota Press).

Mansbridge, J. (1993) 'Feminism and Democratic Community', in J. Chapman and I. Shapiro (eds), *Democracy and Community: Nomos XXXV* (New York: New York University Press), 337–62.

Moulton, J. (1989) 'A Paradigm of Philosophy: The Adversary Method', in A. Garry and M. Pearsall (eds), *Women, Knowledge, and Reality: Explorations in Feminist Philosophy* (New York: Routledge), 3–20.

Nozick, R. (1989) *The Examined Life* (New York: Simon & Schuster).

Nozick, R. (1993) *The Nature of Rationality* (Princeton: Princeton University Press).

Nussbaum, M. (1990) *Love's Knowledge: Essays on Philosophy and Literature* (Oxford: Oxford University Press).

Nussbaum, M. (1995a) 'Human Capabilities, Female Human Beings', in M. Nussbaum and J. Glover (eds), *Women, Culture, and Development: A Study of Human Capabilities* (Oxford: Clarendon Press), 61–104.

Nussbaum, M. (1995b) 'Emotions and Women's Capabilities', in M. Nussbaum and J. Glover (eds), *Women, Culture, and Development: A Study of Human Capabilities* (Oxford: Clarendon Press), 360–95.

Nye, A. (2004) *Feminism and Modern Philosophy* (New York: Routledge).

Phelan, S. (2001) 'The Lines of Reason', *Hypatia* 16:2, 75–9.

Prokhovnik, R. (1991) *Rhetoric and Philosophy in Hobbes's 'Leviathan'* (New York: Garland).

Putnam, H. (1981) *Reason, Truth and History* (Cambridge: Cambridge University Press).

Skinner, Q. (1996) *Reason and Rhetoric in the Philosophy of Hobbes* (Cambridge: Cambridge University Press).

Stocker, M. (1980) 'Intellectual Desire, Emotion, and Action', in A. Rorty (ed.), *Explaining Emotions* (Berkeley: University of California Press), 323–38.

Stocker, M. (1996) *Valuing Emotions* (Cambridge: Cambridge University Press).

Turner, J. (1996) 'The Evolution of Emotions in Humans: A Darwinian–Durkheimian Analysis', *Journal for the Theory of Social Behaviour* 26:1, 1–33.

Velleman, D. (1996) 'The Possibility of Practical Reason', *Ethics* 106:2, 694–726.

Young, I. M. (1987) 'Impartiality and the Civic Public: Some Implications of Feminist Critiques of Moral and Political Theory', in S. Benhabib and D. Cornell (eds), *Feminism as Critique* (Oxford: Polity), 56–76.

3

The social contract

Laura Brace

Introduction

The idea of a social contract as the source of legitimate political authority has played a key role in the development of liberal political thought since the seventeenth century. This chapter provides a brief overview of the social contract tradition and of feminist critiques, and explores the ambiguity of this tradition for feminist theory. In particular, it discusses how feminist theory might take the social contract seriously by analysing it in the multiple contexts of unequal power that derive not from an initial baseline of equality but from historical relations based on force and fraud.

After a brief overview of social contract theory, the chapter focuses on Carole Pateman's influential feminist work *The Sexual Contract* and the debates which it has generated. It then considers the relationship between the sexual and racial contracts. It finds that although feminist critiques have had some impact on analyses of race, this has not produced an effective analysis of the intersections of sex and race to challenge mainstream interpretations of the social contract. It argues both that mainstream writers need to take feminist critiques more seriously than they have generally done and that feminists need to explore the complex and shifting meanings of freedom and individuality if the concept is to realise its radical potential.

Social contract theory: an overview

Social contract theory rests on the idea that political obligation is based on an agreement between rational and equal individuals, rather than on a natural hierarchy. It assumes that individuals will exchange obedience for protection, and so are prepared to give up a portion of their natural rights in order to guarantee their security. The structure of social contract theory begins with a hypothetical 'state of nature', a natural condition without government or legitimate authority. It then moves through the reasoned agreement to obey a sovereign to the formation of the sovereign itself.[1] It is a diverse tradition. Thus in the seventeenth century, Hobbes argued that dissociated individuals would agree to transfer their natural rights to an absolute sovereign as the only way of escaping the 'war of each against all' which was man's natural condition, while Locke, in contrast, argued for limited government based on trust and consent. A century later, Rousseau used the idea of the social contract to develop an argument for popular sovereignty and a collective form of politics, while the late twentieth century political philosopher John Rawls has used it to argue for a liberal, democratic welfare state.

The idea of originally separate, abstract individuals consenting to obey the state was in its initial incarnation a rejection of traditional patriarchy, of divine right and of all forms of tradition-based, naturalised authority. The social contract emphasises the notion of the will, the ability of individuals to act voluntarily, and the capacity for choice and self-creation (Hirschmann 1996:162). This means that social contract theory offers feminism an ambiguous legacy. The enticing possibility of rejecting natural hierarchies is balanced by the dread of not being recognised as an individual, and so being left outside the social contract. Feminist responses to the social contract vary from slightly bemused engagement with a mainstream theory that seems to remain unaware of its own radical potential, to outright rejection of a tradition built on the exclusion of women.

Feminist responses

The diversity of feminist responses to social contract theory reflects the diversity of the tradition itself, divided most obviously between those Hobbesian contractarians who ground moral principles in the rational self-interest of individuals, and Kantians who stress the value of autonomous persons and use contract as a theory of moral justification based on a shared sense of justice. This Kantian approach has been brought up to date by John Rawls's theory of justice. The structure of his argument adapts and develops the structure of the classic social contract, meaning that social contract theory remains central to liberalism. The 'contractarian debate' between Hobbesians and Kantians conducted among philosophers, political theorists, game theorists and legal theorists turns on the problem of collective action, the question of individual and collective rationality, and the issues raised by hypothetical justification. It often remains, despite feminist interventions, abstract and arid ground, a conversation about distributive justice – and only ever about distributive justice – conducted within a very specific corner of modern liberal political philosophy.

Feminist contractarianism demands expansion of the field of social contract theory. It requires constant critical scrutiny in particular of the public/private divide and of the family as a public, political, power-saturated institution (Okin 1989). Even justice-thinking liberal feminists who can work with the notions of reasonableness and fairness that underpin traditional social contract thinking unsettle some cherished categories of the mainstream. T. M. Scanlon, for example, employs the concept of a 'reasonable person' to model the rules for the regulation of behaviour, and feminist contractarians like Jean Hampton are left to point out that 'feminists have good reason to worry about what might seem reasonable in a patriarchal society' (Hampton quoted in Sample 2002:272). Traditional contractarians respond to feminist interventions with a commitment to gender neutrality, especially in their language, but they do little to address what Ruth Sample terms the 'gender caste system' in which 'the fortunes of men and women are arbitrarily determined, or at least strongly influenced at birth' (Sample 2002:276; Okin 1989). They focus instead on questions of equal rationality. In David Gauthier's account of reaching morals by agreement, for example, both parties to the contract are equally rational, so that what is rational for one is rational for the other. As Margaret Moore points out, Gauthier's theory seems to suggest that there is 'a single rational solution to all bargaining problems', rather than that the terms of co-operation are essentially contested in the first place (Moore 1994:218). Moreover, as Raia Prokhovnik's chapter in this volume shows, feminists have identified some deep-seated problems with the very concept of rationality as used within mainstream political theory.

Feminist theory, theory that takes women's experiences seriously and pays close attention to the impact of ideas and practices on women, is unlikely to want to reclaim a concept that relies on the idea that human beings are not the product of their social existence, and is built on the assumption that the fundamental motivations of human beings are presocial, nonsocial and fixed. Once the terms of co-operation are contested, it is at least questionable whether the social contract can be reconstructed in a feminist manner, in John Hoffman's phrase. Carole Pateman, in her ground-breaking 1988 work, the *Sexual Contract*, emphatically argued that the social contract was not a momentum concept with egalitarian potential. Since then, feminists and others have contested her critique. Donna Dickenson (1997) has argued that feminism has been too quick to dismiss contractarianism, and needs to return to an earlier tradition of feminist thinking and campaigning that used the principle of contract to assert female subjectivity and agency in the face of its legal and political denial. In doing so, she reminds us of contract's enticing possibilities.

The sexual contract

Carole Pateman argued that the sexual contract is the repressed dimension of social contract theory, the part of the story that never gets told. The social contract presupposed the sexual contract, and civil freedom presupposed patriarchal right. Modern patriarchy, she argues, has a contractual character. Men and women are husbands and wives before they are fathers and mothers. Patriarchy is the form of political right that all men exercise by virtue of being men. Conjugal power is not paternal, but part of masculine sex-right, 'the power that men exercise as men', not as fathers (1988:22). It is a power that men exercise over women even in the state of nature. It is given a natural basis by all the classic social contract thinkers except Hobbes. Hobbes, as Pateman points out, is an important exception because he begins from the premise that there is no natural dominion of men over women, but nonetheless subscribes to patriarchy in its modern form (Pateman 1991:55–6). Men in the state of nature are free and equal, and any relations based on power and subordination have to be consented to in order to be legitimate. Between men, social relations are conventional and instrumental. This story of conventional and artificial society only makes sense if the sphere of civil society can be purged of the problem of reproduction, if women can be persuaded to give birth and put themselves at a disadvantage in the war of all against all. Otherwise, the social contract would be rather a short story. For the social contract to work, it requires the prior sexual subordination of women to men that gives men control over women's bodies and allows them to overcome 'their crucial inability to assure their own fatherhood' (Dickenson 1997:75) and to reproduce the social contract through the generations. Women, Pateman argues, are born into subjection (1988:41) just at the moment when men are reborn into voluntarism.

Contract, in her account, is the specifically modern means of creating relationships of subordination. Individuals leaving the state of nature through the mechanism of the social contract give up some of their natural freedom in return for increased security. They need to feel safer from each other, more insulated against harm to themselves and to their liberties and estates. Individuals who own a property in their own person contract with one another to respect their property and to recognise each other as property-owners (1988:56). They institute a sovereign with the power to enforce contracts, and so to turn natural individuals into civil individuals (1988:58). Both parties enter the contract on the same basis and for mutual advantage. They exchange obedience for protection. Pateman points out that the peculiarity of this contract is that the party who provides the protection has the right to determine how the party who owes obedience should act in order to fulfil their side of the bargain (1988:59). This is where the coercion gets camouflaged. It looks like an exchange between equals, but it is in fact about the exercise of power. It is a slave contract. The contract is a form of conquest. Because civil subordination originates in contract, it is presented as part of the story of freedom. The 'happy ever after' of the social contract story is, 'as soon as compact enters, slavery ceases'. Pateman argues that, on the contrary, the contract tradition can even accommodate the relation between master and slave (1988:166). The particular freedom gained through contract can be exemplified in slavery. Consent, as Wendy Brown argues, is 'a mark of subordination' (Brown 1995:163).

For Pateman, this is particularly true of the marriage contract. Women must enter into the marriage contract in order to be 'incorporated into civil society' (1988:180), but their incorporation is only partial because they belong to civil society as women, and so as property rather than as individuals. They inhabit a space between the state of nature and civil society, a 'nether world' within which they are neither full market actors nor fully excluded from any civil existence. They are constructed as politically incompetent, as naturally subordinate, and yet as capable of entering the marriage contract. Pateman's central argument is that the way out of this rather shadowy nether world is not more contracts. For her, an alliance between feminism and contract is incongruous: 'The conclusion is easy to draw that the denial of civil equality to women means that the feminist aspiration must be to win acknowledgment for women as "individuals". Such an aspiration can never be fulfilled. The "individual" is a patriarchal category' (1988:184). The individual is masculine, and masculinity means sexual mastery. To be an individual, a person has to possess and have access to sexual property. The individual 'is a man who makes use of a woman's body' (1988:185). Pateman is arguing that women's subordination is secured by contract, so that women's oppression is written into the 'deep structure' of liberalism. It is part of the structure of self-consciousness, humans' conceptions of themselves in relation to other humans, institutions and the non-human environment. As men consent to the social contract 'with the aim of becoming beings individually contracting with one another, they institutionalise a condition in which women become beings consenting to individual men' (Brown 1995:163–4). Liberalism and the social contract could not survive without women inhabiting that subordinate position.

More positive feminist assessment: property in the person

Donna Dickenson argues, against Pateman, that the subjection of women within the private sphere undermines rather than underpins liberal contractarianism's view of the individual (1997:76). Women's oppression, their defeat under patriarchy, is the last vestige of force in politics, and it would be put right by the triumph of liberalism. She insists that it is not the mechanism of contract we should distrust, but its content. The sexual contract is false and flawed not because it is a contract, but because it deals in women's bodies, it exchanges women as objects, and it makes the experience of property different for women and men. The sexual and the marriage contracts are then, in Dickenson's construction, 'crippling internal paradoxes' for liberalism. They weaken rather than sustain the deep structure of liberalism, which requires everything, including the foundations of society, to be open to contract (1997:76).

Pateman argues that: 'Women are property, but also persons; women are held both to possess and to lack the capacities required for contract – and contract demands that their womanhood be both denied and affirmed' (1988:60). For Dickenson, this contains the seeds of an argument that can save liberalism – she calls it 'a Trojan horse *within* liberal gates' (1997:76). Women are property, but also persons, and they are granted enough capacity to enter the marriage contract. For Pateman, this means that the marriage contract both proves women's personhood and justifies their subordination. The marriage contract seamlessly connects the sexual contract to the social contract. For Dickenson, the crucial admission that women are simultaneously property and persons means that women in contractarian liberalism 'continue to hold a property in their persons' (1997:76). A marriage contract that rests on coverture,[2] and so attempts to make the husband and wife into one person, contradicts the basic Lockean principle of property in the person. Husband and wife are not treated as separate individuals, and the contract itself cannot be renegotiated. Such a marriage contract is '*so internally contradictory as not to be a contract at all*' (1997:77). Coverture becomes a kind of backlash against contract. According to Dickenson, Pateman sees women as property, and so risks essentialism in mistaking the historically specific conditions of coverture for universal and inevitable subordination. She fixes meanings that cannot be fixed.

Dickenson's emphasis on women owning a property in their persons means that she can reject the conclusion that 'the individual' is an inescapably patriarchal category. She argues that in order to make this rather bleak assertion, Pateman has to conflate the idea of owning a property in the body with the idea of owning a property in the person. Dickenson reclaims the distinction as crucial. The individual who emerges from her account owns a property in their 'designs, projects and innermost feelings' (1997:78). My labour is not a special kind of property because I own my body, but because it 'represents my agency, a part of my self, my person' (1997:79). People own their actions and their agency, not their bodies. For Dickenson, this 'highlights the room left in liberalism's account of contract for agency and motivation, when we purge it of its repressive connection with ownership of female bodies by men' (1997:79). For her, what is wrong with the sexual contract is that it is sexual, not that it is a contract. This suggestion that 'we' can purge the liberal tradition of its repressive connections implies a fixing of a different sort, one that reconfigures the inside and the outside of the social contract, but keeps their separation intact.

Dickenson's view is that Pateman wrongly implies a necessary connection between all forms of property or contract and women's subordination under liberalism (1997:90). For her, Pateman's reading is ahistorical and stultifying. It is an account that risks denying women's agency, and the positive value that flows from owning a property in the person and from being recognised, acknowledged and affirmed by others as a rational contractor and an active property owner. Dickenson's project is to reclaim these elements of property ownership by directing our attention to Hegel's theory of the educative, developmental role of property. She also advocates an 'openness' to the liberal theory of contract where it emphasises property in the person rather than property in the body (1997:153). She argues in favour of contract 'as an embodiment of mutual recognition, as an enhancement of mutual moral awareness' (1997:171). In her view, when property is constructed in the person rather than the 'sexually tinged' body, then property and contract can stand for ethical agency and moral self-development (1997:171).

I agree with Dickenson that Pateman's approach risks essentialism by assuming that coverture is a reflection of something timeless, static and universal rather than historically specific. We do, as Dickenson urges, need to recover property and the social contract as sites of struggle, as spaces within which women can exercise some moral agency and interact with the world. We need to be able to see women without property as something other than eternal victims or as the objects of property. I worry, though, about her idea that we can purge a whole tradition of its repressive connections with troublesome, sexually tinged bodies, and choose instead to concentrate on 'persons'. I agree with her that there is an important distinction to be made between property in the body and property in the person, and that it is property in the person that underpins the hypothetical social contract. That leaves the crucial problem, though, of who counts as a person. Dickenson seems to be suggesting that we can construct a liberal notion of contract that detaches the answer to this question from the 'bodies' that carry the persons. In her view, if we could only get rid of its sexual dimension, contract could stand as a mechanism for social recognition and moral awareness.

It seems to me impossible to detach social recognition and moral awareness from embodied individuals, and from their struggle with the world. Persons make contracts and have bodies, and the refusal by others to acknowledge and affirm them as rational contractors and active property owners is often inseparable from their embodiment as 'others'. Pateman and Dickenson both concentrate on property in the person, on the 'sexually tinged' body and on the relation between the marriage contract and the social contract. This means that the bodies in question are women's bodies and that subordination is theorised as gendered, and only gendered. I agree that men's citizenship relies on women's subordination, but I think that telling this as the whole story is problematic. It skews the picture for women by assuming that the basis for their exclusion from the social contract always lies in reproduction, and so in the public/private divide and in their unpaid care work. This gets us to think seriously about the ways women are associated with the private and the domestic, and excluded from the amorality of the market. It does not get us to think about other forms of outsiderness for women, those for whom not only unpaid care work but paid work is the problem – single women, poor women, working women whose labour is not taken seriously as work or productive exchange. Elsewhere, I have described these women as 'freelance hustlers', living within an economy of makeshifts and expedients (Brace 2002, 2004). They are denied ethical incorporation into the morality of market society, a morality that is based on the ideal of productive, improving labour, skilled work and membership (of firms, unions, guilds, clubs, etc). The contemporary global care labour market, for example, as opposed to the cloistered domestic sphere that Pateman and Dickenson seem to have in mind, is predominantly occupied by migrants, and by migrant women in particular.

The shift from domestic work to caretaking labour means that care work has become flexible, casual and precarious, taking place well outside the traditional boundaries of a marriage based on coverture. The approaches of both Pateman and Dickenson to the sexual and social contracts focus on a well-defined private sphere that structures women's experiences and risk seeing only the gender divisions that emerge as clearly visible (Graham 1991:69). They are less likely to see the migrant character of affective labour or the plurality and radical diversity of women's relationships to care and to the private sphere. As Evelyn Nakano Glenn argues, 'when we see reproductive labor only as gendered, we extract gender from its context, which includes other interacting systems of power' (1992:33).

Critiquing the mainstream: feminism and *The Racial Contract*

What I find interesting is how difficult this is to correct, how hard it is to explore interacting systems of power together. I want to go on to talk about Charles Mills's work on *The Racial Contract* (1997). In a recent interview, Mills was asked to comment on his work incorporating theories of race into mainstream philosophy. 'What is needed', he argued

> is a self-conscious attempt, following the feminist model on gender, to rethink the main subdivisions in Philosophy in the light of the potential difference that race might make to their conceptualisations, central themes and framing assumptions. If Philosophy is about 'persons' and the world, it needs to specifically address the condition of those persons whose personhood, because of race, has not been recognised. (Carter 2004:1)

The racial contract, in Charles Mills's formulation, has several layers. It is political, moral, epistemological and real. For Mills, it is not a story, or at least not only a story. It is an 'exploitation contract' (1997:9), expressed through the expropriation contract, the slavery contract and the colonial contract. The racial contract is a set of agreements between 'whites' to classify themselves as full persons and 'the remaining subset of humans as "nonwhite" and of a different and inferior moral status' (1997:11). At the same time, the racial contract is 'in effect an agreement to divide among themselves (as common white property) the proceeds of nonwhite subordination' (1997:135). The 'nonwhites' are then synonymous with the propertyless, and they become 'subpersons', so that they have a subordinate civil standing and are not counted as members of the moral community. They are not entitled to social recognition and they are not granted the capacity for moral awareness. The contract to establish society, to transform natural man into civil man at the same time established a racial polity. The 'conceptual partition' is not between the state of nature and civil society but is the transformation of human populations into white and nonwhite men (1997:13). The masculine pronouns here, I think, are not incidental, and I explore some of the implications of this point later. For Mills, race is written into the deep structure of liberalism. It is not an afterthought, 'a "deviation" from ostensibly raceless Western ideals, but rather a central shaping constituent of those ideals' (1997:14). As Pateman argued about gender, race is part of the structure of self-consciousness and of humans' conceptions of themselves in relation to other humans. (For related discussion of the creation of subpersonhood and the exploitation of Black people see Kalpana Wilson's chapter).

Unlike the sexual contract, the racial contract is not prior to the social contract and it is not about consolidating relations of power that already existed in the state of nature. The contract itself brings 'race' into existence. It is the agreement between the powerful, the conventions between men, that constitute some as full subjects and others as subpersons by designating them as white and nonwhite. It has some of the same effects as the sexual contract: it calls the status of the 'individual' as a category into question, and it troubles the notion of consent written into the social contract by revealing the central role of force in establishing the liberal polity. Once again, consent is a mark of subordination. In the racial contract as it is played out, the economic dimension is crucial because it is 'calculatedly aimed at economic exploitation' (1997:32). The polity is partitioned in order to secure legitimate privilege for those designated as white and justify the exploitation of those designated as nonwhite.

Mills argues that the concept of personhood has to include the concept of a 'subperson' – someone who is not an inanimate object, and not entirely outside the imagined moral community, but is not fully a person (Mills 1998:6). Such a subperson is defined in contrast to those who own themselves, and so are able to exercise the kind of property in the person described by Dickenson, owning their own designs, projects and innermost feelings. Subpersons are assumed to have less mental capacity, no real history and no real contribution to make to civilisation. Crucially, for their place within the social contract, they are individuals '... who in general can be encroached upon with impunity' (1998:7). They are not fully recognised as persons, their self-ownership is qualified and their sense of belonging is precarious, but unlike the dangers inherent in Pateman's account, it is clear that they do not cease to be individuals altogether. Subpersonhood also has the interesting effect of troubling the self-ownership of those who are granted full personhood. Whiteness itself becomes a precarious category with permeable boundaries of belonging and identity. It is not fixed, but unfixed by the idea of the racial contract, and the inside/outside dichotomy is not a stable boundary. White privilege may remain a constant, but whiteness itself is fluid and contestable, fractured and inseparable from notions of self-possession (Jacobson 1998). Changing patterns of migration created internal divisions and implicit rankings, seen in the US in the nineteenth century in the treatment and experience of Irish and Italian migrants and Jews, who found that their 'variegated whiteness' was a status that could be lost or called into question by their association with nonwhite groups (Jacobson 1998:41, 57). They could be marked as Black by local custom when they lived and worked as farm labourers, or small tenants for example. Some groups are fit to be white, while others are coded as unfit, a process that is still at work in white Europeans' experience of becoming 'othered' as they migrate from east to west.

This precariousness and instability seems to me a more productive way of thinking about gender, as well as race, than one that fixes gender by confining women to the private sphere and to their reproductive bodies. It makes visible what it means to be 'not-woman', ungendered and unsexed when they fail to present themselves as heterosexuals, for example, and so as clearly fitted for the woman's sphere (Calhoun 2000:34). It helps to get at the spaces between the public and the private, the work that doesn't count as labour, the belonging that entails no honour, the property in the person that has not been properly purged of its connections with sexually tinged bodies. It also troubles the too-straightforward power relations of Pateman's sexual contract, the naturalising of male sex-right as the power that men exercise as men. The racial contract and particularly the notion of subpersonhood should lead us to question whether that can mean the power of all men over all women all of the time.

Mills's analysis should help us to unpack the relations of power and privilege, so that we are not stuck with women as passive victims of subordination and men as patriarchal individuals, frozen into their roles. The racial contract, with its insistence that it is real, disrupts the possibility that the story of the social contract can have an ending. Instead, in different constellations of race and gender, in the performativity of both, it is constantly renegotiated, its boundaries shift, personhood is a fluid, probationary and confusing category. I do not mean that it is easy to cross over from subpersonhood to personhood, but that in different historical situations it may be possible to exercise a property in the person as a market actor without automatically experiencing social recognition or moral awareness. Some people, freelance hustlers or migrant workers, for example, may make contracts that do not insulate themselves from others, that do not bring them acknowledgment and affirmation from others, but do nevertheless grant them partial incorporation into the social contract.

The racial contract, then, when it deals in precariousness, in variegation and in fitness for self-government, has enormous potential for thinking through the interlocking systems of oppression that underpin the social contract and make up the totalising theory of consent. The trouble with Mills's theory of the racial contract is the distinction he draws between liberal ideals and their betrayal by whites in the historical practices of liberalism. His project is as liberal as Dickenson's, and they share the problematic goal of purging liberalism of its repressive elements. The problem with the racial contract, in the end, is its inability to accommodate diversity and difference. It suffers from some of the same drawbacks as the sexual contract. As Anthony Bogues points out in his review of *The Racial Contract* for *Constellations* (2001), the expropriation, slavery and colonial contracts were all systems of exclusion and exploitation, but they were not all the same. The racial contract is a static construct, one that ends up detaching ideals from human historical practice. 'My focus on race in this book', Mills says in his acknowledgments, 'should not be taken to imply that I do not recognise the reality of gender as another system of domination' (1997:xi), but it is, in his view, 'another system'. In the interview with Ginger Carter, Mills was asked to comment on the ways in which his work has been influenced by feminist theory. He pointed out that *The Racial Contract* was inspired by *The Sexual Contract*. He described how he took Pateman's argument that the social contract is a male contract that subordinates women, whilst claiming to be inclusive of everybody, and applied the argument to race. In applying it, he 'claimed that we also need to differentiate the "men", since it is really white men who become equal in the modern period' (Carter 2004:1).

As Mills says in discussing the book he and Pateman are currently writing together, up until now she has focused largely on gender and he has focused largely on race. The book is an attempt to 'bring the two contracts into dialogue with one another, since the ultimate goal, obviously, would be a synthesis of the two', addressing the complexities of intersectional identities (Carter 2004:2). I am not sure that this ultimate goal is all that obvious, either from reading Pateman and Mills or from thinking about gender and race. The rigidity of thinking this through in terms of two separate contracts that have to be brought into reluctant dialogue with one another raises at least two problems. The first is that women of colour fall through the cracks, into the awkward silences, and the second is that the boundaries of the social contract are too rigidly drawn around the idea that compact enters and slavery ceases.

The intersections of sex and race

I find it revealing that Charles Mills focuses on the racial contract as dividing up the spoils of nonwhite subordination between men, and that what he takes from Pateman is the need to differentiate the men. I would like to go on to unpack this in the light of his aspiration to address the complexities of intersectional identities. In her discussion of the way identities intersected around Mike Tyson's rape trial in 1992, Kimberle Crenshaw points to the Black and antiracist community support that was extended to Tyson but not to his black accuser Desiree Washington. Tyson, she argues, was embraced and defended as a victim of racism. His place in the racial contract was determined by the contest between black men and white men over access to women. Racism, she concludes, is consistently portrayed 'in terms of the relative power of Black and white men' (Crenshaw 1990–91:1278). It is about men's differential access, rather than the differential protection of women. The discourses around rape are about men, not about how the rape of Black women by Black men is treated less seriously than the rape of white women by white men. The racialised dimension of intraracial rape somehow disappears, and the experience of black women gets lost from view, obscured under another 'dimension of disempowerment' (1990–91:1249). Black women's experience of racism is seen 'only . . . in terms of white male access to them' (1990–91:1277).

The boundaries of valuation

In her exploration of 'intersectional identities', Crenshaw argues that the prevailing structures of domination shape the various discourses of resistance (1990–91:1243). When the resistance discourses persist in treating race and gender as essentially separate categories, they risk reproducing and reinforcing the existing structures of domination. Black women, she argues, end up 'erased by the strategic silences of antiracism and feminism' (1990–91:1253). In being forced to choose the either/or of race and gender, black women's identity is pushed to 'a location that resists telling' (1990–91:1242). Her examples of this erasure come from her focus on domestic violence and rape. She describes how the LAPD refused to release their statistics on domestic violence broken down by race, citing the fears of both antiracist and feminist campaigners of presenting domestic violence as a minority problem. Once it was identified as such, feminists would no longer be able to present domestic violence as a universal and serious issue, and antiracists would find stereotypes of black men as naturally violent unhelpfully reinforced, and the integrity of their community undermined. Attempts to politicise domestic violence, to bring it under the remit of the social contract, involved convincing white people that it is a universal problem, not a minority problem, but *their* problem, one that affects elite white women and not just the 'other', the poor, black, degraded woman constructed as the stereotypical, archetypal victim (1990–91:1260). In the process, what happens to black women is 'silenced as much by being relegated to the margin of experience as by total exclusion' (1990–91:1261). This is a qualitatively different sort of camouflage for coercion, one that is not about being banished to the 'nether world' of a well-defined private sphere that structures women's experiences, but about being marginalised by the social, sexual and racial contracts and put into a kind of suspended animation.

Intersectionality involves not only thinking about how categories are socially constructed in the first place, through the sexual and racial contracts, but also how those categories come to have social and material meanings and consequences. The focus then is not so much on the story of origins, or on bringing the two separate contracts into dialogue, but on thinking through how the racial and social contracts continue to determine how power clusters around certain categories, and on how 'the descriptive content of those categories and the narratives on which they are based have privileged some experiences and excluded others' (Crenshaw 1990–91:1298). Exploring how these privileges and exclusions work requires situated readings of the sexual and racial contracts, and strategic readings of their intersections. Class, gender and race are 'problematic variables', and they come into existence in and through each other. As Anjali Arondekar argues in her review of Anne McClintock's *Imperial Leather*, 'these categories ... do not derive their signification from one fixed point of origin, but instead are "articulated", unfolded from uneven and often opposing locations' (Arondekar 1996:2). This means that what is required is 'constant structural scrutiny', and an awareness of the dangers of conflating different structures of oppression. This project of sustained critical inquiry, Arondekar argues, quoting Spivak, needs to be undertaken in a spirit of daily maintenance and 'unlike a surgical operation, should not be expected to bring about a drastic recovery or change' (1996:4). In their analysis of the sexual and racial contracts, Pateman, Dickenson and Mills seem to me to be trying to offer a diagnosis that requires a surgical operation to put right, rather than recognising the 'impossibility of fixing lines, keeping people in separate places, stopping slippage' (Hall 2002:10).

This is not only about the missing black women, it is about the boundaries of the social contract, and about the impulse to turn the sexual and the racial contracts into exclusive categories, engaging in 'the drawing of bright lines and clear taxonomies' (Williams 1991:8). The social contract is centrally about 'the making of selves through the making of others' (Hall 2002:20), and that makes it another site of struggle, and an ongoing process. Patricia J. Williams adds another dimension of disempowerment to the idea of owning a property in the person when she talks about unowned slaves as disowned, the way that 'the unowning of blacks' and other freelance hustlers put them 'beyond the bounds of valuation' (Williams 1991:21), outside what she calls 'the marketplace of rights'. Black people, she says, have been perpetual tenants, sharecroppers and lessees. Everything around them is owned by others; they live in a 'limbo of disownedness' (1991:72).

The social contract is then about drawing the boundaries of valuation, putting the dispossessed on the outside, and allowing 'the passersby of the dispossessed' to form a social compact to structure their own expectations and to give them a sense of being legitimate (1991:28, 152). For these passersby, where no harm is intended to others, their property in the person allows them to assert their subjectivity and agency, winning acknowledgment of themselves as individuals. The contract becomes, as Hegel and Dickenson said it would, an embodiment of mutual recognition and an enhancement of mutual moral awareness. The question then is how that mutual recognition and moral awareness are sustained through the shared complicity of leaving the dispossessed on the outside, in limbo, not owning their designs, projects and innermost feelings, but being governed by the intentions of others (1991:72). The passersby, those with the power to determine the boundaries of valuation, feel safe from each other by insulating themselves from the dispossessed, and so they continue to determine how others should act in order to fulfil their side of the bargain. In a global society where everything is open to contract, the social contract reproduces itself through a transnational, globalised frame, where the question becomes, who are the relevant subjects for justice (Fraser 2004)?

Conclusion

Feminist frustration at the lack of mainstream attention paid to the question of who counts as a relevant subject of justice is palpable. One response is to refuse to engage with the social contract at all, to turn to the ethic of care in the place of justice thinking. Traditional male-dominated social contract theory continues to subject the social contract, and contractual relations in general, to formal and abstract analysis, separate from 'the social, psychological and discursive constructions of gender', and so 'their purely formal analysis is only another example of a mystifying and masculine approach' (Coole 1994:207). As Ruth Sample argues, this is not about 'imputing any ill will or active strategising' to mainstream liberal political philosophers, but it does allow us to see what is wrong with the social contract (Sample 2002:276). It is a mechanism which allows liberal political philosophers to take advantage of the caste systems not only of gender, but also of race by not facing the question of who qualifies as a person in the first place, and then by assuming that it is possible to distinguish clearly between those on the inside and those on the outside.

I worry that Pateman, Dickenson and Mills are all telling stories with unconvincing endings, linked to the happy ever after of 'whenever compact enters, slavery ceases'. Pateman's argument that contract is slavery, Dickenson's that contract is freedom, and Mills's contention that we can close the gap between the ideal of the social contract and the reality of the racial contract all assume that it is possible and productive to distinguish clearly between contract and slavery, that we can draw 'bright lines between those with full personal autonomy and those without it' (Beckles 1996:583). As a result, they all miss the crucial point that decolonisation did not lead straight to total freedom, and an 'end to slavery often ushered in not freedom, but bondage in its various, adaptable guises' (Walvin 1996:179).

The social contract is still about the making and re-making of selves through the making and re-making of others in complex formations, and it is to this complexity, variety and adaptability that we need to pay attention. As Shane Phelan argues about community, there are dangers inherent in trying to fix the limits of the social contract, to give it an existence outside our attempts to construct the boundaries of valuation safely around ourselves (Phelan 1996:243). Traditional social contract theory manipulates and reconstructs the notions of freedom and individuality so that they apply exclusively to economically privileged white men. In their reworkings, both Pateman and Mills leave freedom and individuality strangely untouched, fixed with the same meanings they have for social contract thinkers. The individual remains a patriarchal category for Pateman and a viable ideal for Mills. It is only through unfixing the meanings of freedom and individuality, acknowledging their precariousness and understanding the complexity of their interactions with social categories based on gender, race and class that we can find a way of arguing that they could be otherwise.

Key writers and further reading

The key texts in the social contract tradition are Hobbes' *Leviathan*, Locke's *Second Treatise* and Rousseau's *Social Contract*, which needs to be read with his *Discourse on the Origin of Inequality* to understand his account of the state of nature. The edited collection by Boucher and Kelly (1994) provides a useful overview of the issues involved in mainstream social contract thinking.

As discussed in this chapter, the most influential feminist discussion of the social contract is undoubtedly Pateman (1988). Dickenson (1997) and Mills (1997) both offer important responses to the idea of the sexual contract. For an interesting discussion of current feminist thinking about contractarianism, see Sample (2002).

Notes

1 The holder of sovereign power need not be an individual, it can be a body of people, such as a parliament.
2 'Coverture' was defined by William Blackstone in his *Commentaries on the Laws of England* (1765). It describes the legal process whereby the husband and wife became one person in law, so that the legal existence of the woman was suspended during the marriage, or incorporated into that of her husband. In other words, she was 'covered' by him, and lived under his protection.

Bibliography

Arondekar, A. (1996) 'The Problem of Strategy: How to Read Race, Gender, and Class in the Colonial context', *Postmodern Culture* 6:3, http://muse.jhu.edu/journals/postmodern_culture/v006/6.3r_arondekar.html.

Beckles, H. (1996) 'The Concept of 'White Slavery' in the English Caribbean during the Early Seventeenth Century', in J. Brewer and S. Staves (eds), *Early Modern Conceptions of Property* (London and New York: Routledge).

Bogues, A. (2001) 'Review of the Racial Contract by Charles Mills', *Constellations* 8:2, 267–85. Quotations from www.politicalreviewnet.com.

Boucher, D. and Kelly, P. (1994) (eds) *The Social Contract from Hobbes to Rawls* (London: Routledge).

Brace, L. (2002) 'The Tragedy of the Freelance Hustler: Hegel, Gender and Civil Society', *Contemporary Political Theory* 1:3, 329–48.

Brace, L. (2004) *The Politics of Property: Labour, Freedom and Belonging* (Edinburgh: Edinburgh University Press).

Brown, W. (1995) *States of Injury* (Princeton: Princeton University Press).

Calhoun, C. (2000) *Feminism, the Family and the Politics of the Closet* (Oxford: Oxford University Press).

Carter, G. (2004) 'Interview with Dr Charles Mills', www.uahexponent.com/media/paper462/news/2004/04/01/News/Interview.With.Dr.Charles.Mills-649138.shtml?norewrite&sourcedomain=www. uahexponent.com.

Coole, D. (1994) 'Women, Gender and Contract: Feminist Interpretations', in D. Boucher and P. Kelly (eds), *The Social Contract from Hobbes to Rawls* (London: Routledge), 191–210.

Crenshaw, K. (1990–91) 'Mapping the Margins: Intersectionality, Identity Politics, and Violence Against Women of Color', *Stanford Law Review* 43, 1241–99.

D'Agostino, F. (2003) 'Contemporary Approaches to the Social Contract', *Stanford Encyclopedia of Philosophy*, http://plato.stanford.edu/entries/contractarianism-contemporary.

Dickenson, D. (1997) *Property, Women and Politics* (Cambridge: Polity Press).

Fraser, N. (2004) 'Gender Equality and Social Change', paper presented to CRASSH Gender Symposium, 5 March, Cambridge.

Glenn, E. N. (1992) 'From Servitude to Service Work: Historical Continuities in the Racial Division of Paid Productive Labor', *Signs* 18:1, 1–44.

Goldberg, D. T. (1998 edition; 1993) *Racist Culture: Philosophy and the Politics of Meaning* (Oxford: Blackwell).

Graham, H. (1991) 'The Concept of Caring in Feminist Research: The Case of Domestic Service', *Sociology* 25:1, 61–78.

Hall, C. (2002) *Civilising Subjects* (Cambridge: Polity).

Hirschmann, N. (1996) 'Rethinking Obligation for Feminism', in N. J. Hirschmann and C. Di Stefano (eds), *Revisioning the Political* (Boulder CO: Westview Press), 157–81.

Jacobson, M. F. (1998) *Whiteness of a Different Color: European Immigrants and the Alchemy of Race* (Cambridge MA: Harvard University Press).

Lubasz, H. (1977) 'Marx's Initial Problematic: The Problem of Poverty', *Political Studies* 24:1, 24–42.

Mills, C. W. (1997) *The Racial Contract* (Ithaca NY and London: Cornell University Press).

Mills, C. W. (1998) *Blackness Visible: Essays on Philosophy and Race* (Ithaca NY and London: Cornell University Press).

Moore, M. (1994) 'Gauthier's Contractarian Morality', in D. Boucher and P. Kelly (eds), *The Social Contract from Hobbes to Rawls* (London: Routledge), 211–25.

Okin, S. M. (1989) *Justice, Gender and the Family* (New York: Basic Books).

Pateman, C. (1988) *The Sexual Contract* (Cambridge: Polity Press).

Pateman, C. (1991) '"God Hath Ordained to Man a Helper": Hobbes, Patriarchy and Conjugal Right', in M. L. Shanley and C. Pateman (eds), *Feminist Interpretations and Political Theory* (Cambridge: Polity Press), 53–73.

Phelan, S. (1996) 'All the Comforts of Home: The Genealogy of Community', in N. J. Hirschmann and C. Di Stefano (eds), *Revisioning the Political* (Boulder CO: Westview Press), 235–51.

Sample, R. (2002) 'Why Feminist Contractarianism?', *Journal of Social Philosophy* 33:2, 257–81.

Walvin, J. (1996) *Questioning Slavery* (London: Routledge).

Williams, P. J. (1991) *The Alchemy of Race and Rights* (Cambridge MA: Harvard University Press).

4

Sovereignty

John Hoffman

Introduction

Sovereignty involves the self-government of the individual. It is true that the concept of sovereignty is often linked to male violence and domination. In *Beyond the State*, I link sovereignty with the state and dismiss both as incoherent and contradictory (Hoffman 1995). I shall say later why I think that the state is a problematic institution but I now take the view that the link between sovereignty and the state can and should be severed. Sovereignty, I will argue, is too important a concept to be treated as part of the state.[1]

Hence I make the case for reconstructing the concept in a feminist manner, and I shall try to explain what I mean by reconstructing. Concepts like freedom, equality, autonomy and obligation have been subject to reconstructive analysis (that is, reworked so as to become feminist) and so, I think, should the concept of sovereignty. Reconstructing a concept involves developing that concept in such a way that an alternative to the present can be explicitly posed. Not all concepts can be reconstructed – as we will see, concepts that imply division and exploitation (like patriarchy, class, etc.) cannot be part of an emancipated society, and I will attempt to link the notion of reconstruction with what I want to call a momentum concept, a concept that can progress but has no stopping point. I will try to reconstruct sovereignty so that it becomes a momentum concept, a concept with an egalitarian potential that is infinite in character.

Sovereignty has long been associated with the state. While mainstream discussion of the concept has generally ignored feminism (see for example Ashley 1988), this association has led feminists to identify it with patriarchy and domination, and they have therefore given it a hostile reception. To reconstruct sovereignty it needs to be detached from the state so that it can contribute positively to the emancipation of women. The state, I will argue, is an institution that claims a monopoly of legitimate force for a particular territory, and this makes the institution itself incoherent and contradictory. The state claims that which it does not and cannot have. As long as sovereignty is contaminated by statist theory and practice, it cannot be linked to the autonomy and freedom of the individual – of both women and men. This argument rests upon a distinction between state and government: the state involves organised violence, government negotiation and compromise.

This distinction between state and government translates into a distinction between force and constraint. While the notion of force is inimical to the exercise of sovereignty, the same is not true of constraint. Constraints, I will argue, compel people to change their behaviour in ways that are compatible with agency and autonomy. Order is possible without the state but not without government: violence can be dispensed with (as a way of tackling conflicts of interest) but not constraint.

This will bring me to an overall assessment of liberalism. In my view, feminism builds upon liberalism but cannot accept liberal premises as they stand. The individual is important but not as she or he is presented in traditional liberal theory. The individual must be analysed as a complex product of relationships. A relational approach, as presented here, does not suppress individuality but argues for a notion of the individual that is not only universal, but concrete. We are all individuals (hence the notion is universal) and individuality has to be developed (hence the notion is concrete). Relationships come out of history, so I will argue that a relational view of sovereignty seeks to be both absolute and relative. It is absolute because sovereignty is (and has always been) our capacity to govern our own lives, but it is also relative because sovereignty can only manifest itself through historical and constraining relationships. We are always moving towards sovereignty, although we never 'reach' it. Force destroys sovereignty since force destroys the relationships upon which sovereignty depends.

I will also say something about the relationship of care. This has traditionally been assumed to be 'selfless' and feminine in character. In fact, it is neither: care is a dimension of all relationships. Care can be empowering provided we move beyond the traditional 'choice' or dualism between autonomy, on the one hand, and commitment, on the other. We can and must be both autonomous and committed. The problem, as always, is the way in which the liberal tradition abstracts individuals from social relationships, and thus ignores the manner in which our sense of being individuals actually emerges.

We see this abstraction in the traditional liberal treatment of property. Liberalism is right to stress that individuals have property in their bodies as well as minds. But this property 'belongs' both to the individual and to society so that individuals need to treat both themselves and the bodies of others in a socially responsible and developmental fashion. To present the argument in a nutshell: we can only reconstruct the notion of sovereignty as self-government when the concept of sovereignty breaks with the abstract approach of the liberal tradition, and with what I think of as the dualisms of the state.

The traditional view: sovereignty and the state

Feminists have generally been critical of the state, and particularly those aspects of the state (in my view its essential properties) linked to force and repression. It is the association between state and sovereignty that causes many feminists to see sovereignty as an idea of domination and repression. Jones in *Compassionate Authority* (1993), for example, identifies the 'sovereignty trap' with statist concepts and practices, and argues that feminism must therefore reject the idea of sovereignty. Sylvester (1994) speaks of 'sovereign leviathans' (authoritarian sovereign states), Peterson (1992) refers to sovereignty as a 'masculinised deity' while Hutchings and Shildrick speak of 'sovereign individuals' as those that dominate and oppress (cited in Hoffman 2001:22).

It is true that Simone de Beauvoir in her *Second Sex* vacillates. She tends to see sovereignty as the attribute of men who dominate women. Sovereignty is equated with male privilege. The term involves violence and sometimes religion. There is a particularly powerful characterisation of sovereignty as a statist quality when she speaks of isolated and solitary women exchanging their servitude for a sovereign liberty while leaving the framework of a patriarchal society intact (1972:369). But if sovereignty normally denotes domination and repression in *The Second Sex,* it does not always do so. Sometimes de Beauvoir argues that women who assert their sovereignty liberate themselves, rather than becoming masters of men, and on one occasion at least, she equates sovereignty with autonomy (1972:359–60). Such a view has links with some interpretations of the concepts of agency and empowerment as discussed in later chapters of this volume.

The identification of sovereignty with the state (and repression) is, however, understandable when we remember that traditionally and conventionally, the state is linked to sovereignty. In James's account, the notion of the 'sovereign state' is almost pleonastic – that is, the state (and only the state) can be sovereign (James 1986). Indeed, some have even argued that a theory of sovereignty is impossible in international relations because there is no world state!

I define the state (following the celebrated definition of the sociologist Max Weber) as the institution that claims a monopoly of legitimate force, and it is in this claim to have a monopoly that I see the state's claim that it is a sovereign body – an institution with supreme, ultimate, power. I have been criticised for a 'rather essentialising analysis of the state' and 'reducing' the existence of states to a claim to exercise a monopoly of legitimate force. Why can't we, a critic asks, conceive of the state in more positive terms (Kandola 2001:150–1)?

But the definition that I critically utilise is not reductionist nor 'essentialising', since a reductionist or essentialist definition would argue that the state only consists of a single attribute and that the others are of no consequence. The state is not only about force: it is about force that claims to be legitimate, a force that is monopolised and territorially focused. These other attributes are important. They distinguish the force of the state from, say, the force of a robber or a brigand. But force is still the crucial property of the state. The view of the state, that it uses force *and* is also legitimate, assumes that legitimacy and force are of equal importance to the state, whereas (as I will show later) the use of force makes the question of legitimacy problematic. It is true that Rousseau speaks of forcing people in a legitimate polity to be free, but we rightly feel that this is a rather unpersuasive view of the state. We need to specify which attributes are central and which are secondary. In my view, Weber is right to see force as basic or central (Hoffman 1995:36–7).

Is this a negative view of the state? It certainly is, and I think that it is better to argue that when states act positively (by providing aid and resources, for example), they act in ways that are not statist as such but are *governmental*. Government involves the resolution of conflict through negotiation and arbitration, whereas states, strictly speaking, use force to tackle conflicts of interest. This distinction between government and state is important for three reasons.

Firstly, it helps to explain how humankind for most of its existence has settled conflicts of interest without an institution claiming a monopoly of legitimate force. Even today international society has order and is law-governed even though it has no overarching state. Secondly, the distinction between state and government shows the incoherence of the state. The state is an institution that claims something that it cannot possibly have. A state claims a monopoly of legitimate force, but ironically it is only because 'competitors' (that is, criminals, terrorists, etc.) contest the state's claim to have a monopoly of legitimate force that the state exists at all. A state that really did have a monopoly of legitimate force would have no reason to exist. Think of a state in which everyone acted peacefully and regarded all the laws as legitimate. It would be wholly redundant!

Thirdly, a 'negative' definition of the state makes it possible to make sense of the thesis (central to Marxist theory) of the 'withering away' of the state. This argument has (understandably) been discredited by the authoritarian character of Communist Party states, but it is an important one nevertheless. A stateless society is not some kind of mystical 'anarchy' that suddenly arrives but is rather a society in which conflicts of interest are dealt with not by force, but by social pressures. A dualistic theory of the state – that the state is some kind of 'balance' between force and consensus – cannot focus on the problematic character of force as a method of conflict resolution. Force actually suppresses conflict by elevating the victor and crushing the 'enemy' so that using force actually prevents conflict resolution. If we equate (as I think we should) politics and government, we come to the apparently paradoxical conclusion that the state actually works against political solutions to problems!

Thus, in my view, the increase of welfare provision in society can only be deemed statist if it increases the dependence of women upon their husbands and the state. Pateman (1989:200) is right to resist the argument that the 'welfare state' constitutes a form of public patriarchy, since welfare provision might empower women by providing them with resources that help them to resist the domination of men. (For related points see Mercy Ette's chapter in this volume.) To the extent that it does this, the state is acting governmentally, in my terminology. The 'welfare state' is a complex amalgam of the statist and the governmental. It uses force against people while helping them.

Ackelsburg speaks of the need for a state that is 'genuinely responsive to, and representative of the interests, of all its citizens' (Hoffman 2001:91). But although a liberal state is preferable to a non-liberal (explicitly authoritarian) state, it is naïve to take the state at face value and accept its claim to embody the interests of everybody as though it really did. The use of force to tackle conflicts of interest is an inherently exclusionary process, so that it is impossible for the state to represent all its citizens. Not only is it absurd to speak of the target of force being 'represented' (as though one authorises force against oneself), but all who live in the shadow of the state obey norms in the knowledge that these norms are backed by force. How can anyone be sure that they obey laws for purely moral reasons when they know that force will be used if these laws are broken? This is why I would argue that it is impossible to speak of anyone being free while the state exists.

The state is inherently patriarchal in character. States dominate women not as a result of an unfortunate accident, but because patriarchy is in the nature of the state. Why is this? I want to suggest three reasons. In the first place, states are generally run by men. This is, I think, a pretty manifest 'empirical' observation. Secondly, as Lerner (1986) has argued, male domination is only possible because states exist – historically the birth of patriarchy is linked to the rise of the state. And thirdly, the patriarchal nature of the state arises from the gendered nature of force itself. Force is not neutral: it is linked to male domination. Of course, women can use force, but they are acting patriarchally when they do so. Because the state ultimately relies upon force to tackle conflicts of interest, it subscribes to a oneness, a monolithicity that excludes the pluralism that is crucial if the interests of women are to be recognised as distinct from those of men. Historically, states explicitly excluded women from ruling: now the exclusion is implicit (at least in liberal states). In my view, a feminised state is a contradiction in terms.

A critique of the traditional view of the state is crucial to a critique of sovereignty. It is impossible to coherently reconstruct the notion of sovereignty unless we detach it from the state, since the problems with the traditionalist notion of sovereignty arise precisely from its long association with the state. Those who criticise sovereignty are criticising its statist character: to feminise sovereignty, we have to break its linkage with the state.

Reconstructing the concept

Feminists of the second wave dismissed 'malestream' concepts and 'unmasked' classical political thinkers. Classical political thinkers either submerged their patriarchal prejudices in abstractions, like the 'individual' or 'men' (think of Machiavelli, for example) or they made assumptions that traditional commentators considered natural and normal, and unworthy of remarking upon. Of course, feminists have always assumed that an emancipated society is possible, since there would be little point in attacking patriarchal political theory if a post-patriarchal order is out of the question. For this reason it can be said that a concern with reconstructing political concepts has always been implicit. But this concern has, more recently, become explicit as feminists have concerned themselves with reworking earlier concepts in order to argue for an emancipatory alternative to a society dominated by men.

The question arises: which concepts can and should be reconstructed, and which cannot? Reference is sometimes made to 'revisioning' political theory but this 'revisioning' might be seen simply as a process of 'engendering' – that is, bringing to the fore the way in which a particular concept affects men and women. To reconstruct a concept involves rather more than 'revisioning' it. Reconstructing a concept means transforming it so that it can contribute positively to the struggle for a post-patriarchal society. Those concepts that cannot help to realise a post-patriarchal society (and are barriers to its development), for example, patriarchy, the state, violence, must be discarded. This is not to say that they should be ignored, but we do need to look beyond them, rather than reformulate them.

Elsewhere I have argued (2001:23–6) that reconstructed concepts can be presented as momentum concepts, on the grounds that they have a potential for egalitarianism and are emancipatory in character. The momentum concept is progressive – it embodies a logic of transformation – whereas concepts that cannot be reconstructed are static – they obstruct rather than contribute positively to transformation. The notion of momentum helps to emphasise that the process of emancipation or transformation is infinite in character, so that it would be wrong to imagine that a concept like equality or freedom can actually be 'realised' in some grandly culminating point of history.

Yet some feminists who see the importance of reconstruction in general, do not see the importance of reconstructing the notion of sovereignty in particular. They have assumed that sovereignty is a 'malestream' concept that cannot be reclaimed or reconstructed.

Sovereignty and force

Women particularly suffer from force, whether this is domestic or international. As the UN Report at the Beijing Conference puts it, 'Violence against women is pervasive in all societies, cutting across boundaries of class, ethnicity, religion, age and a society's level of development' (cited by Bryson 1999:4).

While the notion of state sovereignty is tied to force, force is inimical to a reconstructed notion of sovereignty. It is often argued that force is only problematic when it is illegitimate or arbitrary, but a moment's thought will reveal that force itself cannot be other than illegitimate or arbitrary. For the notion of legitimacy implies limits, and that which is arbitrary is unpredictable. Although attempts to limit force and make it predictable are laudable and should be encouraged; strictly speaking, force always defies limits and cannot be applied in a wholly predictable fashion. Liberals are right to juxtapose force and freedom, since they see that when force is resorted to, a person cannot be said to be autonomous. Agency is undermined by force, for while Rousseau is correct to argue that force cannot produce morality, he is scandalously wrong to suggest that a person can be 'forced to be free' (1968:52, 64).

Obviously force itself is a complex concept, but I prefer a 'physicalist' definition that identifies force with the infliction of harm. Abuse is a form of force, whereas rudeness (though it may well cause force) is not force as such since it leaves agency (a person's freedom to choose) intact. (For a related discussion see Kalpana Wilson's chapter on agency in this volume.) However, I do see force and violence as broadly synonymous. Anyone who has been on the receiving end of state force will see the distinction between force and violence as unconvincing. Not so, the distinction between force and constraint.

Some make a distinction between force and coercion. Hinsley argues, for example, that in a stateless society, authority relies upon 'psychological and moral coercion' rather than force (1986:16). In much of my writing, I found this distinction persuasive but I would now prefer to defend the conventional view of coercion as the credible threat of force. What is impossible, however, is to conceive of a society without constraining pressures to maintain order. Indeed, the distinction between state and government noted above translates into a distinction between force and constraint. It is true that Marx allows of coercion by capitalists where no force is involved, and John Stuart Mill speaks of the individual being subject to the moral coercion of public opinion rather than the force of the state (cited in Hoffman 2001:171–2). Coercion is, however, linked closely to force, since the threat to use a force that is not credible (think of a child shooting with a water pistol) cannot be called coercion.

This is why I see coercion as more or less linked to force, and as something that we should seek to avoid. Constraint is another matter. Constraints arise where a person is 'compelled' to act through pressures that are structural and impersonal. Marx's comment that people enter into relations that are independent of their will certainly implies constraint. Constraint is unavoidable and exists in all societies. Marx speaks of the existence of a 'public power' in stateless societies (Marx and Engels 1967:104), and this (like power in general) points to the existence of constraint. Mill, for his part, refers to 'natural penalties' (Mill 1974:144) to which all individuals are subject simply because they live in society. These arise when a person pursues their own interest in a way that impacts negatively upon another: for example, a person who was once religious finds that since she has become an atheist her friends no longer want to have coffee with her. As Mill's term suggests, these penalties are surely constraining in character.

It is because we are captive to the classical liberal idea that freedom implies an absence of relationships that we find it difficult to accept that constraints are a condition for, and not a negation of, the exercise of free will. The classical anarchist argument, that it is possible to govern oneself or for a community to govern itself without constraint, is not persuasive. Sovereignty, therefore, is undermined by force but requires constraint, since without the latter it is impossible to resolve conflicts of interest between individuals, between societies or indeed within the individual her – or himself. A clear distinction between force and constraint is crucial if we are to target force as a barrier to sovereignty (and thus government).

Of course, this is not to say that force itself will immediately disappear from human affairs. Force arises because common interests are insufficiently cohesive to allow differences and disputes to be negotiated. Women, who have been the victim of force, may well seek the employment of counter-force to protect themselves but the use of force in these circumstances, while entirely understandable, can never be legitimate, and can only be defended as a way of allowing a breathing space for policies that will cement common interests. Those who commit the crime of rape are, it is certainly true, insufficiently punished. But punishment in itself cannot really resolve the problem. A counter-force can at best succeed in suppressing patriarchal domination: it cannot eliminate it.

Feminism and relationships

Feminists have rightly challenged the abstract character of liberalism, and its notion of the abstract individual. They have seen abstraction as an activity that extinguishes difference. Abstraction in this pejorative sense is linked to violence: it erases the identity of particular individuals and can easily be used to naturalise and normalise male domination.

It is, however, of great importance to stress that in challenging liberalism, one is neither inverting it nor rejecting it. Anarchists tend to invert liberalism; authoritarians reject it. We do not see the idea of relationships as displacing the individual, but on the contrary, the relational approach makes the idea of the individual much richer and more concrete. The uniqueness of the individual does not stand in opposition to the relationships into which she or he enters, for their relationships make individuals what they are. Relationships are not, therefore, a barrier to uniqueness: rather it should be said that they explain and express uniqueness. It is true that classical liberalism privileges the individual over relationships, but nothing is gained by inverting this position and privileging relationships over the individual.

Hence notions associated with liberalism like 'rights', autonomy and privacy need to be reconstructed, not rejected. (Ruth Lister's chapter in this volume can be seen as a contribution to this process.) Sovereignty, as I define it, is a post-liberal, not an anti-liberal concept. By this I mean that sovereignty is a concept that embraces but goes beyond liberalism. It is sometimes suggested that relationships are dependencies that undermine the autonomy of the individual. But this sets up a dualism between autonomy and dependency, and like all dualisms it is false. The autonomous self, it has been well said, is already connected (Minnow and Shanley 1997:102, 105), since it is only through our relationship with others that we can act as free individuals. A relational approach does not contradict the importance of agency: on the contrary, it seeks to explain it (see Kalpana Wilson's chapter in this volume).

Offen identifies a 'relational' approach with a view that stresses difference – but difference is here construed in traditional terms. Relational feminism, in her view, emphasises the distinctive character of women as a group with child bearing/nurturing capacities. It belongs to a continental European tradition that she distinguishes from the 'individualistic' feminism of Anglo-American culture, and she argues that both traditions need to find a place in a feminism that focuses on the importance of self-sovereignty (1992:76, 78, 85). This is surely correct, although in my view both traditions need to be reconstructed. As Offen defines them, they are each one-sided – each expressing the limitations of the liberal tradition. A relational approach has to be created that incorporates but goes beyond the liberal tradition.

The sovereign individual is a person who respects and works with others, just as these others respect and work with themselves. Hence sovereignty implies plurality, since individuals enter into a multiplicity of different relationships, both with themselves and with others. A person does not have one 'ultimate' identity but has many ways of expressing themselves. The notion of conflict is, it seems to me, built into the notion of a relationship. We often mistakenly assume that conflicts are clashes that involve violence, but conflicts can also arise when tension rather than violence is involved. In fact, it is only these latter conflicts that can be resolved (rather than suppressed) since to resolve a conflict, social pressure rather than force needs to be employed.

Conflict arises from difference, and it is impossible to have a relationship without differences between the parties being apparent. If two people were identical in every respect, they could not be related to one another. But difference is not the same as division. Divisions are 'differences' that can only be settled with force, whereas differences are relational and can only be resolved through social sanctions. When force is used, one party becomes a 'thing' and an inter-personal relationship is destroyed. Sovereignty involves difference and conflict, but not force.

As a concept, sovereignty is absolute – but it is also relative. It is absolute because individuals can govern their own lives, but sovereignty is also a relative concept, since individuals – unlike gods! – are part of history and therefore continually change. Were sovereignty 'purely' absolute, it would be outside of history. Were sovereignty 'purely' relative as a concept, it could be argued that every individual is as sovereign as every other. Sovereignty would merely lie in the eye of its beholder. This is why I argue that sovereignty is both absolute and relative.

Defining sovereignty as self-government means that it is a state of autonomy towards which we progress as barriers to sovereignty are removed – force, patriarchy, repressive hierarchy. However, we never actually 'reach' it. To realise sovereignty once and for all would be to privilege some particular point in time. Such a position is an absurdity because it flies in the face of the character of relationships as historical constructs. This is why I refer to sovereignty as a momentum concept – it has a progressive character. We move towards sovereignty – it is an absolute goal – but since we are relational beings, we can never arrive at a station that declares 'You are now totally sovereign, there is no further progress to go!'

Sovereignty, care and reproductive rights

Feminists have rightly concerned themselves with the concept of care. It might be thought that the obligation to care for children or the elderly makes sovereignty impossible since it appears that the carer has lost her or his autonomy in devoting themselves to others.

Care has been traditionally seen as something that is exclusively the prerogative of women. But this is not the problem with care – it is the problem of patriarchy and inequality. Bubeck is right to argue that the performance of care needs to be seen 'as part of what it means, or it implies, to be a member of a political community' (1995:35). (For development of this point see Ruth Lister's chapter in this volume.) Care is a dimension of relationships, and therefore care can only be said to contradict sovereignty by those who perceive sovereignty as the absence of relationships – who see sovereignty as an abstract autonomy, a freedom to act without constraint. Of course, patriarchal prejudice arises from the fact that women give birth to children, but while this may be relevant in explaining why, for example, many women oppose war and violence, it is quite wrong to assume that the biological capacity to give birth makes women, rather than men, into 'natural' carers.

The care relationship has traditionally been taken to mean that carers lose their self-interest and merge themselves with the reality of those for whom they care. But Brace is right to point out that this is an abstract position. It is a one-sided 'communitarianism' and a rejection of the importance of the individual. It is a position that is anti-liberal rather than post-liberal in character. We need a notion of sovereignty that allows us to 'imagine and re-imagine ourselves on our own terms'. Brace refers to Nedelsky's comment that the image of skin rather than walls better captures the concept of a relationship, and she notes wryly that 'we need to reclaim some kind of sovereignty from the ideal of selflessness, otherwise we are going to find far too many people getting under our skin' (1997:151–3).

Hirschmann warns that a feminist theory of obligation (and thus of care) does not seek 'to replace a male-model rights orientation, or consent, with a female, care-centred notion of obligation simpliciter' (1992:306). The liberal distinction between obligation and consent involves one of those either/or propositions and is a mystification of human activity. Of course, consent is crucial to sovereignty, but it is not contradicted by the existence of obligation, for no relationship is possible unless the linkage with others endows both rights and imposes duties. The idea that a person can have rights *without* duties, can consent *without* obligation, enjoy freedom *without* necessity, assumes that people live in a world in which there are no relationships and thus constraints. Such a world can only be the classical liberal concept of a state of nature, and indeed long after liberals have apparently accepted that humans are social in character, they continue to privilege agency over structure. They take the view that a person can be free in a vacuum, in a world without context. Men are deemed to have the agency, while women are prisoners of the structure. You can only privilege agency over structure if you assume that individuals are self-contained atoms, that they are not part of relationships already. We must, as Hirshmann puts it, go 'beyond such oppositions' (1992:306), since these oppositions prevent the construction of sovereignty as an emancipatory and egalitarian concept.

The liberal tradition establishes the notion that the individual has property in her or his person. Enjoying this bodily integrity is crucial to freedom and to sovereignty. The problem with the liberal tradition is that the body of the individual is treated abstractly. It is assumed that the body 'belongs' simply to the individual, and because it is their property, they are entitled to do as they please with it. Mill had begun to break significantly with the liberal tradition when he argued that the individual cannot be free to sell themselves into slavery: they cannot be free to alienate their freedom (1974:173).

The implication of this is extremely interesting. The body of the individual is theirs but only to develop, not to destroy. While it is true that individuals are sovereign over their own bodies, this sovereignty has to be relationally conceived. Hence the body of the individual also 'belongs' to society at large, since bodies like minds are moulded by the relationships that people have both with themselves and those around them. The liberal tradition, taken to its logical conclusion, implies a sovereign right to self-destruction – a sovereign entitlement not to be sovereign. An impossible paradox. The liberal position also implies that since the body is abstractly conceived, some may own the bodies of others. Hence, even when liberals reject outright slavery, they still see the bodies of women as the property of men so that a woman's right to bodily integrity is subject to predatory attacks and possessive attitudes of all kinds.

Daniels (1993) rejects the notion of 'fetal rights' – the idea that an unborn child has rights, an idea used by anti-abortionists to deny women reproductive autonomy. Daniels argues (in my view, quite rightly) that this notion is contrary to a woman's self-sovereignty. Women cannot be sovereign unless they enjoy bodily integrity, but bodily integrity interpreted in a relational rather than an atomistic manner. Our right over our body arises not because our bodies are private property that we can dispose of as we please, but because our bodies belong both to ourselves and to society at large.

The notion of foetal rights can only arise as the result of an abstract, liberal approach. Liberals assume that if things are the same, then they cannot be different and if they are different, they cannot be the same. Of course, the foetus is the same as a birthed individual in the sense it has life and like all forms of life (particularly ones so close to humanity), it is tragic and unpleasant to extinguish it. But it does not follow that because we have something in common with a foetus, we are not also different, and it is surely grotesque to assume that foetuses (like other non-human beings) have rights, simply because humans have rights. Women, like people in general, cannot do what they like to their bodies, but they surely have the right to terminate pregnancies where these are deemed to threaten their well-being and development. Daniels argues eloquently for a culture of compassion and a 'demasculinized' public world (1993:131, 138–9). Daniels demonstrates that feminism has had an impact on the way sovereignty is defined, but her notion of self-sovereignty needs to exert a wider influence on those who continue to identify sovereignty with domination and repression.

To work towards a world in which men are not privileged over women, we need a notion of sovereignty that is relational in character and breaks with the use of force as a means of tackling conflicts of interest.

Conclusion

Although some male writers on the state, such as Bob Connell (1990) and Rob Walker (1999), are clearly influenced by feminism, they do not tackle the question of sovereignty; those, such as Ashley (1988), who write about sovereignty seem to ignore feminism. Much feminist thought too still tends to identify sovereignty with the state and hence sees it as inherently patriarchal. Unlike, say, ideas of freedom, autonomy and authority, the concept is not reconstructed but rejected.

Sovereignty is a pluralistic concept. It embraces the individual, the group, the community, the nation and the world at large. Each 'level' impacts upon the other, so that it is impossible for one to be sovereign at the expense of, or in abstraction from, the other. In my view, feminising sovereignty involves not only the awareness of this plurality, but an appreciation of the masculinist character of force with its monopolistic and exclusionary properties. Because the state is an institution that uses force to tackle conflicts of interest, sovereignty needs to be detached from the state, defined as an institution that claims a monopoly of legitimate force. The state is not the same as government. Indeed, it is the confusion of state and government that makes it impossible to focus on the patriarchal character of the state. A distinction between state and government enables us to look towards the development of a stateless society in a realistic manner. The link between state and sovereignty – though deeply embedded in so much of the literature – is a fallacious one, and it accounts for the fact that sovereignty itself is often depicted in patriarchal terms.

Sovereignty is both an absolute as well as a relative concept. We move towards sovereignty over our lives as we govern ourselves to an increasing extent. That is the absolute dimension of sovereignty. But as historical beings, we can only increase sovereignty in a particular context so that it is impossible to realise sovereignty in a finite and complete way. Hence it is a relative concept as well. Liberalism speaks of individuals as 'sovereign' but treated this sovereignty in an abstract and statist manner. To feminise sovereignty, the concept needs to be reconstructed, so that it is both rooted in, but goes beyond, the liberal tradition.

Mainstream political theory is not only dominated by men, but by men with patriarchal views. Feminist theory is seen as irrelevant and usually ignored, or where it is not ignored, it is treated with condescension and scorn. This is a great pity. For feminists (who need not be but usually are women) raise critical questions about political theory. They speak for those who have been marginalised and excluded by the state, and it is feminism that has made it possible to argue that the process of critical conceptual reconstruction should not stop with concepts like freedom and autonomy, but should press on to include notions of sovereignty and the state. Feminists have often been unwilling to extend their critical approach to the state and to the question of sovereignty, but the reconstruction of the concept of sovereignty flows from the logic of feminist analysis.

Patriarchy, it has to be said, distorts the lives of both men and women, even though it is true that men are apparent beneficiaries of patriarchy and women the victims. In the same way, feminism is a democratic doctrine that concerns itself particularly with the emancipation of women, but in a relational world it is impossible for women to become free without ridding men of the pseudo-freedom that has made them into tyrants and bullies for thousands of years – indeed, since the state developed, and sovereignty was wrongly presented as domination and superiority.

Key writers and further reading

Very little has been written directly on feminism and sovereignty except for my *Gender and Sovereignty* (2001). Jones (1993) offers a negative view of sovereignty, while Daniels (1993) looks at the notion of self-sovereignty. Negative and positive views of sovereignty and women can be found in S. de Beauvoir's classic *Second Sex* (1972). The feminist International Relations literature is worth consulting, particularly Pettman (1996) and Sylvester (1994). The key debate here is whether sovereignty is an inherently patriarchal concept or can be used positively to affirm women's autonomy.

In terms of mainstream literature, Bartelson (1995) and Weber (1995) are difficult but interesting post-structuralist accounts. Walker and Mendlovitz (1990) contains fascinating material. James (1986) is a widely read realist account, while Hinsley's *Sovereignty* (1986) is a classic. So in a different way is Ashley (1988). Newman (1996) makes a number of analytical distinctions that deserve thought. The key debates here are whether the term should be abandoned and the question of its relation to the state. I have looked at these questions in my *Sovereignty* (1998), and material on the issue of sovereignty and Northern Ireland, South Africa and Chile, globalisation, the state, the British parliament, the European Union, ecology and the self can be found in J. Hoffman and L. Brace (1997).

Note

1 I am persuaded by my colleague in the Department of Politics at the University of Leicester, Dr Laura Brace, that sovereignty is one of the concepts that should be reclaimed. We produced an edited volume, *Reclaiming Sovereignty* (London: Pinter, 1997). Needless to say, the title was Laura Brace's idea!

Bibliography

Ashley, R. (1988) 'Untying the Sovereign State: A Double Reading of the Anarchy Problematique', *Millennium* 17:2, 227–62.

Bartelson, J. (1995) *A Genealogy of Sovereignty* (Cambridge: Cambridge University Press).

Beauvoir, S. de (1972) *The Second Sex* (Harmondsworth: Penguin).

Brace, L. (1997) 'Imagining the Boundaries of a Sovereign Self', in L. Brace and J. Hoffman (eds), *Reclaiming Sovereignty* (London: Pinter), 137–54.

Bryson, V. (1999) *Feminist Debates* (Basingstoke: Macmillan).

Bubeck, D. (1995) *A Feminist Approach to Citizenship* (Florence: European University Institute).

Connell, R. (1990) 'The State, Gender and Sexual Politics: Theory and Appraisal', *Theory and Society* 19, 507–44.

Daniels, C. (1993) *At Women's Expense* (Cambridge MA: Harvard University Press).

Hinsley, F. (1986) *Sovereignty* (Cambridge: Cambridge University Press).

Hirschmann, N. (1992) *Rethinking Obligation* (Ithaca and London: Cornell University Press).

Hoffman, J. (1995) *Beyond the State* (Cambridge: Polity).

Hoffman, J. (1998) *Sovereignty* (Buckingham: Open University Press).

Hoffman, J. (2001) *Gender and Sovereignty* (Basingstoke: Palgrave).

Hoffman, J. and Brace, L. (1997) (eds) *Reclaiming Sovereignty* (London: Pinter).

James, A. (1986) *Sovereign Statehood* (London: Allen and Unwin).

Jones, K. (1993) *Compassionate Authority* (New York and London: Routledge).

Kandola, J. (2001) 'Review of J. Hoffman's *Sovereignty*', *International Feminist Journal of Politics* 3:1, 149–51.

Lerner, G. (1986) *The Creation of Patriarchy* (New York: Oxford University Press).

Marx, K. and Engels, F. (1967) *The Communist Manifesto* (Harmondsworth: Penguin).

Mill, J. S. (1974) *On Liberty* (Harmondsworth: Penguin).

Minnow, M. and Shanley, M. (1997) 'Revisioning the Family', in M. Shanley and U. Narayan (eds), *Reconstructing Political Theory* (Cambridge: Polity), 84–108.

Newman, M. (1996) *Democracy, Sovereignty and the European Union* (London: Hurst).

Offen, K. (1992) 'Defining Feminism: A Comparative Historical Approach', in G. Bock and S. James (eds), *Beyond Equality and Difference* (London and New York: Routledge), 69–88.

Pateman, C. (1989) *The Disorder of Woman* (Cambridge: Polity Press).

Pettman, J. (1996) *Worlding Women* (London: Routledge).

Rousseau, J.-J. (1968) *The Social Contract and Discourses* (London: Dent).

Sylvester, C. (1994) *Feminist Theory and International Relations in a Postmodern Era* (Cambridge: Cambridge University Press).

Walker, R. (1999) 'Citizen After the Modern Subject', in K. Hutchings and R. Dannreuther (eds), *Cosmopolitan Citizenship* (Basingstoke: Macmillan), 171–200.

Walker, R. and Mendlovitz, S. (1990) *Contending Sovereignties* (Boulder and London: Lynne Reiner).

Weber, C. (1995) *Sovereignty* (Cambridge: Cambridge University Press).

5

Citizenship

Ruth Lister

Introduction

Citizenship is frequently described as 'an essentially contested concept' (Gallie 1956) that, for all its familiarity, defies easy definition. Typically, its key elements are taken to comprise: membership of a community; the rights and obligations that flow from that membership, including in particular political obligations; and equality of status. It can be understood as both a status and as a practice. Some formulations confine it to the relationship between individuals and the state. Contemporary citizenship theory is more likely to follow the feminist scholars Pnina Werbner and Nira Yuval-Davis in conceptualising it more broadly to embrace 'a more total relationship, inflected by identity, social positioning, cultural assumptions, institutional practices and a sense of belonging' (1999:4).

Citizenship, perhaps more than any other political concept, was traditionally understood as 'just something for the boys'. This chapter starts by outlining briefly the feminist critique of traditional formulations of citizenship in the 'malestream'. This critique has led to a rich feminist literature, which has, in differing ways, attempted to 're-gender' citizenship so that it better fits the 'girls'. This re-gendering raises a number of dilemmas. The chapter will focus on two central ones: whether a woman-friendly model should be ostensibly gender-neutral or explicitly gender-differentiated; and the status of the private sphere in relation to citizenship. In terms of the impact of feminist analysis, the chapter will conclude by arguing first, that it has contributed to a conceptualisation of citizenship that is more sensitive to difference and diversity; and second that, with some exceptions, it *has* influenced the mainstream debate.

Citizenship in the 'malestream': the feminist critique

Historically, the two dominant models were that of the citizen-political actor (in the civic republican tradition) and citizen-the-rights-bearer (in the liberal tradition). Civic republicanism has its roots in classical Greece, where political participation as civic duty and the expression of the citizen's full potential as a political being represented the essence of citizenship. Contemporary civic republicanism similarly emphasises civic duty, the submission of individual interest to that of the common good and the elevation of the public sphere in which the citizen is constituted as a political actor. The prioritisation of obligations and the wider common good is found, too, in communitarianism, which represents an offshoot of the civic republican tradition. Communitarianism also places great emphasis on belonging and on common cultural identity, values and norms.

In contrast, the liberal model places the individual and 'his' rights at the centre of its philosophy of citizenship. Although rooted in seventeenth century liberalism, the classic contemporary exposition of this model was provided by T. H. Marshall after the Second World War. He identified three elements: civil, political and social rights. In his account, civil rights, according each individual equal status before the law, formed the platform upon which political and social rights were in turn built in an evolutionary development. (This evolutionary account has been disputed by feminists and others for its Anglo-centric and male bias and for ignoring the conflicts sometimes involved in the development of citizenship rights.) Since Marshall wrote, neo-liberals have contested the validity of the extension of rights beyond the civil and political spheres to include the social rights provided by the welfare state.

Both the main citizenship traditions were constructed within a male template. Prior to the late twentieth century feminist critique, malestream theorisation of citizenship tended to ignore the gendered nature of this template and the ways in which women's gradual achievement of civil, political and social rights often followed a different pattern from men's. To the extent that women's earlier exclusion was acknowledged, it tended to be dismissed as an historical aberration now more or less effectively remedied. So, for example, Adrian Oldfield claims that it does not 'require too much imagination to extend the concept of the "citizen" to include women'; leaving aside Machiavelli and even allowing for the 'citizen-soldier', there is, he asserts, 'nothing aggressively male' about the concept (1990:59).

Feminist analysis, in contrast, has illuminated how, in both theory and practice, despite its claims to universalism, citizenship has been quintessentially male and it has been a false universalism that citizenship upheld. Thus, women's exclusion (and the chequered nature of their inclusion) far from being an aberration has been integral to the theory and practice of citizenship. It has operated at two levels. At what we might call the surface level, in the civic republican tradition the active participation of male citizens was predicated on the exclusion of women who sustained male participation by their labour in the private sphere. In the liberal tradition, married women's legal subordination helped define their husbands' status as citizen heads of household.

At a deeper level, it reflected an essentialist categorisation of men and women's qualities and capacities, rooted in the public–private dichotomy. On the 'public' side stood the disembodied citizen who displayed the necessary 'male' qualities of impartiality, rationality, independence and political agency. This was upheld by the 'private' side to which embodied, partial, irrational, emotional and dependent women were relegated.

The wider feminist challenge to the public–private dichotomy and to narrow definitions of 'the political', which have underpinned much traditional political theory, has been central to feminist critiques of 'malestream' citizenship theory.[1] In most cases, it has not been a question of arguing for the complete dissolution of the categories 'public' and 'private' but for the re-articulation of the relationship between the two within a broad conception of the political, which is not confined to any particular sphere of action.

At the heart of this re-articulation stands the status accorded to unpaid care work in relation to the rights and responsibilities of citizenship and, related to that, the gendered division of domestic labour and time (see also Valerie Bryson's chapter). More fundamentally feminist theorists have also developed critiques of malestream articulations of rights and obligations.

Rights and obligations

There is no single feminist position on rights (Hobson and Lister 2002). Many feminist campaigns have involved demands for equal rights with men or for rights particular to women, notably reproductive rights. Liberal feminist activists, in particular, have used the language of rights. A number of feminist theorists, not just those labelled liberal, also underline the value of rights claims, particularly in the context of political struggles of marginalised groups such as Black women or disabled women. Feminists working in the field of international development have contributed to a conceptualisation of rights as shaped through struggle and have underlined their value to women in a development context. An example is Shireen Huq, in an article about an activist women's organisation in Bangladesh, which uses a rights discourse. She argues that 'for feminists, a rights-based approach offers the opportunity to contest notions of unequal worth embedded in many cultures and given statutory recognition in their laws; and to demand that notions of citizenship be extended to women and be reconceptualised accordingly' (2000:74).

Others, notably Scandinavian feminist researchers, emphasise the inter-connectedness of civil, political and social rights. Social rights are particularly valued by socialist feminists. They can, though, be wary of rights-talk because of the dangers of abstracting rights from their historical and political context and of ignoring the gap between formal rights and 'really existing citizenship', which depends on the ability to access and exercise rights (Molyneux 2000:122).

Socialist feminists also share with others, particularly relational feminists, a dislike of rights' individualistic quality, especially as interpreted in the United States. Steeped in liberal individualism, the rights-bearer is perceived as a self-sufficient 'cerebral rather than physical being', independent of social relationships in general and caring relationships in particular (Bryson 1999:12). This has been described as male 'political solipsism' by Alison Jaggar (1983, cited in Bryson 1999). Radical feminism's critique of rights stems also from its analysis of patriarchal power relationships. Rights cannot be divorced from such relationships and they therefore reflect dominant male values. Many of the debates within feminism around rights have been played out over the issue of reproductive rights (Bryson 1999). This has contributed to new formulations of rights, which 'reflect an "embodied" rather than a disembodied understanding of what it is to be human, and hence an embodied, rather than abstract, view of citizenship' (Kabeer 2005:11).

This more embodied view of citizenship also underpins much feminist theorising on citizenship obligations and responsibilities, which have come to dominate Western political discourse on citizenship in recent years. An important example is Nancy J. Hirschmann's essay on 'Rethinking Obligation for Feminism' (1996). Hirschmann criticises the construction of obligation associated with social contract theory (see Laura Brace's chapter and also the discussion in John Hoffman's chapter), rooted in individual consent and choice. She does not reject the notion of obligation outright but instead suggests an alternative conceptualisation of it, which 'does not depend on explicit choice and takes care and responsibility as central elements of a moral schema that has existed at least as long as the social contract' (Hirschmann 1996:162–3). Further, she posits that

> a theory that began with connection would try to determine how to carve out a space for the self without violating the imperative of care. By placing obligation at the center, and making freedom something to be justified and explained, the importance of relationship to human life is brought out of the shadows of the sequestered private realm and into the public discourse of political theory. (ibid: 170)

Selma Sevenhuijsen has developed such a conceptualisation more specifically in relation to citizenship, making a clearer distinction between obligation and responsibility, which tend to be used interchangeably in everyday political discourse. In a critique of the formulation of obligations in Anthony Giddens' *The Third Way*, she identifies as problematic 'the ease with which legalistic notions of rights and obligations are pasted onto notions of responsibility' (Sevenhuijsen 2000:27). The philosophical distinction between obligations and responsibilities is critical to Sevenhuijsen's argument: obligations are generated externally whereas responsibilities derive from the individual herself in relation with others.

This distinction, she maintains, reflects the different ontological and philosophical foundations of the two concepts. She suggests that the construction of citizenship obligation in third way politics derives from

> a wish to build the bridges between individuals and society that seem necessary when one takes the detached autonomous individual right holder as the subject of normative argument. Obligations are then derived from rights in an urge to mitigate or counter the detachment that may arise in a society of atomistic, self-governed individuals. Conversely, the feminist ethic of care takes the idea of self-in-relationship as a point of entry for thinking about responsibility and obligation. The moral subject in the discourse of care always already lives in a network of relationships, in which s/he has to find balances between different forms of responsibility (for the self, for others and for the relationships between them). (ibid: 10)

This position underpins Sevenhuijsen's reconceptualisation of citizenship, grounded in an ethic of care and the responsibilities to which it gives rise, which she offers as a corrective to the dominance of paid work as the primary citizenship obligation in contemporary government policy in many industrialised societies. This is one example of what we might call the 're-gendering of citizenship', to which I now turn.

Feminist dilemmas in re-gendering citizenship

A central question posed by this collection is whether the selected concepts can simply be extended to include women, or whether, instead, they must be radically transformed or even abandoned. Such questions have driven much feminist writing on citizenship. There are some who would abandon the concept, as quintessentially exclusionary. This position is rarely articulated in print, although Gillian Pascall (1993) has expressed deep ambivalence about a concept which has been so problematic for women. Likewise, Anne Phillips has warned that 'in a period in which feminism is exploring the problems in abstract universals, citizenship may seem a particularly unpromising avenue to pursue' (1993:87).

Nevertheless, many feminists have gone down that avenue, contributing to a rich seam of scholarship. Why? One reason is that, like Everest, it is there. Moreover, it is there in a prominent position in both academic and political debate. As the rationale for this book indicates, 'man-made' concepts such as citizenship cannot simply be left to 'the boys' to play with. Their implications for the rest of us are too important. Moreover, citizenship is seen as a concept with real potential value for feminist analysis and politics. It has contributed to the theorisation of women's political, economic and social position. According to Yuval-Davis, feminists in a number of countries, have found the notion of citizenship to be the most appropriate political mobilization tool in the post-Beijing era' (1997:22).

She and Werbner suggest that it 'provides women with a valuable weapon in the fight for human, democratic, civil and social rights' (Werbner and Yuval-Davis 1999:28). As such, it has also been deployed by a range of social movements in which women are active and in which they claim full citizenship as, for example, Black women, disabled women, lesbian women. A number of feminist citizenship theorists have thus highlighted the importance of political agency, which provides the link between conceptions of citizenship as an active participatory practice and as a set of rights, which are the object of struggle (Siim 2000; Lister 2003). However, it should also be noted that the concept of agency is itself critiqued by some feminists, as discussed by Kalpana Wilson in this volume.

Given the contested nature of citizenship as a concept, it is not surprising that the issue of how to re-gender it is itself a source of debate. At the heart of the debate is the question I have posed elsewhere: 'is the goal an ostensibly gender-neutral conception of citizenship which enables women to participate as equals with men in the public sphere ... or an explicitly gender-differentiated conception which recognises and values women's responsibilities in the private sphere?' (Lister 2003:9). The chapter will first discuss the two models that flow from this formulation and then explore some difficult issues raised by the relationship of citizenship to the private sphere.

Equal or different?

The two broad approaches to the re-gendering of citizenship, which can be identified in the literature, are rooted in the long-standing equality vs difference debate. This debate has centred on whether women's claims to full citizenship should be based on their equality with men or on their particular qualities and responsibilities. On the one side is what might be called an 'ostensibly gender-neutral model'. It is gender-neutral because it treats gender as irrelevant to the allocation and exercise of citizenship rights and obligations. However, it is appropriate to add 'ostensibly' because, as Judith Squires (1998) pointed out in an astute book review, I and others had shown how it is not really gender-neutral at all.

Indeed, this is the main criticism of the model. It takes the existing male template of citizenship as given and simply attempts to ensure that women have equal access to and status within it. In particular, it emphasises women's full and equal participation with men in formal politics as a matter of equality and justice, competition on equal terms in the labour market and equal social rights (all constructed on a male model).

On the other side is an 'explicitly gender-differentiated model', which critiques the male template and which recognises women's particular concerns and contribution and, in particular, values their care responsibilities in the private sphere. Historically, the attempt to forge a gender-differentiated model was rooted in maternalist arguments for treating motherhood as the equivalent of a male civic republicanism grounded in active political participation and the ability to bear arms. Mothers' contribution to citizenship was to raise the next generation of citizens. In contemporary feminism, proponents of maternalism have, in different contexts, focused on improving the material conditions of women as mothers and on enhancing their political position and projecting their values into political life as a legitimate basis for women's citizenship from a position of moral superiority.

Other feminists have rejected maternal thinking as the basis for citizenship, in part on the grounds that it reinforces 'a one-dimensional view of women as creatures of the family' (Dietz 1985:20). Another argument is that it projects the kind of 'sexually segregated norms of citizenship' that Kathleen B. Jones has warned against when constructing a woman-friendly polity (1988:18). As Carole Pateman (1989) has reminded us, it is just such sexually segregated norms that have served to subordinate and marginalise women as citizens. This has led a number of feminists, sympathetic to some of the values promoted by maternalism, to argue for a non-maternalistic conceptualisation of difference around the broader notion of care and an ethic of care, which is not confined to women or mothers.

The case for an ethic of care as a resource for political citizenship has been put by feminists such as Diemut Bubeck (1995), Selma Sevenhuijsen (1998) and Fiona Mackay (2001). The argument is that the private concerns, values, skills and understandings associated with the practice of caring can all enhance public practices of citizenship. 'Responsibility, trust, being adaptable and accommodating to other's differences, toleration for our own and others' human frailty, and how to sustain and repair relationships' can all, according to Fiona Williams, be seen as 'civic virtues', which contribute to social cohesion. Care is therefore 'part of citizenship' she argues (Williams 2004:76). This view was endorsed in a study of female local politicians in Scotland who expressed the belief that the 'practical strategies and intellectual skills which arise from the practice of caring such as attentiveness, connectedness, responsibility and reciprocity can be "transformed" and transferred to a wider context of politics' (Mackay 2001:186–7).

One arena particularly conducive to such practices is that of informal, typically community-based, politics, often grounded in concerns which derive from women's responsibilities for care. A significant theme of feminist citizenship analysis has been to argue that such politics constitute an important arena of citizenship.

However, it is in relation to social citizenship where the momentum for incorporating care into thinking about citizenship has been stronger. The case has been made by a number of feminist analysts for including 'care in the definition of citizenship, so the rights to time to care and to receive care are protected' (Knijn and Kremer 1997:357). Although such analysts attempt to avoid the essentialism of some maternalist thinking, the fear remains that, unless and until a more equitable gendered division of domestic labour is achieved, such formulations could nevertheless serve to trap women in traditional gender roles within the private sphere and marginalise them as public citizens. Moreover, disabled feminists have challenged the very language of care in the context of adult care. Jenny Morris, for example, argues that 'the common assumption that disabled people are "in need of care" ... undermines other people's ability to see us as autonomous people'. This, in turn, creates 'an attitudinal barrier to citizenship participation' (Morris 2005:25).

In a famous passage, Carole Pateman (1989) encapsulates the difficulties that these two models pose as 'Wollstonecraft's dilemma'. She sees the two as incompatible: either women conform to the male citizenship model or they continue with their tasks as carers, which are not and cannot be adequately valued by that model. This is, though, perhaps too pessimistic and politically paralysing a conclusion. We can aim for a gender-inclusive model of citizenship that incorporates care as an expression of citizenship in line with the gender-differentiated model but not at the expense of undermining progress towards gender equality, so that the ostensibly gender-neutral model cannot totally be discarded. Such a synthesis needs to be within a framework of diversity (see below and elsewhere in this volume). Pivotal to the synthesis is the disruption of the public–private divide discussed earlier. This throws up another set of dilemmas for the feminist reinterpretation of citizenship.

Citizenship and the private sphere

I have argued elsewhere that it is 'within both the public and the private spheres and the interrelationship between the two, as governed by the sexual division of labour and time, that the practical barriers to women's citizenship lie' and that 'both women and men's citizenship would be enriched, if the value to citizenship of caring responsibilities in the private sphere were acknowledged and if those responsibilities were shared more equitably between the sexes' (Lister 2003:119).

At the same time, when writing specifically about political citizenship I have drawn a distinction between citizenship politics, located in the public sphere, and 'what feminists have rightly identified as the personal politics which can also take place in the "private" or "intimate" sphere'. I argued that 'not all politics necessarily counts as citizenship, for the latter, in its political sense, implies active political participation, albeit broadly defined' (ibid: 29). I then used Anne Phillips's (1993) example of the difference between campaigning in public for men to do their fair share of housework and simply sorting out the division of labour within one's own home. I suggested that 'in the case of the former, we are acting as citizens, in the case of the latter, which is nevertheless significant for citizenship, we are not'

(2003:30). I therefore accepted that 'the terrain of political citizenship action is the public sphere while underlining how it cannot be divorced from what happens in the private, which shapes its contours and is the proper object of citizenship struggles' (ibid). I also emphasised how 'actions in both public and private spheres can interact to enhance the capacity to act as a citizen' (ibid).

There are a number of aspects of this position which are open to challenge and which, indeed, have been challenged, by, for instance, Raia Prokhovnik (1998), John Hoffman (2004), Andrew Dobson (2003) and Paul Kershaw (2005). The last two authors are examples of male theorists whose work is deeply and explicitly influenced by feminist thinking on citizenship.

One argument that I have tried to take on board is that, in emphasising the centrality of shifting the gendered division of labour in the private sphere as the basis for promoting women's citizenship in the public sphere, there is a danger of perpetuating the valuing of paid forms of work over unpaid care work and of treating care as simply a barrier to citizenship rather than as also an expression of citizenship in its own right and as a practice of inherent value. Nevertheless, I am aware that that tension still exists in my own and others' writings; it is a tension which reflects the underlying tension between the two models of citizenship outlined above. As Paul Kershaw observes, the feminist literature identifies care-giving 'as both a site of rich reward and a deep source of discrimination. This ambivalence motivates the need to develop a policy blueprint that accommodates the finding that caregiving can be a practice that is inherently valuable both socially and privately, but which ultimately requires redistribution ... in order to minimize discrimination' (Kershaw 2005:13).

A related argument concerns the status of the private sphere as a locus for citizenship. Prokhovnik argues that 'it is *not* that women need to be liberated from the *private* realm, in order to take part in the public realm as equal citizens, but that women – and men – already undertake responsibilities of citizenship in both the public and the private realms' (1998:84). She also suggests that 'feminists can recognize that citizenship involves whatever ethically-grounded activities, undertaken by women in the private as well as the public realms, are *relevant* to *their* lives' (ibid:96). (For development of this argument in the context of democratisation in Chile see Georgina Blakeley's chapter in this volume.)

In similar vein, Dobson contends that 'far from being a lesser realm than the public ... the private sphere may be a crucial site of citizenship activity' (2003:54). He challenges the distinction made by Anne Phillips and myself between campaigning for men to do a fair share of housework and sorting out the division of labour in one's own home. His argument is that, from an ecological perspective, this would mean 'for example that campaigning for recycling centres is citizenship, but composting in one's own garden is not' yet all 'green actions in the home have a public impact' (ibid:136). Hoffman takes the position that 'the term *political* is interchangeable with the term *citizen*'; therefore it is not valid to exclude 'the politics of the personal or intimate sphere' from citizenship (Hoffman 2004:67). He gives a rather different example of the public impact of private actions: 'If women are dominated or humiliated by men (or their partners) in the bedroom, this surely has an effect on their capacity to participate in more conventionally defined public arenas' (ibid).

Kershaw conflates the social and the political in the notion of the 'sociopolitical' to make the case for care-giving as a form of active citizenship. Drawing in particular on the care practices of African American women, he challenges me to broaden my 'vision of the socio-political further': 'Once the sphere of the family and other fictive kin relations is recognized as a significant domain for identity politics, as well as for refuge, resistance, and activism, a definition of active citizenship that excludes domesticity entirely from the terrain of citizenship becomes less tenable' (Kershaw 2005:121).

There are a number of related issues at stake in what these critics are saying. The first is whether 'the political' and 'citizenship' are 'inter-changeable', as suggested by Hoffman (2004). My own view is that they are not, as illustrated in the housework argument above. That what happens in the domestic sphere can have consequences for the capacity to act as a citizen 'in more conventionally defined public arenas' (ibid: 67), as Hoffman argues and as I have also acknowledged (Lister 2003:30), does not mean that political actions in the domestic sphere themselves constitute citizen-ship. Moreover, to treat 'the political' and 'citizenship' as interchangeable implies that political action which infringes the citizenship rights of others, for instance harassment of unpopular minority groups, still counts as citizenship (for a discussion see Lister 2003:32–3). Rather, as Prokhovnik argues, citizenship has 'a moral basis', which points to 'the exercise of citizenship [as] ethical association' (1998:86).

Another question raised by the criticisms outlined above is whether it is valid to make a distinction between political and other forms of citizenship. Such a distinction underlies what might seem like a contradiction in my position: that, on the one hand, care does represent an expression of citizenship but that, on the other, care and other activities in the private sphere do not constitute *political* citizenship understood as active political participation. In contrast, Kershaw's notion of the 'sociopolitical' denies any such distinction. Or perhaps what is at issue is how we define political citizenship? Or is the key the distinction that Dobson implicitly makes between actions in the home that do or do not have a public impact? That in turn raises the question as to how we define public impact. Kershaw's argument, as I understand it, is premised on the assumption that in certain circumstances care-giving does have a wider public impact. He cites the work of the Black feminist, Patricia Hill Collins, which

> suggests that domestic care has the potential to function as a form of resistance to oppression that stretches well beyond the particular homes in which the work is performed because it contributes to a broader project of community development. *Qua* cultural workers, mothers contribute significantly to the project of 'group survival' by transmitting an ethnocentric worldview to the next generation. (Kershaw 2005:116)

I find myself torn between a commitment to an expansive and inclusive conceptualisation of citizenship on the one hand and a sense that boundaries do have to be drawn somewhere between what does and does not constitute citizenship on the other. Moreover, I believe that it is still valid to distinguish between political and social citizenship actions/responsibilities, even if some actions fuse the two in the 'sociopolitical'. So, even if care does, as argued earlier, provide a resource for political citizenship (and represents a responsibility of social citizenship), that does not mean that the act of caring is of itself an act of political citizenship.

Nevertheless, Kershaw's arguments are persuasive in suggesting how, in certain circumstances, the practice of caring might represent political citizenship and that therefore it is not valid to assume *a priori* that political citizenship cannot be practised within domestic spaces. Perhaps one conclusion to be drawn from his work, together with that of the other authors discussed, is that the key determinant of whether or not an action constitutes citizenship should be *what* a person does and with what public consequences, not *where* they do it. While there are no simple answers, what this discussion illustrates is how feminism has unsettled the tight boundaries around citizenship drawn in earlier malestream writings, leaving them more fluid and open to contestation.

The impact of feminist citizenship theory

As stated above, any resolution of the tension between equality and difference based conceptions of citizenship needs to be within a framework of diversity. In very different ways, Chantal Mouffe (1992) and Iris Young (1990) have conceptualised citizenship from feminist perspectives, which explicitly foreground diversity and the differences that exist within the categories 'woman' and 'man'. Such an approach can be found in many, though not all, feminist writings on citizenship (see, for instance, Yuval-Davis and Werbner 1999). It has contributed to a more differentiated theorisation of citizenship in much, though by no means all, of the wider citizenship literature also.

A good example is the Introduction by Engin Isin and Bryan Turner to their *Handbook of Citizenship Studies*, which provides an overview of the field. They point to the number of scholars, writing from a range of perspectives who are exploring and addressing concepts of sexual citizenship, ecological citizenship, diasporic citizenship, differentiated citizenship, multicultural citizenship, cosmopolitan citizenship and Aboriginal citizenship. These studies, taken together, have already made an impact on social and political thought and practice . . . The importance of accommodating some form of differentiated citizenship and the inadequacy of modern liberal citizenship are now widely accepted. (Isin and Turner 2002:2)

That they are so is arguably in large part due to the impetus provided by feminist analysis.

While it is impossible to keep up with everything published in what Isin and Turner refer to as 'the spectacular growth of the field of citizenship studies' (ibid), new theoretical texts and textbooks – and also writings on citizenship in the international development field – typically reflect to a greater or lesser extent elements of the feminist input into thinking about citizenship. A good example of someone who has taken the feminist critique as a starting point is Ken Plummer. In *Intimate Citizenship* he explains that 'the idea of intimate citizenship builds upon, but certainly does not replace . . . feminist citizenship and sexual citizenship' (2003:60). He conceptualises intimate citizenship as 'public discourse on the personal life' (ibid:68) and offers it as 'a potential bridge' between the public and private spheres (ibid: 15). Another is Paul Kershaw, a political theorist, mentioned earlier. He states in the Introduction to his book on care and citizenship that the normative framework, which he employs, is 'unabashedly feminist'; and the volume reflects a careful reading of the feminist literature on citizenship (2005:9).

However, not all accounts of the feminist position are as well grounded as Kershaw's. An example is Pattie et al's 'major empirical study of citizenship in Britain' (2004:dustjacket). A discussion of contemporary debates about citizenship does include a page or so about the feminist contribution to these debates. However, the authors identify as problematic that feminist perspectives on citizenship see it 'exclusively as a matter of extending or creating rights' and ignore the responsibilities and obligations from which 'rights cannot be divorced' (Pattie et al, 2004:16). This is a rather extraordinary assertion in light of the vibrant feminist debates about the nature of citizenship responsibilities and obligations discussed above. Nor are these debates reflected in Richard Dagger's important volume, *Civic Virtues* (1997), which addresses the relationship between rights and responsibilities, although he does engage with Iris Young on questions of difference and autonomy.

There is, more fundamentally, reluctance among some malestream theorists to countenance any association of citizenship with the private sphere. David Marquand (1991), for instance, has responded to the feminist case by arguing that it is unreasonable to expect the notion of citizenship to address questions concerning the private sphere of the home and family. In his widely publicised most recent book, *Decline of the Public: The Hollowing-Out of Citizenship*, he warns those who use the feminist slogan 'the personal is political' that 'if the personal is politicized, or the political personalized, the public and private domains are both likely to be twisted out of shape' (2004:80).

Marquand is not alone in asserting the irrelevance of the private sphere to citizenship. Matthew Almond (2005), who looked at expert and lay understandings of good citizenship, conducted a delphi study of experts in the field of citizenship as part of his research.[2] The statements 'cares for elderly or infirm friends', 'cares for elderly or infirm relatives' and 'is a good parent' were not generally associated with good citizenship on the grounds that these are private not public sphere activities. Interestingly, however, these were the only statements on which opinions were divided along gender lines. A gender analysis revealed that it was only the male experts who considered that caring activities had nothing to do with good citizenship. Interestingly, too, lay respondents often spoke in terms redolent of the 'ethic of care' in formulating *their* ideas about good citizenship. For them, the interpersonal dimension of good citizenship was paramount: 'care' and 'helping others' were repeatedly mentioned as key elements of good citizenship.

Conclusion

This chapter has offered a relatively optimistic interpretation of the influence of feminist analysis on thinking about citizenship. Yet, as with any analysis of feminism's impact, the verdict has to be mixed. It is still possible to read texts and listen to politicians speak about citizenship and think that the feminist critique might as well never have happened. That does not detract, though, from the importance of the work of feminist scholars worldwide who have developed a feminist (and differentiated) theory and praxis of citizenship, which challenges the idea that citizenship is 'just something for the boys'.

Key writers and further reading

The literature on citizenship is huge. Much of it refers back to T. H. Marshall's post-war classic (1950), discussed in this chapter. Good general introductions can be found in Faulks (2000) and Dwyer (2004), both of which pay some attention to feminist perspectives. Isin and Turner's *Handbook* (2002) provides a wide-ranging contemporary overview of the field. Explicitly feminist accounts are provided by Voet (1998), Hobson and Lister (2002), Lister (2003) and Siim (2000), who compares the UK, France and Denmark. Yuval-Davis and Werbner's (1999) edited collection offers a more internationalist feminist perspective and Sevenhuijsen (1998) and

Kershaw (2005) theorise citizenship in relation to care. In addition to these texts, the work of a number of prominent feminist authors affords important insights into gendered citizenship. These include Pateman (1989), Young (1990), Mouffe (1993), Phillips (1993) and Yuval-Davis (1997).

Notes

1 It should, however, be noted that not all feminists subscribe to this position on the implications of the public–private divide for citizenship. In particular, for many women in Central and Eastern Europe the private, domestic, sphere represented a site of solidarity against a totalitarian state under state socialism (Einhorn 1993, 2006) and for many Black women it offers a bulwark against racist oppression (Glenn 1991).
2 The Delphi Technique is designed to sample a group of knowledgeable individuals in order to gain a consensus of opinion on a particular topic without bringing them together face to face.

Bibliography

Almond, M. (2005) *An Investigation into the Meanings of Good Citizenship*, PhD thesis, unpublished (Loughborough: Loughborough University).

Bryson, V. (1999) *Feminist Debates: Issues of Theory and Political Practice* (Basingstoke: Macmillan).

Bubeck, D. (1995) *A Feminist Approach to Citizenship* (Florence: European University Institute).

Dagger, R. (1997) *Civic Virtues* (Oxford: Oxford University Press).

Dietz, M. (1985) 'Citizenship with a Feminist Face: The Problem with Maternal Thinking', *Political Theory* 13:1, 19–37.

Dobson, A. (2003) *Citizenship and the Environment* (Oxford: Oxford University Press).

Dwyer, P. (2004) *Understanding Social Citizenship* (Bristol: The Policy Press).

Einhorn, B. (1993) *Cinderella Goes to Market* (London: Verso).

Einhorn, B. (2006) *Citizenship in an Enlarging Europe: From Dream to Awakening* (Basingstoke and New York: Palgrave).

Faulks, K. (2000) *Citizenship* (London and New York: Routledge).

Gallie, W. B. (1956) 'Essentially Contested Concepts', *Proceedings of the Aristotelian Society* 56, 167–98.

Glenn, E. N. (1991) 'Racial Ethnic Women's Labor: The Intersection of Race, Gender, and Class Oppression', in R. L. Blumberg (ed.), *Gender, Family and Economy: The Triple Overlap* (London and New Delhi: Sage).

Hirschmann, N. J. (1996) 'Rethinking Obligation for Feminism', in N. J. Hirschmann and C. Stefano (eds), *Revisioning the Political* (Boulder: Westway Press), 157–80.

Hobson, B. and Lister, R. (2002) 'Citizenship', in B. Hobson, J. Lewis and B. Siim (eds), *Contested Concepts in Gender and Social Politics* (Cheltenham and Northampton MA: Edward Elgar), 23–54.

Hoffman, J. (2004) *Citizenship Beyond the State* (London: Sage).

Huq, S. P. (2000) 'Gender and Citizenship: What Does a Rights Framework Offer Women?', *IDS Bulletin* 31:4, 74–82.

Isin, E. F. and Turner, B. S. (2002) 'Citizenship Studies: An Introduction', in E. F. Isin and B. S. Turner (eds), *Handbook of Citizenship Studies* (London: Sage), 1–10.

Jaggar, A. (1983) *Feminist Politics and Human Nature* (Brighton: Harvester).

Jones, K. B. (1988) 'Towards the Revision of Politics', in K. B. Jones and A. G. Jónasdóttir (eds), *The Political Interests of Gender: Developing Theory and Research with a Human Face* (London: Sage), 11–32.

Kabeer, N. (2005) 'Introduction. The Search for Inclusive Citizenship', in N. Kabeer (ed.), *Inclusive Citizenship* (London and New York: Zed Books), 1–27.

Kershaw, P. (2005) *Carefair. Rethinking the Responsibilities and Rights of Citizenship* (Vancouver and Toronto: UBC Press).

Knijn, T. and Kremer, M. (1997) 'Gender and the Caring Dimension of Welfare States: Toward Inclusive Citizenship', *Social Politics* 4:3, 328–61.

Lister, R. (2003) *Citizenship: Feminist Perspectives*. 2nd edn (Basingstoke and New York: Palgrave).

Mackay, F. (2001) *Love and Politics* (London and New York: Continuum).

Marquand, D. (1991) 'Deaf to Duty's Call', *New Statesman and Society* 25 January.

Marquand, D. (2004) *Decline of the Public: The Hollowing-Out of Citizenship* (Cambridge: Polity Press).

Marshall, T. H. (1950) *Citizenship and Social Class* (Cambridge: Cambridge University Press).

Molyneux, M. (2000) 'Comparative Perspectives on Gender and Citizenship: Latin America and the Former Socialist States', in J. Cook, J. Roberts and G. Waylen (eds), *Towards a Gendered Political Economy* (Basingstoke: Macmillan), 121–44.

Morris, J. (2005) *Citizenship and Disabled People* (London: Disability Rights Commission).

Mouffe, C. (1992) 'Feminism, Citizenship and Radical Democratic Politics', in J. Butler and J. W. Scott (eds), *Feminists Theorize the Political* (New York and London: Routledge), 369–84.

Mouffe, C. (1993) *The Return of the Political* (London and New York: Verso).

Oldfield, A. (1990) *Citizenship and Community: Civic Republicanism and the Modern World* (London: Routledge).

Pascall, G. (1993) 'Citizenship – A Feminist Analysis', in G. Drover and P. Kerans (eds), *New Approaches to Welfare Theory* (Aldershot: Edward Elgar), 113–28.

Pateman, C. (1989) *The Disorder of Women* (Cambridge: Polity Press).

Pattie, C., Seyd, P. and Whiteley, P. (2004) *Citizenship in Britain* (Cambridge: Cambridge University Press).

Phillips, A. (1993) *Democracy and Difference* (Cambridge: Polity Press).

Plummer, K. (2003) *Intimate Citizenship: Private Decisions and Public Dialogues* (Seattle and London: University of Washington Press).

Prokhovnik, R. (1998) 'Public and Private Citizenship: From Gender Invisibility to Feminist Inclusiveness', *Feminist Review* 60, 84–104.

Sevenhuijsen, S. (1998) *Citizenship and the Ethics of Care* (London and New York: Routledge).

Sevenhuijsen, S. (2000) 'Caring in the Third Way', *Critical Social Policy* 20:1, 5–37.

Siim, B. (2000) *Gender and Citizenship* (Cambridge: Cambridge University Press).

Squires, J. (1998) 'Citoyennes?', *Imprints* 2:3, 263–75.

Voet, R. (1998) *Feminism and Citizenship* (London: Sage).

Werbner, P. and Yuval-Davis, N. (1999) 'Introduction: Women and the new Discourse of Citizenship', in N. Yuval-Davis and P. Werbner, *Women, Citizenship and Diffference* (London and New York: Zed Books), 1–38.

Williams, F. (2004) *Rethinking Families* (London: Calouste Gulbenkian Foundation).

Young, I. M. (1990) *Justice and the Politics of Difference* (Oxford: Princeton University Press).

Yuval-Davis, N. (1997) 'Women, Citizenship and Difference', *Feminist Review* 57:1, 4–27.

Yuval-Davis, N. and Werbner, P. (1999) *Women, Citizenship and Difference* (London and New York: Zed Books).

6

Representation[1]

Sarah Childs

Introduction

Talking about political representation is far from easy: as an essentially contested concept there are multiple, if not competing, definitions in play. Yet, unless it can be first agreed what is meant by political representation, talking about women's political representation is likely to prove even more problematic. The claim, for example, that women are numerically under-represented is empirically true: the global average for the percentage of women in national parliaments is 17 per cent, and nowhere are they elected in proportion to their percentage in the population.[2] But should this matter? Numerical representation is only one conception of representation, and women's numerical under-representation has until recently rarely aroused any interest. Representation in western democracies is more usually taken to refer to geographic representation: elected representatives 'represent' a particular and finite locality – the local constituency, the region or (in some proportional electoral systems) the whole nation. Furthermore, in party democracies the dominant means through which political interests are aggregated is via political parties. In such contexts, representation refers also, if not primarily, to party representation. Accordingly, it is not con-sidered to be an issue that parliaments are disproportionately constituted by middle-aged white men, for it is assumed that voting behaviour is determined not by the sex (or race or age) of the candidate, but by whether the particular candidate stands closest to the voter or, at the minimum, is the candidate most likely to defeat the voter's least preferred candidate (Phillips 1995:1–2, 25).

From a feminist perspective, however, traditional conceptions of representation seem insufficient and unsatisfactory. Feminists have called attention to the numerical under-representation of women in politics, arguing that this is neither natural nor just, and have suggested that women's political presence also matters for symbolic and, more contentiously, for substantive reasons: women's concerns will be imperfectly represented when women are absent from our political institutions. While such arguments are still often neglected, mainstream writers are at least beginning to acknowledge the existence of feminist arguments and concerns.

This chapter begins with a discussion of Hanna Pitkin's *The Concept of Representation* (1967). This seminal book discusses and draws on the contributions of some of the 'great men' of political theory which are discussed in more detail in Georgina Blakeley's chapter in this volume. More importantly, Pitkin's work has structured subsequent mainstream *and* feminist discussions. In this chapter Pitkin's ideas are subjected to the following question: what do her differing conceptions of representation, and especially her preferred definition, offer to discussions of women's political presence? The chapter then turns to feminist engagements with the concept of representation, with Anne Phillips's work without doubt the most influential contribution (Phillips 1991, 1995, 1998). In these more recent reconsiderations, conceptions downplayed or dismissed by Pitkin are reclaimed and significant nuances added to our understanding of her preferred conception of representation as 'acting for' (substantive representation). The chapter closes with a brief discussion of feminist political scientists' empirical research into the complicated relationship between women's descriptive and substantive representation *in practice*. It advocates a shift away from a focus on *when,* to a focus on *how,* the substantive representation of women occurs.

Traditional theories of political representation: Hanna F. Pitkin

Pitkin defines representation, drawing upon the word's etymological origins, as making present again (Pitkin 1967:8). But, she acknowledges, 'except in its earliest [Roman] use ... this has always meant more than a literal bringing into presence, as one might bring a book into the room' (ibid). Representation means then 'the making present *in some sense* of something which is nevertheless *not* present literally or in fact' (Pitkin 1967:8–9). But even this more expansive definition remains problematic for Pitkin. To state that 'something is simultaneously both present and not present' is paradoxical, as she admits, and begs additional questions, namely in what sense can the 'something' be considered present when 'in fact it is not'? And, 'who is [doing the] considering'? (Pitkin 1967:9)

Choosing to explore the concept of representation through looking at its ordinary usage – considering the family of words on the root 'represent' and its close synonyms – Pitkin develops a four-part typology of representation:

1   Formalistic representation;
2   'Standing for': descriptive representation;
3   'Standing for': symbolic representation;
4   Representing as 'acting for'.

Formalistic representation

Formalistic representation refers to the formal bestowing of authority (the right) onto a person to act for others. In this conception the represented (those for whom the representative is acting) become responsible for the consequences of the representatives' actions as if they had done them themselves (Pitkin 1967:38–9, 42–3). However, Pitkin finds the author-isation definition inadequate because it assumes that 'as long as he has been authorised *anything* that a man does is representing' (Pitkin 1967:39, emphasis added). In a similar fashion she rejects 'accountability theories' of formalistic representation, where the representative is 'someone who is to be held to account ... for what he does' (Pitkin 1967:55). Once again, there is no guarantee that the representative will act *for* the represented; that they might be removed from office at the end of their term cannot guarantee the quality of representation as it occurs (Pitkin 1967:59).

'Standing for': descriptive representation

Descriptive (or microcosmic) representation refers to a notion of correspond-ence between a representative's characteristics and the represented: the representative 'stands for' them, by virtue of a correspondence or connection between them (Pitkin 1967:61). This conception is particularly troubling for Pitkin. Firstly, she considers the apparent transparency of descriptive representation misleading. Representative art is 'never a replica', neither is a map absolutely accurate (some depict 'land', others 'topography' or 'economic trade regions') while mirrors reflect 'only visual features' (Pitkin 1967:66–72). In a similar fashion she asks the question, whom should our political fora represent: 'The one who is typical and average in every conceivable respect, including intelligence, public spiritedness, and experience' (Pitkin 1967:76)? Pitkin also wonders whether the characteristics that warrant representation are always self-evident and constant (Pitkin 1967:87).

Secondly, Pitkin questions the link between characteristics and actions, concluding that there is 'no simple correlation' (Pitkin 1967:89). Thirdly, Pitkin contends that a man (sic) can 'only be held to account for what he has done' and 'not for what he is'. This means that neither representation as acting for nor representation as accountability is possible within descriptive representation (Pitkin 1967:90; McLean 1991:175). Finally, Pitkin worries that descriptive representation 'almost inevitably' means that there is a concentration on the composition of our political institutions (who is present), rather than its activities (what they do) (Pitkin 1967:226).

'Standing for': symbolic representation

According to Pitkin, symbols represent something or someone because they 'stand for' and 'evoke' its referent – the flag representing the nation, for example. But symbols are, in her view, often arbitrary, with no obvious connection to what is being symbolised (Pitkin 1967:97). This means that the only criterion of what constitutes a symbol is 'people's attitudes and beliefs' (Pitkin 1967:100). Thus, in politics, the criterion of symbolic representation is whether the representative is believed in (Pitkin 1967:102). This, however, renders the basis for symbolic representation 'emotional, affective, irrational psychological responses' (cited by Squires 1996:16). Once again, there is no room in symbolic representation for representation as acting for the represented (Pitkin 1967:102), and with no rational criteria for judging it Pitkin finds this conception wanting; open to manipulation the representative can simply make the represented feel represented.

Representing as 'acting for'

In everyday language, Pitkin reminds us, representatives are said to act 'on behalf of others', 'in their place' and 'in their interest' (Pitkin 1967:17). Moreover, she asks us to acknowledge both that people behave differently when they are acting on behalf of someone else and that we have expectations of how a person will act if they are acting on our behalf (Pitkin 1967:118). Distinguishing between mandate (under explicit instruction) and independence (acting in the best interests of the represented) theories of representation, Pitkin considers the proper relationship as one in which the represented is 'logically prior' – the representative must be responsive to the represented 'rather than the other way around' (Pitkin 1967:140). This implies that 'normally' the wishes of the represented and the action of the representative will converge but that when conflict occurs the representative should provide an explanation for their actions (Pitkin 1967:163–5).

Feminist engagement with Pitkin

'Acting for' representation is for Pitkin the true meaning of representation (Pitkin 1967:224): the representative system must look after the public interest and be responsive to public opinion, except insofar as non-responsiveness can be justified in terms of the public interest (ibid). However, her confidence that this is the true and only definition of representation has not gone unchallenged, even in the mainstream literature (Birch 1971; Judge 1999). And with sex and gender added into the mix, the limitations of Pitkin's conceptualisations become clear. As discussed in the following sections, feminists have been particularly anxious to stress the importance of 'descriptive' representation and have devoted considerable efforts to exploring the relationship between descriptive ('standing for') and substantive ('acting for') representation. These feminist reconceptions of representation are complex; readers may find it helpful to consult Table 1 (p. 88), where the main differences between Pitkin and feminists are highlighted.

Formalistic representation

Pitkin's rejection of formalistic theories of representation as an adequate notion of representation, however, stands the test of time (Pitkin 1967:58). In both its authorisation and accountability forms it fails to enable an evaluation of the activity of representation – the relationship between the represented and the representative – as it occurs. For this reason formalistic representation has little to offer discussions of women's political representation. While it might be the case that particular representatives (men or women) claim that they *will* act or *have* acted in particular ways on particular women's issues, in party democracies it is difficult to hold representatives to account for one particular issue among all the others they are associated with (Voet 1992:397). To be sure, a representative's position on abortion (either pro- or anti-) might 'trump' their other policy positions, enabling voters who feel strongly about abortion to give or deny them their vote on that basis. But what if the represented have to evaluate between apparently contradictory policy positions on women's concerns for example, a representative who is both pro-state funded childcare provision and against the minimum wage (which in practice disproportionately benefits women). For whom should they vote?

The concept of formalistic representation has, though, one important feature: it reveals the identity (sex) of our representatives. In this way it supports the important activity of counting and recording the numbers of women in our political institutions. Even if this is limited in what it can tell us about why women are numerically under-represented or why their numbers increase or decline in particular places at particular times, it is important that the numbers of women elected to parliaments around the world are documented.

Representing as 'acting for'

Representation as acting for – Pitkin's preferred conception – at least initially, looks to resolve our concern with women's descriptive and substantive representation. For the representative relationship to be operating, representatives must be, according to Pitkin's conception, responsive to women. If they are not – irrespective of whether they are male or female – then they are failing in their (acting for) representation. However, there is little agreement as to what Pitkin's notion of the representative being 'logically prior' and responsive to the represented actually means in practice (Pitkin 1967:140; Birch 1971:15–16; Rao 1998:29, 31). Moreover, with party representation cross-cutting, acting for, representation it is likely that individual representatives' desire to act for women will be circumscribed. So, this conception seems unable to account for the actions of a representative who, forced by party discipline, votes neither in the apparent interests of the represented nor with their own judgement but with their party (Judge 1999:71; Birch 1971:97). It might be argued, of course, that the represented should have been aware of their representative's party identity when they voted for them and should not feel aggrieved at their actions (Pennock 1968:24) and, in any case, women can subsequently, like all electors, act to vote out a representative who has not acted for them (ibid).

'Standing for': symbolic representation

If symbols, as Pitkin claimed, can be arbitrary it also should not matter if our political representatives are disproportionately male, for they can still symbolically represent women. Yet, the form the symbol takes may be more important than Pitkin allows. Could the British Union Jack be transformed into one constituted by pink and green butterflies, as the British fashion designer Paul Smith did in 2004, and still represent the UK (cf Duerst-Lahti and Verstegen 1995:216–17)? Similarly, can a political institution constituted of men really symbolically represent women in their absence? Note further that, according to Pitkin, the criterion of symbolic representativeness is *feeling* represented and that she was highly critical of this (Squires 1996:86). A conclusion that women are symbolically represented when they believe they are, even if all the representatives are men, is surely as unconvincing now as the general principle was for Pitkin in the late 1960s.

'Standing for': descriptive representation

Although 'probably' the most contested of all the definitions of representation (Phillips 1991:63), descriptive representation is now highly fashionable. Nonetheless, Pitkin's criticism of descriptive representation continues to resonate. The case against is pretty straightforward. It might be unfortunate that, when push comes to shove, the bodies in our parliaments are overwhelmingly male but this does not really matter: with universal suffrage, individuals choose to vote for representatives that best represent their views – views which are neither determined by, nor contained in, particular sexed bodies.

And even if one accepts the principle that our political institutions should reflect our societies, critics ask, just like Pitkin, how is it possible to determine which characteristics should be represented (Judge 1999:45)? The case for descriptive representation on the basis of sex might hold but what about other, more questionable (at least in the critics' view), characteristics? (See for example Phillips 1991; Voet 1992.) Designing electoral mechanisms to deliver descriptive representativeness is also said to be problematic (Judge 1999:45). Sex quotas may be workable (indeed they have been successfully implemented in many countries and parties throughout the world), but, again, critics assert, what about other mechanisms for other characteristics? Are all-Black shortlists possible *in practice* (Duerst-Lahti and Verstegen 1995:221; Phillips 1995)?

Pitkin's conclusion that an over-emphasis upon the composition of political bodies prevents a proper focus upon the activity of representation also remains a strong criticism of descriptive representation (Judge 1999:22;

Phillips 1998:226; Phillips 1995:3; Darcy et al 1994:17; Voet 1992). However, a careful reading of *The Concept of Representation* shows that Pitkin herself chose to downplay the idea that elected bodies are determined to some (unsubstantiated) degree by those who constitute them even while she was aware that advocates of descriptive representation are concerned about ensuring descriptive representation 'precisely because they expect the composition [of a political forum] to determine the activities' (Pitkin 1967:63 cited in Judge 1999:22). Indeed, concepts of descriptive representation played a part in the extension of the franchise to previously excluded categories of people – which begs the question of why it was thought necessary to extend the franchise to the working classes and women if rich white men were representing them in the first place (Birch 1993:72; Judge 1999:22–3; cf Voet 1992).

A distinction between two forms of descriptive representation, the microcosmic and the selective, is helpful here. Mansbridge acknowledges the concern that microcosmic representation, 'achieveable only by lottery or another form of representative selection', might throw up 'legislators with less ability, expertise' and 'possibly commitment to the public good' than those selected through election (Mansbridge 1999:631). However, selective descriptive representatives 'need not be significantly less skilled' than other representatives because they are as likely to have 'chosen politics as a calling', been selected through competitive mechanisms and have demonstrated the necessary skills (whatever they may be) for politics (ibid). Furthermore, the argument that the presence of women will be deleterious for our politics is on very weak ground: sex is *not* a determinate of ability (Darcy et al 1994:17–18). Thus, even if the argument holds that small farmers are better represented by politicians than small farmers, it does not hold for women. Women selected to fulfil quotas need not be the less able or less expert women that Pitkin or other critics of descriptive representation fear (Mansbridge 1999:633).

Nonetheless, and again following Pitkin, advocates of women's presence must contend with the criticism that women's descriptive representation is in fact illusory (Voet 1992:392); women who become representatives will be, by definition, different from those they represent – at the minimum by dint of their being representatives, but also because they are likely to be more educated, more middle class and members of the dominant ethnic group (not least because women who are less qualified or atypical are less likely to be selected as candidates and elected as representatives) (Parry et al 1992). As the chapters in this volume by Georgina Blakeley and Mercy Ette show, this pattern has been clear in Chile and Nigeria. However, this argument is not specific to women's representation – all representatives are, on these terms, distinct from those they represent.

The most damning critique of descriptive representation remains however, Pitkin's conclusion that there is no simple correlation between representatives' characteristics and action. If women representatives cannot be trusted or made to act in a way that is responsible and responsive to women (Rao 1998:25) – remember there is no room in descriptive representation for representing as acting for nor means of holding representatives to account (Voet 1992:393) – there will have to be other grounds on which to argue for women's political presence, ones that are not linked to substantive representation. Such arguments are discussed in the following section.

Feminist concepts of political representation

Anne Phillips: the politics of presence

The argument for women's political presence is one example of a wider claim for a politics of presence made by other disadvantaged groups (Phillips 1995). The normative case is argued on four grounds. Firstly, presence is important in terms of symbolic representation; secondly, it is premised upon the need to tackle exclusions that derive from party representation; thirdly, it is argued that disadvantaged groups need more aggressive advocates; and finally, presence is said to be needed to ensure a transformation of the political agenda.

In symbolic terms, the presence of the formerly excluded demonstrates that they are the equals of those who were previously included because, contrary to traditional understandings of symbolic representation, particular bodies need to be physically present to symbolise their equality (Phillips 1995:40, 45; Mansbridge 1999:636). Their inclusion is also likely to have the effect of enhancing the legitimacy of political institutions as more people identify with (by seeing themselves in) particular political spaces (Phillips 1995:40, 65).

The second argument for a politics of presence looks to the limitations of party representation. Here, the represented must choose between a limited number of parties (Phillips 1995:44). Inevitably, certain issues will be left out of the parties' agendas (packages). In addition, a particular party's position on one policy area, for example privatisation, may well be a poor indicator of another, for example sexual or racial equality (Phillips 1995:41–2). At the same time, and even where party cohesion is strong, representatives still have some room to act free of their party identity. For this reason (and to ensure that women's and other groups' concerns are strongly articulated) it matters who our representatives are (Phillips 1995:43).

The third argument – disadvantaged groups' need for aggressive advocates – is not a claim that no one ever acts on behalf of others. But rather, and as Phillips makes clear, the presence of the previously excluded may be necessary to ensure the assertive articulation of their concerns.

The fourth argument for the politics of presence – the politics of transformation – refers to the idea of a broadening of the political agenda and builds on the previous case. It focuses upon the realm of preferences not yet formulated, articulated or legitimated on the political agenda and therefore unable to be part of the packages of political ideas (Phillips 1995:44, 176; Mansbridge 1999:634–6). In such circumstances it is important that representatives with different perspectives and concerns are present.

Women's political presence

These arguments feed into the feminist case for women's political presence, which is made on four related bases. Firstly, principles of justice. Now rarely contested, women's absence from our political institutions is increasingly regarded as *prima facie* evidence of injustice (Phillips 1995:65). Second is the role model effect. The presence of women representatives (just like women in any other hitherto male-dominated occupation) should engender women's numerical representation as women see representatives who look like them 'doing politics'; some may even gain direct experience working for women representatives (Clark 1994:100). Third is the realist argument that women's interests are discounted in the absence of women's political presence;[3] and finally, there is a claim that women have a different relationship to politics, one in which women will introduce a different set of values and concerns.[4] These last two arguments are two sides of the same coin – suggesting a relationship between descriptive and substantive representation, although they also cover the argument that suggests that women prefer a more consensual rather than confrontational style of politics (based either on women's biology or the practices of the second wave feminist movement) (Phillips 1991). The claim that women should be present in politics because of a relationship between descriptive and substantive representation is the most prominent and contested argument for women's political presence.[5] Although it might be a necessary argument to employ in order to secure women's greater numerical representation, as it has the power to mobilise women to participate in politics (Mackay 2001:3), the argument that women should be present in politics because, once there, they will act for women, especially when crudely portrayed, seems to be both reductive (reducing women representatives' attitudes and behaviour back to their bodies) and essentialist (presuming that women are a category who share a set of essential attributes) (Mackay 2001:10; Young 1990b:87).

In *The Politics of Presence* Phillips turns away from such a strong interpretation and advocates, as an alternative, gender parity. She does this because she holds that there is no 'empirical or theoretical plausibility' to the idea that women share experiences or that women's shared experiences translate into shared beliefs or goals. Neither does Phillips consider it likely that women will organise themselves into a group with group opinions and goals that can be represented (Phillips 1995:53–5). Women, in short, are too diverse. However, she maintains that women do have concerns that derive from their gendered experiences and that these will be inadequately addressed in political fora dominated by men. Consequently, gender parity continues to contend that women should be present in politics because they are more likely to act for women but, crucially, this is not a guarantee that they will (Phillips 1995:158, 56; 1998:233–5).

The complicated relationship between women's descriptive and substantive representation

Arguments for women's presence, even when premised on gender rather than sex, as in Phillips' case, still need to contend with a number of complicating counterpoints. The first derives from the theoretical and practical problems thrown up by contemporary feminist understandings of women's differences (Reingold 2000; Squires 1999; Dodson 2001). The second questions the basis upon which women substantively represent women in practice.

That women constitute a group in society seems to make intuitive sense. If we look outside there are 'women' who appear to us distinct from 'men'. At the same time, women are also different from each other, at the very least in terms of social class, race, ethnicity and sexuality. Yet working with recognition of women's differences causes problems for theorists of women's substantive representation: if women have multiple identities and experience the world in different ways, the basis upon which women can act for other women seems by necessity either to succumb to essentialism or be underpinned by a denial of those differences (Voet 1992:71). Indeed, postmodern views of representation go one step further in that they challenge the possibility of 'authentic representation' at all: each woman must be her own 'politician/presenter' (Vickers 1997:40–1, 43).

A number of feminist theorists hold, however, that such postmodern propositions should be contested. In contrast, they contend that the substantive representation of women remains possible. For one thing the proposition that there really are no women's interests *per se* confounds those who seek to count and measure women's interests as politically articulable and salient (Trimble 2004:9). Furthermore, and as Cynthia Cockburn notes, it is important that differences between women are not 'read as delegitimating' the claim for women's political presence based on women's gendered differences from men (Cockburn 1996:17). It is also rather ironic that women's 'representational claims are declared inauthentic' precisely at the moment when women are recognised as 'subjects' and therefore able to demand political presence (Vickers 1997:41–2).

In holding on to the idea that the representation of women (in all its dimensions) is possible, the work of Jane Mansbridge and Iris Marion Young is instructive. Mansbridge argues, in a similar way to Phillips, that descriptive representation denotes gender (shared experiences) and not sex (visible characteristics) (Mansbridge 1999:637, 629). Moreover, her understanding of women's 'shared experiences', the basis upon which women representatives act for other women, is premised upon a belief that, while they may not have shared the same particular experiences, women representatives share 'the outward signs of having lived through' the same experiences. This gives women representatives 'communicative and informational advantages' and enables them to 'forge bonds of trust' with the women they represent based on their gendered experiences (Mansbridge 1999:641).

Furthermore, Mansbridge's arguments for women's descriptive and substantive representation are underpinned by an explicit rejection of women's essentialism. She asks three questions whose answers determine the case for descriptive representation: 1) What are the features of the existing electoral process that have resulted in lower proportions of certain descriptive groups in the legislature than in the population? 2) Do members of that group consider themselves able adequately to represent themselves? And, 3) Is there any evidence that dominant groups in the society have ever intentionally made it difficult or illegal for members of that group to represent themselves? If the answer to the first question suggests discrimination and the suppression of interests and answers to the second and third questions are positive then the group 'appears to be a good candidate for affirmative selective representation' (Mansbridge 1999:639).

Young similarly talks in terms of a shared women's perspective (Young 2002:137). Women's social perspective is derived from women being 'similarly positioned' in society and means that women have affinity with one another and 'are attuned to particular kinds of social meanings' (Young 2002:123, 136–7). Young provides an illustration of how her concept contends with women's differences through the example of American women legislators coming together to demand an enquiry into allegations of sexual harassment (Young 2002:140). Although the women legislators agreed that the issue should be addressed, this did not mean that their views on sexual harassment *per se* and/or the guilt or innocence of the Senator in question were shared.

Despite these two more theoretically sophisticated responses to the challenge of women's differences, such conceptions of women's substantive representation have not gone uncontested. Laurel Weldon cuts to the chase: 'If she is white, straight, middle class mother, she cannot speak for African American women, or poor women, or lesbian women, *on the basis of her own experience* any more than men can speak for women merely on the basis of theirs' (Weldon 2002:1156).[6]

Women's perspectives cannot reside 'completely in any individual' woman but are created when women interact with other women 'to define their priorities' (Weldon 2002:1154–7). Without engaging with other, and different, women an individual representative is forced into relying on their own limited and partial experience. It appears, then, that women's differences mean that there can be no set of women's policy positions or recommendations, only an 'agenda of topics for discussion or list of problem areas' (Weldon 2002:1157). Yet Weldon's ideas do not seem to be so distant from Phillips, Mansbridge and Young. For a start, her example of women's shared concern for childcare is arguably akin to Young's example of the women legislators' concern with sexual harassment. While women may be (are likely to be) divided over the issue of childcare – with those seeking paid childcare desirous of lower wages and those women providing the care seeking higher wages, for example – Weldon recognises that both groups of women 'confront the issue of the relationship between motherhood and work' (ibid). Furthermore, although she argues that women's perspectives come from women interacting with one another, Weldon also admits that an individual woman representative can 'articulate a truncated version of the group perspective' 'without interacting' with other women '*if* she is so inclined' (Weldon 2002:1158, emphasis added). Although this 'truncated version' is inadequate, her statement, nonetheless, implies that there is some kind of (albeit imperfect) relationship between women's descriptive and substantive representation. Otherwise, how can one explain why some women representatives are '*so* inclined' to act for women (cf Reingold 2000:35–6)?

What is needed for women's substantive representation to occur is, then, not the presence of just any women (some of whom may not see themselves as part of, or with obligations to, the group women) but the presence, in Suzanne Dovi's terms, of 'preferable descriptive representatives' (Dovi 2002:729–34). Such representatives experience a sense of belonging to, and have strong mutual relationships with, women (Dovi 2002:736, 729). They share aims with women – that is, they would want to see women's 'social, economic and political status' improved – and experience a 'reciprocated sense of having [their] ... fate linked' with women (Dovi 2002:736–7). Preferable women representatives also recognise differences between women and acknowledge that women may have 'different conceptions of what is necessary' to achieve women's aims (Dovi 2002:737). But there are limits: a woman representative who does not share either 'policy preferences' or 'values' with women could not be said to share their aims (Dovi 2002:737–8). Like representatives generally, women representatives should sometimes act as trustees and at other times act as delegates (Dovi 2002:734).

It is, to be sure, not the case that electing more women to our political institutions automatically delivers Dovi's preferable women representatives. It is quite possible that a parliament could be filled with women representatives who choose either not to identify with women or, even if they do, may not interpret this identification in feminist terms. But this should not trouble us too much: admittedly, most gender and politics scholars are likely to be seeking the *feminist* substantive representation of women – that is, our 'preferable descriptive representatives' will be feminist women acting in feminist ways; but others' 'preferable descriptive representatives' may be more traditional women.

The relationship in practice

Feminist political scientists investigating the relationship between women's descriptive and substantive representation in practice have often relied upon the concept of critical mass. According to its proponents, the presence of a 'critical mass' of women explains increased attention to women's concerns and gendered changes to existing parliamentary practices, while the absence of a 'critical mass' accounts for why women do not appear to have made a difference thus far. There is, though, a contemporary crisis of confidence in the concept, in large part the consequence of mis-readings of the key early contributions (Kanter 1977; Dahlerup 1988). In particular, there has been a failure to appreciate Kanter's three claims that suggest a number of possible outcomes that follow women's enhanced numerical representation (Childs and Krook 2006a):

1 With increased relative numbers, women might 'form coalitions and affect the culture of the group';
2 With increased relative numbers, women might 'begin to become individuals differentiated from one another'; and
3 With increased absolute numbers, even with a small shift in relative numbers, women might develop 'a close alliance and refuse to be turned against each other [due to] strong identification with the feminist cause or with other women' (Kanter 1977:209, 238).

Because the likelihood that women representatives will act for women is dependent upon a range of different variables (inter alia, gender identity, party, newness and institutional norms), gender and politics scholars would do better to investigate *how* the substantive representation of women occurs rather than trying to determine the percentage of women that constitutes the 'critical mass' or identifying all the possible variables that mediate the impact of numbers (Childs and Krook 2006a). Accordingly, researchers should be engaged in detailed analyses that trace the attitudes and behaviour of representatives over time in order to uncover the respective roles of women as 'critical actors' in the substantive representation of women.

This approach raises important questions about methods. Put simply: how can we know when women have made a substantive difference? Perhaps the most problematic issue concerns the search for sex differences. While observed differences between women and men are an indication of the substantive representation of women, the absence of such differences does not necessarily mean that women are not effecting change. Factors beyond the preferences of female representatives may interfere with their opportunities to act for women or dilute their impact due to changes in the behaviour of male representatives. In this regard it is useful to distinguish between the feminisation of the political agenda (where women's concerns and perspectives are articulated) and the feminisation of legislation (where output has been transformed), as the articulation of women's concerns constitutes an attempt to substantively represent women even where this has little or no effect in terms of legislative output. Finally, it should be acknowledged that demonstrating a direct causal relationship between the presence of women and broad feminised change is probably impossible. As Lovenduski (2005) has noted, we cannot be absolutely sure that women representatives are making a difference, only that a difference is being made and women are part of the process. There is, though, highly suggestive and consistent evidence both in the UK and elsewhere (Childs, et al 2005). The UK case studies reveal, for example, that there are sex differences in attitudes between women and men representatives, particularly in respect of women's concerns, as well as instances of different parliamentary behaviour. There is also evidence that women in the 1997 and 2001 parliament had a feminised effect on legislation, with the case studies of the Sex Discrimination (EC) Act and reducing VAT on sanitary products (Childs 2004; Childs et al 2005).

Conclusion

Feminist theorists have spent considerable time and effort reconsidering the concept of representation over the last decade or so. The limitations of mainstream conceptions of representation are clear: the classic typology is gender blind. In particular, Pitkin's preference for representation as 'acting for' belies the fact that liberal democracy has, thus far, proved resistant to any substantial representation of women (Phillips 1991:18–19). Women remain under-represented numerically in all parliaments of the world and their concerns remain nearer the margins than the centre of politics. Yet such observations would have been unimaginable without a feminist reworking of the concept. Times have changed: demands for women's numerical represen-tation are being heard around the world and there are now few public critics of women's claims. That our parliaments should better reflect, at least in terms of sex and race, our society is widely accepted although fewer are supportive of the necessary measures – such as quotas – that would deliver parity of representation. The feminist claim that there is a link between descriptive and substantive representation is more strongly contested. Indeed, there are significant debates *among* feminist theorists and feminist political scientists. The relationship, to be sure, is not straightforward: an appreciation of the theoretical challenges thrown up by contemporary understandings of gender identity as well as an acknowledgement of women's differences and the political contexts within which women representatives act 'on the ground' mediate any relationship. Contemporary theoretical and empirical research that seeks to answer the question of, *how* the substantive representation of women occurs is likely to prove fruitful in capturing the critical actors and processes involved.

Despite a growing community of gender and politics scholars and a burgeoning theoretical and empirical literature on representation, politics – the discipline – often appears hesitant in embracing our research.[7] A recent survey of British politics textbooks, for example, found few pages devoted to women's descriptive representation – a finding that suggests that gender and politics analyses have yet to become part of the discipline's 'conventional wisdom' (Childs and Krook 2006a; Moran 2006). On a more positive note, British gender and politics scholars are now recognised as 'an organised voice' in the discipline and our work on women's representation is published in mainstream omnibus journals and edited books on British politics (for example, *British Journal of Politics and International Relations; Politics; British Politics*). Perhaps more importantly, it is also beginning to invite critical reaction from beyond its own research community (see the exchange of articles in *Politics* 2006, for example), suggesting that we are not just speaking to the converted.

Key writers and further reading

The concept of representation has long been a concern of mainstream political theory: early writers include Thomas Hobbes, Edmund Burke, the Utilitarians and J. S. Mill. Their work is discussed in various texts: in Pitkin's seminal *The Concept of Representation* (1967), which is an accessible if quite long book that should be read in the original, as well as by Birch (1971; 1993) and Judge (1999). A central issue in much of the traditional literature is the trustee–mandate debate: whether the representatives should follow the wishes of their constituents or act as the representatives see those interests/ interests of the nation.

Anne Phillips' *The Politics of Presence* (1995) is, as the chapter suggests, the key feminist contribution. Not only does it set out the bases upon which women's political presence might be made but it also explores the relationship between women's descriptive and substantive representation. In addition to reading Phillips first hand, the work of Mansbridge (1999), Dovi (2002) Weldon (2002) and Young (1990a, b and 1997) provides a comprehensive introduction to the theoretical contributions of, and debates among, contemporary feminists. The edited collection by Sawer, Tremblay and Trimble (2006), *Representing Women in Parliament*, contains chapters analysing women's descriptive and substantive representation in the UK (Westminster, Scotland, Wales and Northern Ireland), Australia, Canada and New Zealand.

Table 1 Conceptions of Representation

Representation	Definition	Pitkin	Feminist
Formalistic Representation	The person upon whom the authority to act for others has been bestowed; or the person who is to be held to account	No guarantee that the representative will act for the represented	Agrees with Pitkin's criticism
Standing For: Descriptive	There is a correspondence between the characteristics of the representative and the represented	It is not clear which characteristics should be represented; there is no simple correlation between characteristics and actions; representative cannot be held to account for 'what he is'; risks an over-emphasis on composition of political fora	Composition of political fora matters; there may not be a simple correlation between characteristics and actions but (at least for many feminists) there is some kind of relationship between representatives' behaviour and their gender
Standing For: Symbolic	Representatives 'stand for' and 'evoke' the represented	Symbols are often arbitrary; symbolic representation relies upon the represented believing that they are represented; there is no room for representation as 'acting for'	The form of the symbols is more important than Pitkin implies; it is unconvincing to argue that women *are* represented when they *think* they are
Representing as 'Acting For'	Representatives act on behalf of and in the interests of the represented	This is the true definition of representation; the represented are 'logically prior' to the representative	Pitkin's definition is unable to evaluate the activity of representation as it occurs; it struggles to take account of gender – many feminists link women's descriptive and substantive representation

Notes

1 This chapter draws extensively on the first chapter of S. Childs (2007) *Women in British Politics* (London: Routledge).
2 The National Assembly for Wales – which is sex-balanced – does not qualify as a national parliament (www.ipu.org).
3 The concept of interest has a long and distinguished history of feminist engagement (Sapiro 1998; Diamond and Hartsock 1998; Jonasdottir 1990). For reasons of clarity Cockburn's definition of concerns is employed: to speak of women's concerns points to issues that bear on women, without in any way presupposing what position any given group of women would take on them (Cockburn 1996: 14–15).
4 In her later work Phillips reframes the fourth point and makes reference to a revitalisation of democracy that bridges the gap between representation and participation (Phillips 1998: 238).
5 This is not to say that the symbolic dimension of women's representation is unimportant or that it should be treated as unrelated to women's descriptive and substantive representation. However, this dimension has received considerably less attention in the literature.
6 See Dodson (2001), Weldon (2002) and Young (2002) for discussion of women's substantive representation through means other than, or in addition to, women representatives.
7 See Childs and Krook (2006a, 2006b) and Moran (2006) for a fuller discussion of the impact of gender and politics research on the British politics mainstream.

Bibliography

Beetham, D. (1992) 'The Plant Report and the Theory of Political Representation', *Political Quarterly* 63:4, 460–7.
Birch, A. H. (1971) *Representation* (Basingstoke: Macmillan).
Birch, A. H. (1993) *The Concepts and Theories of Modern Democracy* (London: Routledge).
Bochel, C. and Briggs, J. (2000) 'Do Women Make a Difference?', *Politics* 20:2, 63–8.
Carroll, S. J. (1994) *Women as Candidates in American Politics* (Bloomington and Indianapolis: Indiana University Press).
Childs, S. (2004) *New Labour's Women MPs* (London: Routledge).
Childs, S. and Krook, M. L. (2006a) 'Gender and Politics, the State of the Art', *Politics* 26:1, 18–28.
Childs, S. and Krook, M. L. (2006b) 'Gender, Politics and Political Science: A Reply to Michael Moran', *Politics* 26:3, 203–5.
Childs, S., Lovenduski, J. and Campbell, R. (2005) *Women at the Top* (London: Hansard Society).
Clark, J. (1994) 'Getting There: Women in Political Office', in M. Githens, P. Norris and J. Lovenduski (eds), *Different Roles, Different Voices* (New York: Harper Collins), 99–110.
Cockburn, C. (1996) 'Strategies for Gender Democracy', *European Journal of Women's Studies* 3:7, 7–26.

Dahlerup, D. (1988) 'From a Small to a Large Minority', *Scandinavian Political Studies* 11:4, 275–99.

Darcy, R., Welch, S. and Clark, J. (1994) *Women, Elections and Representation* (Lincoln and London: University of Nebraska Press).

Diamond, I. and Hartsock, N. (1998) 'Beyond Interests in Politics', in A. Phillips (ed.), *Feminism and Politics* (Oxford: Oxford University Press), 193–223.

Dodson, D. L. (2001) 'Acting for Women', in S. J. Carroll (ed.), *The Impact of Women in Public Office* (Bloomington: Indiana University Press), 225–42.

Dovi, S. (2002) 'Preferable Descriptive Representatives', *American Political Science Review* 96:4, 729–43.

Duerst-Lahti, G. and Verstegen, D. (1995) 'Making Something of Absence', in G. Duerst-Lahti and R. Mae Kelly (eds), *Gender Power Leadership and Governance* (Ann Arbor: The University of Michigan Press), 213–38.

High-Pippert, A. and Comer, J. (1998) 'Female Empowerment: The Influence of Women Representing Women', *Women and Politics* 19:4, 53–66.

Jonasdottir, A. G. (1990) 'On the Concept of Interest, Women's Interests, and the Limitations of Interest Theory', in K. B. Jones and A. G. Jonasdottir (eds), *The Political Interests of Gender* (London: Sage), 33–65.

Judge, D. (1999) *Representation* (London: Routledge).

Kanter, R. M. (1977) 'Some Effects of Proportions on Group Life', *American Journal of Sociology* 82:5, 965–90.

Lovenduski, J. (2005) *Feminizing Politics* (Cambridge: Polity).

Mackay, F. (2001) *Love and Politics* (London: Continuum).

Mansbridge, J. (1999) 'Should Blacks Represent Blacks and Women Represent Women?', *Journal of Politics* 61:3, 628–57.

McLean, I. (1991) 'Forms of Representation and Systems of Voting', in D. Held (ed.), *Political Theory Today* (Cambridge: Polity), 172–96.

Moran, M. (2006) 'Gender, Identity and the Teaching of British Politics: A Comment', *Politics* 26:3, 200–2.

Norris, P. (1996) 'Women Politicians: Transforming Westminster?', in J. Lovenduski and P. Norris (eds), *Women in Politics* (Oxford: Oxford University Press).

Parry, G., Moyser, G. and Day, N. (1992) *Political Participation and Democracy in Britain* (Cambridge: Cambridge University Press).

Pennock, R. J. (1968) 'Political Representation: An Overview', in J. R. Pennock and J. W. Chapman (eds), *Representation* (New York: Atherton Press), 3–27.

Phillips, A. (1991) *Engendering Democracy* (Cambridge: Polity).

Phillips, A. (1995) *The Politics of Presence* (Oxford: Clarendon Press).

Phillips, A. (1998) *Feminism and Politics* (Oxford: Oxford University Press).

Pitkin, H. F. (1967) *The Concept of Representation* (Berkeley, Los Angeles: University of California Press).

Rao, N. (1998) 'Representation in Local Politics: A Reconsideration and Some New Evidence', *Political Studies* 46:1, 19–35.

Reeve, A. and Ware, A. (1992) *Electoral Systems* (London: Routledge).

Reingold, B. (2000) *Representing Women* (Chapel Hill: University of North Carolina Press).

Sapiro, V. (1998) 'When are Interests Interesting?', in A. Phillips (ed.), *Feminism and Politics* (Oxford: Oxford University Press), 161–92.

Sawer, M., Tremblay, M. and Trimble, L. (2006) *Representing Women in Parliament* (London: Routledge).

Squires, J. (1995) 'Rethinking Representation', Paper presented to the Political Studies Association Annual Conference, York University.

Squires, J. (1996) 'Quotas for Women', in J. Lovenduski and P. Norris (eds), *Women in Politics* (Oxford: Oxford University Press), 73–90.

Squires, J. (1999) *Gender in Political Theory* (Cambridge: Polity).

Swers, M. L. (2002) *The Difference Women Make* (Chicago: University of Chicago Press).

Trimble, L. (2004) 'When do Women Count?', Paper presented to Women and Westminster Compared' conference, June, Ottawa.

Vickers, J. (1997) 'Towards a Feminist Understanding of Representation', in J. Arscott and L. Trimble (eds), *In the Presence of Women* (Toronto: Harcourt Brace), 20–46.

Voet, R. (1992) 'Political Representation and Quotas', *Acta Politica* 27:4, 389–403.

Weldon, S. L. (2002) 'Beyond Bodies: Institutional Sources of Representation for Women in Democratic Policymaking', *Journal of Politics* 64:4, 1153–74.

Young, I. M. (1990a) *Justice and the Politics of Difference* (Princeton, New Jersey: Princeton University Press).

Young, I. M. (1990b) *Throwing Like a Girl and Other Essays in Feminist Philosophy and Social Theory* (Bloomington and Indianapolis: Indiana University Press).

Young, I. M. (1997) *Intersecting Voices* (Princeton, New Jersey: Princeton University Press).

Young, I. M. (2002) *Inclusion and Democracy* (Oxford: Oxford University Press).

Web pages

www.ipu.org

7

Democracy and democratisation

Georgina Blakeley

Introduction

This chapter focuses on democratisation, grounding this in an initial discussion of democratic theory. This chapter therefore rejects the current gulf separating the literature on democratisation from that on democratic theory (see Allison 1994). This separation denotes a more general split between theory and practice which is best reflected in Dahl's wish to reserve the term democracy for the 'ideal' of democracy while coining a separate term, polyarchy, for that set of 'institutional arrangements that have come to be regarded as a kind of imperfect approximation of an ideal' (Dahl 1971:9).

Following David Beetham's lead, this chapter rejects Dahl's dichotomy. Beetham maintains 'to base our conception of democracy entirely on a set of existing institutions and practices offers no means of addressing the crucial, critical question: how might they be made more democratic?' (1994: 27). If we accept Dahl's dichotomy between normative ideal and empirical reality, the study of democratisation answers, rather than poses, the question of what people in processes of democratisation are struggling to achieve. This is particularly pertinent for women, given that democracy in theory and in practice has historically been based upon their exclusion. Assuming a priori that we know what kind of democracy people are struggling for risks perpetuating women's exclusion.

This chapter begins by examining some key assumptions of democratic theory, albeit in a necessarily cursory fashion given the extensiveness of the field, and some of the now well-established feminist critiques of these assumptions. It finds that although feminism has had some influence on democratic theory, this influence remains patchy and has not extended to the literature on democratisation. Despite the prolific nature of the democratisation literature, the dominant explanatory paradigms have virtually ignored the role of women in democratisation. This chapter redresses this balance by exploring what a feminist analysis of democratisation would entail.

'Malestream' democratic theory and the feminist challenge

Democracy today is generally taken to mean liberal democracy. This broad acceptance, however, should not blind us to the historical and geographical specificity of this particular form of democracy. Nor should it lead us to ignore the extent to which liberal democracy remains contested. Much of this contestation points to divergent theories of democracy. Despite this variety of thought, however, the theorists who comprise the canon of democratic theory remain those 'malestream' theorists who not only have been content to build their theory on the exclusion of half of the world's population but, moreover, have often not even noticed that they have done so!

Representation

Liberal democracy is an indirect and representative form of democracy based on a division of labour between those who rule and those who are ruled. Today's representative form contrasts with the direct democracy of the Greek city-state of Ancient Athens, over two thousand years ago, where the people governed themselves directly. This direct democracy was dependent on a small, homogeneous citizen body that was free to dedicate time to politics. The exclusion of women, 'immigrants' and slaves from the citizenry guaranteed the homogeneity of the citizenry and provided the labour necessary to allow citizens to go about their political business.

This direct form of government did not go uncontested. One of Athens's key political philosophers, Plato, criticised Athenian democracy precisely because it required the direct participation in government of those whom Plato considered unfit to rule, namely the poor and uneducated masses. This distrust of the masses is a constant thread throughout democratic theory. Certainly this distrust of the multitude was uppermost in the mind of James Madison (1751–1836). One of the Founding Fathers of the US Constitution, and the fourth President of the United States, Madison designed a political system for the United States based on the idea of representative republicanism, not democracy. For Madison the distinction between these two forms of rule was paramount: 'The first two great points of difference between a democracy and a republic are: first, the delegation of the government, in the latter, to a small number of citizens elected by the rest; secondly, the greater number of citizens and greater sphere of country over which the latter may be extended' (Madison et al 1987:126). Representation was a practical device for dealing with the size and complexity of the United States and a normative tool which legitimised government by referring to the power of the people while keeping that power at one remove from the business of government. From this point on, representation became synonymous with democracy and, in the words of the Scottish philosopher James Mill (1773–1836), representation was 'the grand discovery of modern times' (1825:16).

While heralding the 'grand discovery' of representation, however, liberal thinkers of the seventeenth and eighteenth centuries were deafeningly silent on who was being represented and by whom. Women, children and those without property were excluded from the suffrage, either because they were seen as lacking the necessary skills for political life or because it was thought that their interests could be sufficiently represented by others. The French philosopher, Rousseau (1712–78), was radical in his beliefs concerning freedom, equality and popular sovereignty, but he believed that only men were entitled to participate in politics because only they had reason to check their 'immoderate passions'; women were not rational and only had their 'modesty' to restrain their 'unlimited desires' (1762:1259). (For a critical discussion of the concept of rationality see Raia Prokhovnik's chapter in this volume.) For James Mill, women did not need to be included in the suffrage because their interests could be adequately represented by their fathers or husbands (1825:21). Liberal theorists who argued for female suffrage, such as J. S. Mill (1806–73), were the exception to the rule. Exclusion, as a defining feature of democracy, lasted well into the twentieth century. Women only gained the right to vote in national elections in Switzerland in 1971 and Kuwait in 2005, while it was only with the 1965 Voting Rights Act that formal restrictions (such as unequally applied literacy tests) preventing Southern Blacks from voting in the United States were finally lifted.

Given women's explicit exclusion from democracy, dating from its origins in Ancient Athens, one of the first tasks of feminist writers on democracy was to highlight the extent and nature of this exclusion (Coole 1993; Okin 1979). In some ways, this was the easy part and it was a task in which malestream writers could participate. Thus, contemporary malestream texts on democratic theory (Dahl 1989; Arblaster 1994; Holden 1993) lament the past exclusion of women. Simply deploring this exclusion as if it were an unfortunate part of democracy's history, however, does little to explain this exclusion and the extent to which it is written into the very fabric of democracy as it is practised today.

Abstract individualism

Today, exclusion is not explicit. There are no legal barriers barring any citizens from full participation in political life. This does not mean, however, that all are able to participate fully in practice. Liberal democracy is made in the image of the 'abstract individual'. As Ruth Lister also argues in this volume, in theory this abstract individualism purports to a universalism that ignores gender and other distinctions; in reality, it posits as standard the white, generally middle-class, male around whom politics and public activity, and much else besides, are then organised. This is a 'one size fits all' approach to politics which either does not care to notice that the structures, procedures and institutions of liberal democracy are not neutral but are fashioned in the image of a white, bourgeois male or, simply assumes, on the basis of our common humanity, that they will be suitable for everyone regardless of difference. This is like trying to force a round peg into a square hole while cursing the peg for being the wrong shape!

While malestream theorists have been happy to note women's explicit exclusion from the polity, they have been less alert to women's *implicit* exclusion. It has been up to feminists, like Mendus, to highlight that liberal democracy is based on the 'male model of normality' against which women are judged different and disadvantaged (1992:212). As Sarah Childs' chapter in this book attests, the under-representation of women throughout the world's democratic assemblies illustrates the extent to which the structures of liberal democracy militate against the full inclusion of women. Thus, far from being a mere historical oversight, women's exclusion from democracy is woven into the fabric of democratic life by positing a 'male model of normality' to which women are expected to conform. This dominant view of male 'normality', juxtaposed to women's difference and hence 'abnormality', explains why women continue to be implicitly excluded though formal exclusion no longer exists. Another factor behind women's implicit exclusion, to which this chapter now turns, is the distinction between the public and private spheres which defines liberal democracy.

Public/private

The distinction between the public and the private spheres is constitutive of liberal democracy. The development of capitalist relations of production and the resulting formal separation between economic power (the private sphere) and political power (the public sphere) made the unique combination of liberal democracy possible. With this separation, formal political equality could be enjoyed within the public sphere without disturbing the exploitative relations between capital and labour, and the inequalities arising from this, within the private sphere.

Marx's powerful critique of liberal democracy centres precisely on this split between the illusory political world of the state and the real economic world of civil society. In the 'Critique of Hegel', Marx argued that the equality of political society was illusory because it remained compromised by the inequalities of the real world of civil society where differences in property and wealth become differences in real freedom and real equality (Marx 1844). Theorists on the left have continued to criticise the public/private split and the illusion that formal political equality remains insulated from the inequalities that exist in the private sphere. Despite Mary Wollstonecraft's (1759–97) 'pioneering inquiry into the nature of the interconnections between the public and private realms' (Held 1996:63), however, it was not until feminism's second wave in the 1960s that the significance of this dichotomy for women began to be taken seriously.

To begin with, Pateman added a further distinction to the public/private distinction which Marx had earlier criticised. Pateman claims that there is not one single public/private distinction, but a double one: the first between the family (private) and civil society (public) and the second, which takes place within civil society itself, between civil society (private/economic) and the state (public/private) (1989:122). For Pateman, because 'the separation between private and public is thus re-established as a division within civil society itself, within the world of men', the distinction with which feminists are most concerned, between the domestic sphere and the public sphere of civil society, simply gets 'forgotten' in theoretical discussion (1989:122). This explains why the participatory theorists of the 1960s and 1970s continued to ignore the domestic realm as a potentially political sphere even when arguing for a broader definition of politics to embrace areas, previously considered to be private, like the work place. Feminists, however, took the premise to its logical conclusion: the expansion of democracy and politics set in motion by the participatory theorists should embrace all spheres of life. Pateman, both in her earlier work on participation and in her later work on feminism, epitomises this shift. In *Participation and Democratic Theory* (1970), Pateman criticised the public/private distinction between civil society and the state and argued for an expansion of democracy to include the industrial realm. In *The Disorder of Women* (1989) she addresses the prior public/private distinction between the family and civil society and argues that the domestic sphere is also political and should therefore be democratised.

It is not easy to move towards a relational way of thinking in order to transcend the public/private dichotomy which not only associates the public sphere with the activity of men and the private sphere with that of women but also values the former over the latter (see Valerie Bryson forthcoming 2007 and Raia Prokhovnik's chapter in this volume). Many feminists such as Phillips worry that 'an overassimilation of the personal and political may endanger what is positive about private life' (1991:103). The slogan 'the personal is political' highlights the interdependence of the public and private spheres but it also carries risks. Phillips argues that the attention to embracing democracy in all spheres of our lives is positive, but cautions 'This positive insistence on the democratisation of everyday life should not become a substitute for a more lively and vital political life' (1991:119).

Feminism's impact on malestream democratic theory

While feminism's impact on malestream democratic theory is incontrovertible, it is also patchy. Held's (1996) oft-quoted *Models of Democracy* is unusual for a textbook on democracy in that, in addition to the usual canon of malestream writers, it discusses Wollstonecraft's *Vindication of the Rights of Woman* and J. S. Mill's much-neglected work,

The Subjection of Women. Held's discussion of the public/private dichotomy is also clearly influenced by feminist thought. Hyland's (1995:220) discussion of the interdependence of political and non-political spheres and 'the intricacies and possible covertness of structures of power and domination' within them also owes much to feminist critiques.

Other theorists, however, appear less indebted to feminist contributions. Holden (1993), for example, confines the feminist critique of liberal democracy to a footnote in a chapter covering the radical critique of liberal democracy; others (Graham 1986; Harrison 1993; Dahl 1989) note the exclusion of women from democratic thought and practice while failing to explicitly acknowledge the feminist critique of democracy even when their discussions, for example of equality, the public/private dichotomy and the individual, overlap with feminist concerns.

If some theorists have continued to ignore the contribution of feminism to democratic theory, feminism's contribution to the literature on democratisation has been marginalised to an even greater extent. This chapter will go on to argue that unless analysts take on board feminist critiques of liberal democracy's abstract individualism, the public/private dualism and the narrow definition of politics which underpins it, the literature on democratisation will remain considerably impoverished.

Malestream approaches to democratisation

Since the start of the Third Wave of democracy which, according to Samuel Huntington (1991), began in Portugal in 1974 and subsequently spread to countries in Latin America, Africa and Eastern Europe, political scientists have attempted to explain this current process of democratisation and the likelihood of its persistence. Despite its prolific nature, however, the literature on democratisation, understood as a three-stage process involving the breakdown of authoritarianism, the transition to democracy proper and the consolidation of democracy, displays a remarkable degree of uniformity in terms of explanatory factors and theoretical perspectives. In particular, the contemporary literature on democratisation is characterised by its voluntarist and positivist nature (see Georgina Waylen 1994 for an extended critique). These two features have particular consequences for feminist scholars wishing to contribute to a more nuanced understanding of democratisation.

The voluntarism which characterises the democratisation literature is evident in the change from structural explanations of democratisation, regarded as too deterministic, to those based on elite agency. This change was heralded by Dankwart Rustow's seminal article in 1970 comparing democratisation in Turkey and Sweden. Rustow criticised the dominance of socio-economic factors in previous studies and changed the explanatory emphasis to elite choices and strategies summed up in the now famous phrase that a country never 'becomes a democracy in a fit of absent-mindedness' (1970:355).

In addition to voluntarism, the democratisation literature is positivist. This is most obvious in the rejection of substantive definitions of democracy in favour of procedural definitions, typified by Schumpeter's definition of democracy as a 'political method', that is to say, 'that institutional arrangement for arriving at political decisions in which individuals acquire the power to decide by means of a competitive struggle for the people's vote' (1992:269). From that point onwards 'rationalistic, utopian, idealistic definitions of democracy' were sidelined at the expense of 'empirical, descriptive, institutional, and procedural definitions' (Huntington 1991:6).

Assessing the malestream

The switch to agency-based explanations has been a welcome change from the structural determinism characteristic of past approaches to democratisation. Similarly, one can defend the adoption of a procedural definition of democracy as an expedient tool of analysis without which no transition to democracy, let alone the longer, more complex process of democratic consolidation, could be classified as complete. What is concerning, however, is the failure of analysts to acknowledge that this positivist and voluntarist focus denotes a particular ontological foundation. In short, analysts fail to perceive the consequences of this positivist and voluntarist focus for what they choose to analyse.

The stress on agency is specific in its emphasis on individual and elite-level agency rather than collective or mass-level agency. Some authors have tried to counter the elite bias within the literature by focusing on the agency of collective actors organised in social movements and associations within civil society. Bermeo (1997) stresses that elites are only able to engage in a strategy of pacts if they can count on the support of the mass actors whom they are supposed to represent. Tarrow uses an 'interactive' framework to draw attention to 'both elite and mass levels and to the interactions between them in the democratisation process' (1995:204–9). This literature, however, tends to concentrate on class-based instances of participation, thereby ignoring the role of other actors such as women. Women, in general, are simply not accorded agency within democratisation. This blindness reflects the fact that those studying democratisation identify only one distinction between the public realm of the state and the private realm of civil society, thereby ignoring Pateman's double distinction, mentioned above, which also includes the domestic realm.

Another consequence of the emphasis on elite agency is that democracy is restricted to the political–institutional sphere alone where politics becomes defined by elite activity. As such, the democratisation literature refers almost exclusively to the establishment of a democratic polity rather than to the establishment of a democratic society. This narrow definition of democracy denotes the positivist nature of much of the democratisation literature. The voluntarist and positivist nature of the current literature on democratisation are thus two sides of the same coin.

The positivist nature of the literature leads to two related problems. First, a narrow, procedural definition of democracy leaves wider questions of economic and social power outside of the analytical framework. Bermeo states that 'it is [even more] troubling to think that demands for the redistribution of property and power cannot go hand in hand and that electoral democracy must be built upon the patience of the poor' (1990:374). Przeworski concludes that 'Democratic institutions are likely to be economically and socially conservatising: this is simply the price which democrats must pay' (1992:134). These authors do not recognise, however, that 'the patience of the poor' and 'the price which democrats must pay' are gendered, with the result that this burden will be born predominately by women. Second, the positivist nature of the literature obscures the fact that the dominant procedural definition of democracy is itself normative. Defining democracy in terms of what exists, rather than on the basis of a set of normative values, implies taking existing circumstances for granted and therefore fails to problematise the status quo. Levine is virtually alone in noting: 'how curious it is to study "prospects for democracy" without serious consideration of democracy itself' (1988:393); most theorists accept without question the dominant Schumpeterian definition of democracy. As noted before, this acceptance of existing circumstances is particularly problematic for women, given that what exists marginalises or excludes women.

Positivism fails to acknowledge that defining democracy in terms of what exists depends itself on the bias of researchers in choosing to define some social phenomena as problems in need of explanation, while other social phenomena will be ignored. The narrow definition of politics, upon which Schumpeter's procedural definition of democracy is based, means that key factors which are problematic from a feminist viewpoint are not seen by mainstream analysts as worthy of explanation: they may simply not be seen at all (see Waylen 1994 and 2003 for similar arguments). The result is a form of democracy which, like the theoretical model on which it is based, implicitly excludes women. Accordingly, the work of feminist scholars on democratisation has consisted of drawing our attention to a number of factors as issues to problematise and to analyse rather than to accept unquestioningly. Three factors will be examined using illustrative examples from the Chilean process of democratisation, which is regarded as a successful example of a pacted transition and a neo-liberal economic success story. The three factors are: women's marginalisation from the public sphere as liberal democracy is re-established; the relationship of women's movements to political society; and the consequences of the neo-liberal economic model which accompanied the Third Wave of democracy. Feminist writers on democratisation see these three factors as issues to problematise in a way that malestream theorists do not. This is because a feminist understanding of these issues is grounded in a more comprehensive understanding of democracy built on well-established feminist critiques of liberal democracy's shortcomings: its abstract individualism, its dependence on the public/private dichotomy and a narrow understanding of politics.

Feminist work on democratisation

Women and the breakdown of authoritarianism

Much of the work on women has concentrated on their role in the first stage of democratisation: the breakdown of authoritarianism. This work is an important correction to the elite-dominated literature. It contributes to our understanding of how transitions come about and the central role of women within that explanation. Indeed, women were often the first actors to oppose non-democratic regimes. In Latin America, women took on key opposition roles because the closure of the public sphere under the military authoritarian regimes meant that political activity had to occur under less conventional guises within the private sphere. A combination of severe repression and the effects of a harsh neo-liberal economic model made it extremely hard for male actors organised in parties and trade unions to act. As the military suppressed traditional channels of political articulation, many areas of social life, such as housing, consumption and religion, became politicised. Domestic issues became central to the struggle against the military regimes and they contributed to redefining the 'political' and inventing new ways of doing politics.

Women's opposition activities were frequently linked to their traditional roles in the private sphere. Human rights organisations, or community organisations fighting to fulfil everyday needs, were seen as a natural extension of women's domestic and maternal roles. This is why women's opposition was so effective. Neither the military regimes, nor often the female participants themselves, perceived women's agency as political. Rai argues: 'The strategies that women have used to challenge non-democratic regimes are often anchored in existing social relations and are powerful because of the inability of those in power to counter this subversion without countering the norms which govern their social rhetoric' (1994:218). This was particularly pertinent under military regimes like Chile where motherhood and the family were seen as sacred. The simple question to which mothers demanded an answer – Where are our Children? – became unanswerable without calling the whole regime into question.

By becoming active in the private sphere, and on the basis of traditional gender roles, Latin American feminism has often been labelled 'maternal feminism' and juxtaposed to Western feminism, although maternal feminism has also been represented in the West, primarily by Ruddick (1989) and Elshtain (1981) (see Ruth Lister's chapter in this volume for a discussion of maternalist arguments in relationship to citizenship). In a similar vein, various authors have distinguished two types of women's opposition organisations. Molyneux (2001) distinguishes between those organisations with practical aims and those with strategic aims; Alvarez (1999) differentiates between those with 'feminine' as opposed to 'feminist' concerns. Those with 'practical' or 'feminine' concerns encompass human rights organisations or community organisations and they are seen as a natural extension of women's domestic and maternal roles. Movements or organisations which have 'feminist, strategic' aims are those which explicitly challenge existing gender power relations.

Some feminists have therefore seen the latter as progressive organisations in comparison to the former, which are seen as reactionary because they are based on traditional notions of women's reproductive and caring roles. By simply extending women's domestic roles from the private to the public sphere, it is argued that such organisations may reinforce traditional gender roles in society. This is, however, quite a static distinction. The potential of the human rights and community organisations to develop, almost as a by-product, the self-awareness and politicisation of the participants should be emphasised. Likewise, the importance of communal shopping or cooking groups, though based on women's traditional domestic roles, lay in the fact that these roles were no longer individual roles performed in private households; on the contrary, they were collectivised activities performed in the public sphere (Larrain 1986 quoted in Chuchryk 1994:69). As discussed in Ruth Lister's chapter in this volume, how these boundaries are drawn affects perceptions of citizenship.

Some authors therefore reject the feminine/feminist distinction. Stephen argues that the lived experiences of women simply do not uphold the feminine/feminist dichotomy (1997:12). Ackelsberg and Breitbart concur. They argue that studying women's political activism challenges the boundaries between public and private spheres, workplace and community, spheres of production and consumption because the daily realities experienced by women point to 'the interpenetration of public and private arenas' (1987–88:168, 173). Certainly, for many groups in Chile, the questioning of authority in one sphere led to the questioning of authority more generally. The collective Mujeres por la Vida (Women for Life) adopted the slogan 'Democracy in Chile and at home', thereby acknowledging the interpenetration of the public and private realms which feminists have highlighted in their critique of democratic theory and practice.

Nevertheless, other analysts argue that regardless of how the dichotomy is experienced by women activists, it can have lasting consequences for women's activism once the transition to democracy is underway and conventional politics reasserts itself. Precisely because women became active politically in the private sphere, and because both men and women saw this activism as non-political, once democracy was restored, both women and men continued to see women's agency as non-political. Women thus found it difficult to maintain their visibility once democracy was restored. Under authoritarianism, when men found it difficult to act politically, women became a 'reserve army' of political labour; once democracy was restored, however, women's political labour was no longer needed. Franceschet argues that because Chilean women based their strategy on their 'difference', this 'inhibited women from demanding power (i.e. access to institutions as individuals) because this conformed to a masculine-defined notion of politics inconsistent with women's different style of practicing politics' (2001:207). Jaquette recognises that 'politicised motherhood' might be an appropriate and rational strategy in the context of repressive, authoritarian regimes, but stresses that 'the argument can still be made that when women participate as mothers, not as citizens in their own right, they reinforce traditional gender roles in societies where male–female distinctions are already well-entrenched' (1994:225).

Friedman (1998) explains the difficulty women face in maintaining their visibility once liberal democracy is restored by borrowing a much-used concept from the social movement literature, namely the political opportunity structure. Tarrow defines the political opportunity structure as 'consistent – but not necessarily formal, permanent or national – dimensions of the political environment which either encourage or discourage people from using collective action' (1994:18). In contrast to most writers, however, Friedman highlights that the concept of the political opportunity structure is gendered at each stage of democratic transition (1998:88). This explains the apparent paradox that women are extremely active under authoritarian regimes but are relatively inactive once democracy has been re-established while, for men, the reverse is true. Women are able to organise under authoritarianism, while men cannot, precisely because their gender labels their activity as non-political. But once democracy is restored this same gender identity continues to condemn women's activity to the non-political sphere. Matear (1996:247) points to the absurdity of this situation in Chile where:

> Under apparently open democratic systems women and men were formally incorporated with the same political rights yet, in practice, they did not have equal representation or access to political positions of power. By contrast, the closed systems of military dictatorships produced high levels of female mobilization in non-institutional politics.

Malestream theorists, however, do not see the absurdity of this situation. Without feminists' understanding of the public/private dichotomy underpinning liberal democracy and the ways in which it renders women's agency invisible, malestream theorists of democratisation do not see the progressive marginalisation of women from the public sphere as liberal democracy is re-established as problematic at all. Malestream theorists similarly fail to problematise the relationship between women and political society to which this chapter now turns.

Women and political society

The difficulty faced by women's movements of responding to the new liberal democratic governments is often encapsulated in the literature in terms of the autonomy vs. integration debate (see Waylen 1994). The mainstream democratisation literature does not problematise the state or political parties whereas feminists have long recognised the problematic and complex role of both the state and parties in sometimes facilitating women's advancement while, at other times, forming a key hindrance. The autonomy vs. engagement debate reflects similar dilemmas in Western feminism of the extent to which feminists should engage with the state and political parties, thereby risking co-option, or the extent to which autonomy should be maintained, thereby risking political marginalisation. Though the terms of the debate may be similar, the context of regions like Latin America is very different. This dilemma is more acute in Latin America where political parties and the state have been weak in terms of their capacity to represent interests and provide services, but strong in terms of their ability to use coercive and clientelist strategies to co-opt disempowered social groups. Thus, although political parties may respond to women as constituencies to be mobilised and whose vote must be courted, particularly if women have been visible during democratisation processes, they remain reluctant to share power.

Those active in civil society thus tend to regard those within political parties and the state with suspicion. Franceschet argues that with the restoration of democracy the majority of women who were active in the opposition remain active at the community level but do not often translate that activity into the formal political sphere. She concludes that 'transitions to democracy present rather narrow windows of opportunity for women to challenge fundamentally gender relations in the formal political sphere' (2001:211). This mirrors the concern of feminists such as Phillips, mentioned earlier, that while concerning themselves with the democratisation of everyday life, women run the risk of leaving the democratisation of the public sphere to men.

Nevertheless some gains have been made: many Latin American countries have institutionalised some of the key demands from the transition period by setting up ministries or government offices for women. Many political parties in the region have implemented quotas either for internal party positions and/or for legislative and executive positions. In contrast to the views of some authors mentioned above, the maternal feminism of Latin America has not prevented women from arguing for electoral quotas. Jaquette remarks that 'US feminists are astounded at the ease with which some Latin American political parties have committed themselves to nominating a certain percentage of women on their lists of candidates' (1994:232). Again, however, context is everything and Jaquette cautions:

> in the Latin American context, quotas will make it easier for men to treat women as a special sector and to enforce a gender division of political labour. Women will be expected to take care of women's issues, leaving the rest to men. And the men can deny any responsibility for women's issues on the grounds that they have already met their obligations by giving women guaranteed representation. (1994:232)

For women, then, political parties may not be the 'crucial mediating mechanism' that Rueschemeyer et al claim in their groundbreaking comparative-historical analysis of democratisation (1992:287). Their analysis emphasises the importance of political parties as intermediaries between the state and civil society, but it ignores the fact that political parties can represent key institutional barriers to women's political activism. This is particularly the case in countries like Chile where parties have traditionally monopolised politics and controlled all access to spheres of decision-making.

For malestream theorists of democratisation, however, this is not an issue worthy of analysis. Without feminists' understanding of abstract individualism, malestream theorists of democratisation remain blind to women's implicit exclusion from traditional channels and structures of political activity, including political parties and the state. In a similar way, malestream theorists fail to problematise the gendered consequences of neo-liberalism, which will be discussed next, given that they remain constrained by a conventional, narrow definition of politics.

Women and neo-liberalism

The final issue, which the democratisation literature fails to problematise, is the neo-liberal model which accompanied the Third Wave of democracy (see John Craig's and Kalpana Wilson's chapters in this volume for a discussion of the consequences of neo-liberalism for women). Due to the narrow definition of democracy adopted, most analysts fail to see neo-liberalism as a political project as well as an economic one. And yet, as Boron argues, 'the ideological success of neoliberalism far exceeds the modest accomplishments – at inordinate social cost – it obtained in the terrain of the economy' (1999:213).

The key consequence of neo-liberalism in Latin America is the extent to which it depoliticises politics and reduces collective, political problems to technical, individual ones. A neo-liberal lens views structural problems like poverty as individual problems which individual endeavour within the market place can solve. Schild argues that the political conscious-raising work shops of the past have been replaced by 'technical training work shops that are geared towards helping poor women access the market and rely on market-based solutions to their problems' (2000:27).

Boron highlights that 'the state has retreated to minimal functions, and former collective goods (health, nutrition, education, housing, occupational training, and so on) have become individual problems that must be solved according to the egotistic rules of the market place' (1999: 220). Boron fails to emphasise, however, the extent to which the retreat of the state primarily affects women. As Jaquette argues, 'women in general have been disproportionately harmed by cuts in government spending that have weakened social safety nets and reduced budgets for health and education' (2001:112). Craske argues that the structural adjustment programmes common to neo-liberal states in the region are gendered in that they rely on women's traditional roles in the domestic sphere of reproducing the labour force in the cheapest way possible while at the same time relying on them to provide low-wage competition in the labour market (1998:114). Unsurprisingly, Craske questions 'how long can people who already work long hours in the reproductive and productive arenas be expected to engage in grassroots political activity in their "spare" time? This has been the triple burden to befall women over the past decades' (1998:114). (See Valerie Bryson's chapter in this volume for a discussion of the issue of time poverty.)

Most Latin American cases reveal that the women's groups that survive the transition process and the return to 'politics as normal' are those of the middle classes, not those of the working classes or the shantytown women who remain on the periphery. While we can point to the greater representation of women within the parties and the state apparatus in most Latin American countries (not least because of the adoption of quotas), this 'new female political class' is not representative of women as a whole. The election of Michelle Bachelet in 2006 as the first female President of Chile, and only the third in the history of Latin America, is undoubtedly an immense achievement that few would have predicted even a few years previously, but while the integration of individual women into the political hierarchy is important, of more significance is the empowerment of women as a group. This, of course, reinforces the limits of the individual as the basis of liberal democracy mentioned earlier. Matear concludes that 'the more lasting barriers to institutional politics therefore may be based not on gender but on social class' (Matear 1996:262). Waylen concurs: 'Relatively few women are active in institutional politics, partly because democratisation has not been accompanied by moves toward the wider social and economic equality that would enable women to participate in greater numbers' (1994:352).

Conclusion

This chapter has argued that the voluntarist and positivist nature of the mainstream democratisation literature is not accidental but denotes a particular ontological foundation that tends at best to marginalise women's activism and, at worst, simply ignores it. A narrow definition of democracy, based on elite agency within the political–institutional sphere, fails to problematise key issues that impact on women's activism. The reason why these issues are marginalised from the mainstream is simple and complex. It is simple because the narrow definition of democracy underpinning the democratisation literature means that these issues are defined as non-political and thus a problem for individuals rather than the state. As such they are simply not the proper subject for analysis. The answer is complex, however, because the ways in which these issues are defined as non-political reflects underlying ontological assumptions which are obvious to those who do not share them but are unacknowledged by those who do. As a result, much of the work that now exists on feminism and democratisation has remained at the margins of the mainstream literature. Waylen, who has led the way on integrating women into the democratisation literature, comments that despite the volume of work on gender and political transitions that now exists 'Although some articles appear in gender and area studies journals, very few are found in the major mainstream comparative politics journals' (2003:157). This isolation contrasts with the greater influence of feminist thought on democratic theory, where edited collections are now more likely, as a matter of course, to include chapters on feminism alongside the more long-standing critiques (Dunn 1992; Blaug and Schwarzmantel 2001).

The gap between democratic theory and democratisation is harmful in general: it fails to problematise existing circumstances and thus has an implicitly conservative bias towards accepting the status quo. But the gap is particularly harmful for women because the status quo is one implicitly based upon their exclusion from democratic life. Women will therefore find it hard to join with Fukuyama in celebrating 'the universalization of Western liberal democracy as the final form of human government' (1989:4). For feminists, this cannot be as good as it gets!

Key writers and further reading

As noted in this chapter, the literature on both democratic theory and democratisation is vast. An invaluable way into the literature on democratic theory therefore is provided by Held's (1996) *Models of Democracy*, which provides a comprehensive overview of both historical and contemporary democratic theorists. Also useful is the reader compiled by Blaug and Schwarzmantel (2001), which is an extensive collection of primary extracts from a wide range of canonical and contemporary theorists. The key feminist writers who have provided major contributions to democratic theory include Phillips (1991), Pateman (1989) and Mendus (1992).

The best starting point for the literature on democratisation is provided by the comprehensive overview of the literature edited by Potter, Goldblatt, Kiloh and Lewis (1997). As this chapter has argued, the feminist writer who has led the way on integrating women into the democratisation literature is Georgina Waylen (1994, 2003). Other key feminist contributions come from Rai (1994) and Jaquette (2001).

Bibliography

Ackelsberg, M. A. and Breitbart, M. (1987–88) 'Terrains of Protest: Striking City Women', *Our Generation* 19:1, 151–75.

Allison, L. (1994) 'On the Gap between Theories of Democracy and Theories of Democratization', *Democratization* 1:1, 8–26.

Alvarez, S. E. (1999) 'Advocating Feminism: The Latin American Feminist NGO "Boom"', *International Feminist Journal of Politics* 1:2, 181–209.

Arblaster, A. (1994) *Democracy* (Buckingham: Open University Press).

Beetham, D. (1994) 'Key Principles and Indices for a Democratic Audit', in D. Beetham (ed.), *Defining and Measuring Democracy* (London: Sage), 25–43.

Bermeo, N. (1990) 'Rethinking Regime Change', *Comparative Politics* 22:3, 359–77.

Bermeo, N. (1997) 'The Power of the People', *Working Paper* No. 97 (Madrid: Juan March Institute).

Blaug, R. and Schwarzmantel, J. (2001) *Democracy: A Reader* (Edinburgh: Edinburgh University Press).

Boron, A. (1999) 'State Decay and Democratic Decadence in Latin America', in L. Panitch and C. Leys (eds), *Global Capitalism Versus Democracy* (Rendlesham: The Merlin Press), 209–26.

Bryson, V. (forthcoming 2007) *The Politics of Time* (Bristol: The Policy Press).

Chuchryk, P. (1994) 'From Dictatorship to Democracy: The Women's Movement in Chile', in J. S. Jaquette (ed.), *The Women's Movement in Latin America* (Boulder, Colorado: Westview Press), 65–107.

Coole, D. (1993) *Women in Political Theory: From Ancient Misogyny to Contemporary Feminism* (Hemel Hempstead: Harvester-Wheatsheaf).

Craske, N. (1998) 'Remasculinisation and the Neo-liberal State in Latin America', in V. Randall and G. Waylen (eds), *Gender, Politics and the State* (London: Routledge), 100–20.

Dahl, R. A. (1971) *Polyarchy, Participation and Opposition* (New Haven: Yale University Press).

Dahl, R. A. (1989) *Democracy and Its Critics* (New Haven: Yale University Press).

Dunn, J. (1992) (ed.) *Democracy: The Unfinished Journey 508 BC to AD 1993* (Oxford: Oxford University Press).

Elshtain, J. B. (1981) *Public Man, Private Woman* (Princeton: Princeton University Press).

Franceschet, S. (2001) 'Women in Politics in Post-transitional Democracies: The Chilean Case', *International Feminist Journal of Politics* 3:2, 207–36.

Friedman, E. J. (1998) 'Paradoxes of Gendered Political Opportunity in the Venezuelan Transition to Democracy', *Latin American Research Review* 33:3, 87–135.

Fukuyama, F. (1989) 'The End of History', *National Interest* 16, 3–18.

Graham, K. (1986) *The Battle of Democracy* (Brighton: Wheatsheaf Books).

Harrison, R. (1993) *Democracy* (London: Routledge).

Held, D. (1996) *Models of Democracy* (Cambridge: Polity Press).

Holden, B. (1993) *Understanding Liberal Democracy* (Hemel Hempstead: Harvester-Wheatsheaf).

Huntington, S. P. (1991) *The Third Wave* (Norman: University of Oklahoma Press).

Hyland, J. (1995) *Democratic Theory* (Manchester: Manchester University Press).

Jaquette, J. S. (1994) *The Women's Movement in Latin America* (Boulder, Colorado: Westview Press).

Jaquette, J. S. (2001) 'Women and Democracy: Regional Differences and Contrasting Views', *Journal of Democracy* 12:3, 111–25.

Levine, D. H. (1988) 'Paradigm Lost: Dependency to Democracy', *World Politics* 40:3, 377–94.

Madison, J., Hamilton, A. and Jay, J. (1987) *The Federalist Papers*, edited by I. Kramnick (Harmondsworth: Penguin).

Marx, K. (1844) 'Contribution to the Critique of Hegel's Philosophy of Right', in K. Marx and F. Engels (1975) *Collected Works, Vol. 3, 1843–44* (London: Lawrence and Wishart).

Matear, A. (1996) 'Desde la Protesta a la Propuesta: Gender Politics in Transition in Chile', *Democratization* 3:3, 246–63.

Mendus, S. (1992) 'Losing the Faith: Feminism and Democracy', in J. Dunn (ed.), *Democracy: The Unfinished Journey 508 BC to AD 1993* (Oxford: Oxford University Press), 207–19.

Mill, J. (1825) *Essay on Government* (New York: Sentry Press).

Molyneux, M. (2001) *Women's Movements in International Perspective* (London: Palgrave).

Okin, S. (1979) *Women in Western Political Thought* (Princeton: Princeton University Press).

Pateman, C. (1970) *Participation and Democratic Theory* (Cambridge: Cambridge University Press).

Pateman, C. (1989) *The Disorder of Women* (Cambridge: Polity Press).

Phillips, A. (1991) *Engendering Democracy* (Cambridge: Polity Press).

Potter, D., Goldblatt, D. Kiloh, M. and Lewis, P. (1997) *Democratization* (Milton Keynes: Open University Press).

Przeworski, A. (1992) 'The Games of Transition', in S. Mainwaring, G. O'Donnell and J. S. Valenzuela (eds), *Issues in Democratic Consolidation* (Indiana: University of Notre Dame Press), 105–52.

Rai, S. M. (1994) 'Gender and Democratisation: Or What Does Democracy Mean for Women in the Third World?', *Democratization* 1:2, 209–28.

Rousseau, J.-J. (1762) *Emile* (www.ilt.columbia.edu/pedagogies/rousseau/em_eng_bk5.html).

Ruddick, S. (1989) *Maternal Thinking* (London: Verso).

Rueschemeyer, D., Stephens, E. and Stephens, J. (1992) *Capitalist Development and Democracy* (Cambridge: Polity Press).

Rustow, D. A. (1970) 'Transitions to Democracy: Toward a Dynamic Model', *Comparative Politics* 2:3, 337–63.

Schild, V. (2000) '"Gender Equity" Without Social Justice: Women's Rights in the Neoliberal Age', *NACLA Report on the Americas* 34:1, 25–53.

Schumpeter, J. A. (1992) *Capitalism, Socialism and Democracy* (London: Routledge).

Stephen, L. (1997) *Women and Social Movements in Latin America* (Austin: University of Texas Press).

Tarrow, S. (1994) *Power in Movement: Social Movements, Collective Action and Politics* (New York: Cambridge University Press).

Tarrow, S. (1995) 'Mass Mobilisation and Regime Change: Pacts, Reform and Popular Power in Italy (1918–1922) and Spain (1975–1978)', in R. Gunther, P. Diamandouros and H. Jürgen Pühle (eds), *The Politics of Democratic Consolidation* (Baltimore: Johns Hopkins University Press), 204–30.

Waylen, G. (1994) 'Women and Democratisation: Conceptualizing Gender Relations in Transition Politics', *World Politics* 46:3, 327–54.

Waylen, G. (2003) 'Gender and Transitions: What Do We Know?' *Democratization* 10:1, 157–78.

8

Development

John Craig

This chapter explores the main feminist contributions to the study of development and assesses their impact on contemporary mainstream development practice and discourse. It begins by providing a brief review of the concept of development and some of the key themes that are considered within the field of development studies. It then turns to review the mainstream of development theory in the 1950s and 1960s, demonstrating that these were, by and large, focused primarily on the male experience of development. The chapter then turns to consider the emergence of feminist development theory in the 1970s and 1980s, focusing in particular on the contribution of the 'Women in Development' (WID), Women and Development' (WAD) and 'Gender and Development' (GAD) approaches. The impact of these ideas on the mainstream of development theory is then explored and assessed.

It will be argued that while feminist interventions have made a significant impact on the mainstream of development theory and practice, the extent of this has been uneven. The incorporation of feminist perspectives in some areas is contrasted with their more limited adoption in others. This is highlighted in the case of privatisation, which has been a key element in orthodox development strategy for nearly two decades, but where little work exists on the gender dimensions of the policy. However, it is suggested that this not only reflects the uneven basis on which feminist perspectives have been incorporated into the development mainstream, but also a narrowing of the scope of the mainstream itself.

Defining development

Development is a contested concept and is subject to multiple uses and definition in both academic and practitioner communities. Alan Thomas (2000a) summarises three ways in which the term has been used. The first usage of the term relates to those historical processes of change that have transformed societies in recent centuries and have been variously characterised as industrialisation, urbanisation and the growth of capitalism or the great social transformation. The extent and impact of these processes have been uneven across the globe and have produced the sharp divide between developed countries (those that had successfully undergone these processes) and underdeveloped countries (those that had not). The countries of Western Europe, North America, Japan and Australasia would generally be seen as constituting the first group, while those in Latin America, Africa and Asia would classically have been classed in the second group.

The effect of this divide was to prompt a range of social groups to undertake actions with the aim of bringing development to those countries that were underdeveloped. These actions give rise to the second usage of the term that is identified by Thomas (2000a:29), which identifies development as 'deliberate efforts aimed at improvement'. The social actors involved in these efforts have been many and varied. They have included local communities, international governmental organisations, business enterprises, voluntary groups, and governments in both developed and underdeveloped countries. Nevertheless, whoever is involved, such actions have always contained within them (either implicitly or explicitly) a vision of the desirable end-state of the development process. It is this which provides the basis for the third use of the term identified by Thomas (2000a), development as a vision.

From this, it can be seen that development is a complex term, encompassing theory and practice, and positive and normative elements. And these differences are not just relevant to academic discourse; the different conceptualisations of development have implications for how those involved in development policy and practice plan and devise their actions and measure the progress achieved. This might be illustrated by comparing the practical issues of how development is measured. Traditionally many development academics and practitioners have distinguished between more and less developed countries on the basis of their per capita national income. This reflected the fact that those countries such as Great Britain, the United States and Japan, that had experienced processes of industrialisation and urbanisation, had higher national incomes per head of population than those that had not. It additionally conceptualised development as being about rising levels of material wealth and linked to the notion that development strategy and practice were concerned with generating high levels of economic growth.

An alternative approach to measuring development is the Human Development Index (HDI), which was developed by the United Nations Development Programme. This differentiates between countries on the basis of not only their national income per capita, but also the levels of literacy and the longevity of the population. In terms of ranking which countries have more development, and which have less, the HDI approach does not differ a great deal from those derived from the national income-based alternative. Countries within Western Europe, North America and Japan are still at the top, while those from Sub-Saharan Africa remain towards the bottom. Nevertheless, the approach explicitly aims to conceptualise development as more than just economic growth and instead implies that development might be promoted through a distinct set of deliberate efforts aimed at delivering improvements in education and health, as well as income (Streeton 1995).

Classic theories

Academic reviews of development theory, such as Preston (1996:310) and Calvert and Calvert (2001:235), often suggest that the mainstream development writers of the 1950s and 1960s simply ignored the role and position of women in the development process. Such claims about the content of classic literatures can sometimes become unfounded orthodoxies and it is useful to revisit some of the classic texts to re-evaluate them.

A good starting point for this examination is Walt Rostow's *The Stages of Economic Growth*, first published in 1960 and subtitled a 'Non-communist Manifesto'. At the time that Rostow was writing this volume, he held the post of Professor of Economic History at the Massachusetts Institute of Technology and was a speech writer for President Eisenhower. Later Rostow would serve as the leading national security advisor to President Johnson and played a key role in developing that administration's Vietnam policy. As a consequence of this, Rostow's work can be seen as reflecting some of the key mainstream policy and academic orthodoxies of the period.

In *The Stages of Economic Growth*, Rostow (1960) provides a grand theory of the process of development, tracing the progress of societies through five stages of growth – from traditional through to the age of mass consumption. The first stage was that of the pre-Newtonian traditional society, a state in which most human societies had existed for most of history. These were not seen as necessarily static societies, but nevertheless they were constrained in their attempts to grow and develop by their relatively undeveloped understanding of the physical world. These traditional societies were distinguished from those which had entered a second stage in which innovations in science and technology had begun to expand the potential for industrial and agricultural transformation. As this process became more generalised, Rostow saw societies entering a third stage of 'take-off' in which year-on-year growth in the economy comes to be regarded as 'normal' and is supported through a high level of re-investment. This take-off is followed by a long period during which high levels of continued investment allow a sustained growth in the economy and allow it to achieve the fifth and final stage of high mass consumption.

There have been many critiques of this approach in the half-century since it was written, but here our main focus is to explore the role accorded to women in this approach. In fact, Rostow (1960) makes reference to women on only one of its 167 pages. This is in the context of his speculations of what will occur as the period of mass consumption develops and scarcity is banished from the human experience in developed countries. Will we, he mused, turn our attentions to the exploration of outer space or 'will man, converted en masse into a suburban version of the eighteenth century country gentleman, find in some equivalent of hunting, shooting and fishing ... sufficient frontiers to keep for life its savour' (Rostow 1960:91).

The use of the term 'man' was apparently, in this context, quite conscious, for Rostow quickly clarifies that 'we doubt that half the human race – that is to say, women – will recognise this problem ... the problem of boredom is a man's problem, at least until the children have grown up' (Rostow 1960:91). At once it is clear that all the social and economic changes that are analysed by Rostow are primarily seen as affecting men. Women, it is presumed, would remain at home as spectators of these revolutionary changes. Indeed it was such assumptions that informed mainstream development practice during the period, which engaged with women primarily as mothers and focused on issues such as nutrition, family planning and child rearing (Moser 1993:58–62).

It is, of course, only fair to turn the same spotlight upon the classical texts of the radical tradition in development theory. Here we might identify the dependency and underdevelopment schools of analysis which developed as a critique of mainstream theorists such as Rostow. These radical approaches emphasised the exploitative nature of the global capitalist economy and the extent to which the development of the richer countries was systematically linked to the underdevelopment of the poorer. Nevertheless, despite this focus on issues of power and inequality between classes and nations, as Hulme and Turner (1990:89) argue, the dependency approach proved little better at focusing on the experience of women. The points might be illustrated by turning to the example of Samir Amin's *Unequal Development* (1976). The text is a tour de force of radical development theory which explores issues relating to the historic processes of underdevelopment as well as exploring the shape of contemporary social formations in the developing world. In its entire 385 pages, reference to women is made on only three occasions. Once this is a passing reference within a discussion of the monetarisation of pre-capitalist societies and twice it is a reference to the role of women in the small-scale food production and trading sectors. At no point is it suggested that the experience of development or underdevelopment might be systematically different for men and women.

Overall, therefore, it would seem a fair assessment that until at least the mid-1970s, the mainstream of both orthodox and radical development theories was primarily focused on the experiences of men and that little consideration was given to the role of women. In that sense, the mainstream of development in this period may be fairly considered to have also been a 'malestream'. We will now turn our attentions to consider the ways in which feminist theorists engaged with this 'malestream' of development theory.

Feminist development theory

It is widely recognised that the key contribution which kicked this off was Ester Boserup's *Woman's Role in Economic Development* published in 1970. At the core of Boserup's argument was an identification of the existing sexual division of labour between men and women and the recognition that this would both influence and be influenced by the process of development. Crucially, Boserup (1970) argued that there would be an overriding tendency for women to be marginalised and excluded from the benefits of development.

This was highlighted in her coverage of the development of industry 'from the hut to the factory' (Boserup 1970:106). Here it is argued that in pre-industrial societies, women frequently play a significant role in the production of traded goods within the home. However, with the development of industries and markets, larger production units, such as factories, are able to benefit from economies of scale and out-compete these home industries. This trend, Boserup (1970) suggested, would adversely affect women in two ways. Firstly, they would be directly affected by the curtailment of demand for their products and suffer the associated fall in income. Secondly, women would also fail to benefit from the new employment opportunities offered by the expansion of factories as this tended to draw primarily male labour.

Boserup (1970) offered two primary explanations for this trend towards predominantly male employment within the factory sector. Firstly, on the demand side, she suggested that employers may prefer to hire male workers. Here Boserup (1970:115–16) cites the potential additional costs of employing women workers related to issues of fertility, childcare and cultural restrictions on the range of work that women may perform. Secondly, on the supply side, Boserup cites women's own reluctance to engage in work outside the home. Among the potential reasons for this were the challenge of combining external work outside the home with their continuing domestic duties (such as childcare) and cultural problems relating to contact with men from outside of their own family.

From this analysis was derived the 'Women in Development' or 'WID' approach to development practice. This approach aimed to address the exclusion of women from the development process by generating policies and strategies that would provide women with new opportunities to engage in the development process and enjoy its benefits.

Within the context of the United Nations Decade for Women (1975 to 1985) and the growing influence of the feminist movement in the countries of the developed world, the WID approach rapidly became adopted by mainstream development institutions and organisations. During the period, many development organisations established special women's policy units or employed special advisors to ensure that they began to factor women into the development of their policies and practices.

The WID approach was, however, challenged in the later 1970s by a second wave of feminist writings on development which became known as WAD ('Women and Development') theories. WAD approaches differed from WID approaches in two fundamental respects. Firstly, whereas WID theorists argued that women were generally excluded from development, WAD theorists argued that they had been integrally involved in the process. However, in further contrast to WID theorists, those writing from a WAD perspective did not characterise this as a necessarily positive experience. Drawing on radical development perspectives, they emphasised the exploitative nature of much of this participation, analysing it within a framework informed by Marxist critiques of capitalism and imperialism. As Bandarage (1984:x) summarised the contrast, 'WID thinkers see free trade and the liberation of women as mutually compatible. For the Marxists, however, the integration of Third World women into free trade represents exploitation, not liberation.'

Those writing from a WAD perspective provided a distinctly different picture to that developed within the WID framework. An example of this approach is the work of Maria Mies. Mies (1986:116) argued that rather than being marginalised, women provided the 'optimal' labour force for global capitalism. The reason for this was that they entered the labour market defined as 'housewives' rather than 'workers'. As such they constituted a form of 'unfree labour' that was subject to super-exploitation. With other writers Mies noted the intensive use of female labour in the emerging industrial sector of countries such as Indonesia, Malaysia and Mexico to evidence her claim.

The Third Wave of feminist engagements with development theory, known as 'Gender and Development' or GAD approaches, arose as an attempt to move beyond these existing literatures. At the centre of this approach were a number of core ideas relating to the conceptualisation of gender, the scope of development and the nature of social change (Rathgeber 1990; Young 1997).

Firstly, GAD followed the conceptual shift made elsewhere in feminist literature in exploring women's position in particular societies as socially constructed, rather than biologically determined. That is to say that the norms, behaviours and expectation associated with either sex will change over time and place. Thus, what might be regarded as men or women's work in one society may not be so regarded elsewhere. As such, any particular constructions of gender are influenced not only by biological factors, but also by a host of social factors such as class, race, age and ethnicity.

This distinction between sex and gender can be regarded as a particularly important thematic element within development studies since by their nature social change made the construction of these roles more apparent. For example, Karen Tranberg Hansen's (1984) article 'Negotiating Sex and Gender in Urban Zambia' explores the processes through which the place of women in the emerging towns and cities of Zambia became defined through conflict and bargaining with both Zambian men and the colonial authorities. Focusing on the dramatic changes in life and livelihood that had occurred in just a few decades, Hansen (1984:238) writes of how 'women and men wrestle with their own definition of what a heterosexual relationship ought to be; and they confront the state over the question of how families ought to make a livelihood'. As such, the parameters are not given, but are instead socially constructed and reproduced through active processes.

A second defining element of the GAD approach was the broader scope of social relationships that were explored. Despite the differences between WID and WAD perspectives, both tended to focus primarily on the economic sphere and issues around women's participation in society as economic agents. By contrast GAD provided a broader focus and aimed to examine 'the totality of social organisation, economic and political life in order to understand the shaping of particular aspects of society' (Young 1997:52).

GAD is further differentiated from WID and WAD through its emphasis on women as social actors within these processes of change, rather than merely passive recipients of an unfolding historical logic. In this sense, the process of development does not necessarily benefit or marginalise women. Rather it presents an evolving pattern of opportunities, pressures and constraints that interact with the individual and collective actions and strategies of men and women. This leads on to a fourth point concerning the complex and potentially contradictory nature of development. It may be that women gain in one area, employment opportunities for example, while simultaneously experiencing greater challenges in another, such as political or civil rights.

Before moving on to assess the influence of these perspectives on mainstream development theory and practice, it is important to note a number of points. Firstly, while it can be tempting to present each of these three waves as superseding those that went before it, this can over-emphasise the degree to which there is a current consensus based on the GAD perspective. While it would be correct to suggest that GAD has emerged as the most influential of these approaches, there are many who remain critical of this approach in academic and practitioner spheres.

Some feminist writers have been critical of the shift in emphasis from 'women' to 'gender'. Mies (1994) argued that the distinction between sex as biologically determined and gender as socially determined can result in a dualistic approach in which biological essentialism can be reinforced rather than discarded. In addition, the terminological move away from the word 'women' can also be accompanied by a more substantive change in emphasis and priorities of development agencies. Policies can become watered down and this can once more result in women becoming invisible in the development process. (For additional criticisms see Kalpana Wilson's chapter in this volume.)

In contrast to the view that GAD represents a de-radicalisation, others have suggested that development agencies have sometimes been reluctant to embrace the GAD approach because it implies a far more dramatic change to their practice (Chant and Gutman 2000). From this perspective, the concept of gender is seen as more difficult to operationalise and integrate into established planning approaches. For this reason, there remains some preference for the WID approach as it is perceived that these practices can be more easily added on to existing activities.

It should also be noted that the bodies of work which make up the WID, WAD and GAD approaches were often not as mutually exclusive as might be suggested by the clear-cut definitions described above. In addition, these three conceptual frameworks were also not the only perspectives to be developed in this period. Others, such as 'Women, Environment and Development' (WED) perspectives also contributed to the debates, although we have not explored these here.

Impact on the mainstream

Having reviewed the contribution of feminist approaches to development theory over the past thirty-five years, we will now turn to consider the extent to which these theories, ideas and approaches have impacted upon the mainstream of academic debate and policy development.

There is certainly evidence that the profile of gender issues in the context of development is higher than it has been in the past. The United Nations Millennium Development Goals, which were adopted in 2000 and which are supported by all member states as well as major development organisations such as the World Bank, include a commitment to 'promoting gender equality and the empowerment of women' (United Nations 2005). In addition, a further goal is to improve maternal health, while other goals, such as that relating to education, make specific mention of gender equality as an aspect of their fulfilment.

The *Human Development Report*, which is published annually by the United Nations Development Programme, includes two gender-focused development indices which sit alongside the main Human Development Index and two further poverty related indices (UNDP 2004). The first of these, the Gender-Related Development Index (GDI) aims to take account of the effect of gender equality/inequality on the level of human development and is calculated by comparing the average life expectancy, literacy rate and level of earned income for men and women in a particular country. By contrast the Gender Empowerment Index (GEM) aims to assess the extent to which economic and political power is held equally between men and women. It draws on additional indicators such as the percentage of parliamentary seats and professional and technical positions held by women, as well as a measure of the relative levels of earned income. Together both the GDI and the GEM provide alternative mechanisms for tracking and measuring the development process which foreground issues of gender equality.

Such high profile commitments by international organisations are the tip of the iceberg. Pearson (2000:383), for example, notes that

> at the beginning of the twenty-first century, the central place of gender issues and gender analysis at the heart of development policy is no longer disputed. The prime importance of understanding gender relations and the ways in which they intersect with markets, with civil society, with organisations, with state structures and state services, with anti-poverty strategies and with resource management and conservation has been amply demonstrated.

This perspective is shared by others such as Jackson (1998:39), who has written of the need to 'acknowledge that gender has been assimilated into development thinking in a comprehensive way', and Kerr (1999), who identifies a broad front of progress in academic and practitioner circles.

There are good grounds, therefore, for identifying a broad consensus that acknowledges that feminist perspectives have made a significant impact on the development mainstream. However, alongside these headline recognitions of progress, many academics and practitioners express reservations at the uneven and partial way in which these waves of feminist theory have been incorporated into the mainstream.

Pearson (2000:402) argues that the incorporation of feminist agendas into the development mainstream has resulted in a process of de-politicisation in which the 'technical efficiency of policy interventions rather than the emancipatory transformation of development agendas' becomes the core concern of those involved. Others, such as Jackson (1998) and Beall (1998), have argued that gender has tended to become subsumed into other elements of the mainstream agenda, such as poverty reduction. The result of this can be that the focus of policy shifts from a concern with women or gender issues as a whole towards a particular focus on the 'problem' of female-headed households as a key target group in poverty reduction strategies.

While the particular association of gender and poverty reflects current concerns with poverty within and beyond the development community, it also reflects a deeper problem of the instrumental integration of women and gender issues into mainstream agendas (Baden and Goetz 1997). The consequence of this instrumentalism can be that 'justifications for attention to gender are in terms of how this will facilitate other development objectives rather than being an end in itself' which are 'taken on board insofar as they are consistent with other development concerns ... and insofar as women are seen to offer a means to these, other ends' (Jackson 1998:40).

Such instrumentalism can be identified in the current gender strategy of the World Bank (2002a). Asserting that 'gender equality is an issue of development effectiveness, not just a matter of political correctness or being kind to women' (World Bank 2002a:1), the paper maps out a 'business case for mainstreaming gender'. This includes the recognition that gender inequality impedes the process of economic growth and poverty reduction initiatives. While this may be correct and may tactically be an effective way to generate support for the strategy, it nevertheless subordinates feminist agendas to the goals of economic growth and efficiency.

A further area of concern that has been highlighted is the potential gap between the adoption of policy stances and commitments by organisations and the actual implementation of policy and practice on the ground. This implementation problem is a generic problem that has been widely observed across many areas of public policy and can arise for a variety of reasons including poor project planning, deficiencies of resources, conflict with other policies and lack of political commitment (Hill and Hupe 2002). It is, therefore, not unique to the context of development or gender issues. Nevertheless, implementation problems have been highlighted by a number of studies, such as Derbyshire (2002) and Moser and Moser (2005), and there is evidence that these are often more acute in gender related policy areas.

The existing literature, therefore, provides something of a qualified verdict on the impact of feminist perspectives on development theory and practice. Notwithstanding the reservation that many writers have on the terms of incorporation, there is nevertheless a general consensus that gender issues have been integrated into the mainstream and that women are no longer invisible actors. There are, however, some areas which have been more resistant to adopting gender analysis and in which women still remain largely invisible and it is to one such area, the study of privatisation, that we now turn.

Privatisation and gender

Privatisation can be broadly defined to encompass policy initiatives that aim to increase the role of the private sector and market mechanism in the allocation of resources within a society, or more narrowly as the transfer of state-owned assets and enterprises to private ownership. By either definition, privatisation has been a major feature of economic policy across the globe during recent decades and in this time has had a major impact on the economies and societies of developing countries. A recent World Bank survey estimated that between 1990 and 2003, around 7,860 privatisations had occurred across 120 developing countries (Kikeri and Kolo 2005). This has resulted in changes in production patterns, employment and livelihoods, and drawing on what we know from WID, WAD and GAD contributions to development theory, is likely to have had a significant differential effect on men and women.

However, when we turn to the literature on privatisation we see little coverage of this. For example, a recent report published by the OECD, *Privatisation in Sub-Saharan Africa: Where Do We Stand?* (Berthelemy et al 2003), makes no reference to women or gender issues in its analysis. This is despite the fact that the report notes that employment and wider social welfare impacts are an important element in assessing the effectiveness of privatisation and explores each of these in considerable detail.

Unfortunately, such gender blindness is the rule rather than the exception when it comes to writings on privatisation and the same invisibility of women and gender issues can be found in reports produced by other development agencies. Examples might include country level studies, country level post-privatisation evaluations conducted for the World Bank, such as Sermelitos and Fusco (2003), and academic studies focusing on the distributional impact of privatisation, such as Birdsall and Nellis (2003) or Bayliss (2002). To turn the issue around, key gender policy documents, such as the World Bank's (2002b) *Evaluation of the Gender Dimensions of Bank Assistance*, can fail to even touch upon the issue of privatisation, despite the fact that the organisation had been a leading supporter of the policy across the globe for the previous decade or more.

There are, however, some rare exceptions to this general trend and a small number of studies do explore the gendered impact of privatisation.[1] Many of these demonstrate that privatisation policies and programmes do have materially different impacts on men and women, for example Geldstein (1997), who explores the gender dimensions of the privatisation of state-owned enterprises in Argentina. As Geldstein (1997:555) notes, the public sector had historically provided an important source of employment for women workers. As such, women were disproportionately affected by the changing employment policies and practices which have been associated with the privatisation process. These affected women in a number of ways. Firstly, many women lost their jobs as enterprises reduced employment levels, particularly in areas in which female employees were concentrated. Those who were retained in employment found that the terms and conditions under which they worked tended to be less favourable and, as Geldstein (1997) notes, this itself had a specifically gendered impact. The flexible working practices of the public sector, which allowed women to combine employment and family commitments, were increasingly replaced with less flexible arrangements which increased the pressures on many women and resulted in changes in the composition of the female labour force. Increasingly, the age profile of women workers shifted, with an increased proportion of female employment accounted for by younger women without family commitments.

Why might this gender blindness in studies of privatisation have occurred? There are perhaps two elements to constructing an explanation. Firstly, the data required for such studies are generally harder to come by than those which are required for many of the other calculations that are more routinely made. For example, data on pricing, profits and aggregate employment levels are generally 'naturally occurring' within the commercial routine of a business. They are commonly reported to stakeholders and are routinely used as a basis for commercial decisions. By contrast, data on the male/female breakdown of employment tend not to be produced as a matter of course and this would present an immediate obstacle to such a study. Indeed, it is an obstacle that Geldstein (1997) notes she herself faced in her study.

An alternative approach to explaining the gender blindness of much of the privatisation literature is to relate the problem to what may be characterised as the narrowing scope of development discourse in recent decades. Here Alan Thomas (2000b) has argued that the scope of development as social transformation has tended to be narrowed down in recent decades with an increased acceptance of the limitations of working within a system of liberal capitalism. In this context, development policy and practice have tended to become more narrowly defined as being concerned with deliberate actions to mitigate the social disruptions of a market capitalist order.

From such a perspective, issues relating to forms of ownership and employment patterns are regarded as being best left to the market to determine. Where the result of this is social distress through poverty and unemployment, these issues are separately addressed through public actions and social policies. The structure of the wider policy framework that may have produced these problems is taken for granted, at least in mainstream political discussion and analysis.

Conclusion

This chapter has argued that over the last three and a half decades, development theory and practice have changed. Feminist ideas, articulated through the WID, WAD and GAD approaches, have influenced mainstream development theory and practices and it is now common for mainstream development actors to take gender issues into account when devising policy strategies and initiatives. In that sense, the mainstream of development is no longer simply a 'malestream'.

However, it has also been argued that the incorporation of these perspectives has been partial and uneven. Some areas of policy and theory have remained relatively resistant to the influence of these ideas while in other areas they have been incorporated on an instrumental basis. This was illustrated by exploring a range of recent academic and practitioner studies of privatisation. Despite the extensive evidence that such policies would be likely to have a differentiated gendered impact, few studies have sought to explore this. However, it was argued that this did not only reflect the terms on which feminist perspectives had been incorporated into the mainstream, but also changes that had occurred within the mainstream itself. Principally, the growing influence of neo-liberal ideas has served to narrow the scope of policy and practice and, through this, reduced the scope for explorations of the gendered nature of development.

Key writers and further reading

There are many books available which provide a good overview of the main schools of thought that have emerged within the mainstream of development studies. Martinussen (1997), Hoogevelt (2001) and Haynes (2005), for example, all explore a range of classic and contemporary themes, debates and issues. Alongside these, much can also be gained from engaging with some of the classic texts such as Rostow (1960), Frank (1969) and Amin (1976).

Key interventions from a feminist standpoint include Boserup (1970), Mies (1986) and Elson (1995). The ideas and perspectives represented in these can be usefully augmented with reference to two collections, Visvanathan et al (1997) and Jackson and Pearson (1998), both of which explore some of the key points of debate. In addition, Simon (2005) also provides a valuable source of reference on both mainstream and feminist development theorists, while Desai and Potter (2002) have brought together a range of perspectives in an inclusive collection of perspectives on development themes and issues.

As argued in this article, little has been written on gender and privatisation. However, two recent collections that provide a diverse range of views on privatisation are Parker and Saal (2003) and Weizsäcker (2005).

Note

1 In addition to Geldstein (1997), the work of Due and Temu (2002) can also be cited as identifying and exploring the gendered impact of enterprise privatisation in a development context. Others, such as Lastarria-Cornhiel (1997), have

examined the creation of private property rights for land, while studies such as Liborakina (2001) and Zollner (2005) have examined privatisation in former command economies. All of these studies identified a differential gendered impact of privatisation.

Bibliography

Amin, S. (1976) *Unequal Development: An Essay on the Social Formation of Peripheral Capitalism* (New York: Monthly Review Press).

Baden, S. and Goetz, A. M. (1997) 'Who Needs [Sex] When You Can Have [Gender]: Discourses on Gender at Beijing', *Feminist Review* 56, Summer, 3–25.

Bandarage, A. (1984) 'Women in Development: Liberalism, Marxism and Marxist Feminism', *Development and Change* 15:4, 495–515.

Bayliss, K. (2002) 'Privatisation and Poverty: The Distributional Impact of Utility Privatisation', *Annals of Public and Cooperative Economics* 73:4, 603–25.

Beall, J. (1998) 'The Gender and Poverty Nexus in the DFID White Paper: Opportunity or Constraint?', *Journal of International Development* 10:2, 235–46.

Berthelemy, J.-C., Kauffman, C. Valfort, M.-A. and Wegner, L. (2003) *Privatisation in Sub-Saharan Africa: Where Do We Stand?* (Paris: OECD Development Centre Studies).

Birdsall, N. and Nellis, J. (2003) 'Winners and Losers: Assessing the Distributional Impact of Privatization', *World Development* 31:10, 1617–33.

Boserup, E. (1970) *Woman's Role in Economic Development* (London: Earthscan).

Calvert, P. and Calvert, S. (2001) *Politics and Society in the Third World* (London: Pearson Education Limited).

Chant, S. and Gutman, M. (2000) *Mainstreaming Men in Gender and Development: Development Debates, Reflections and Experiences* (Oxford: Oxfam).

Derbyshire, H. (2002) *Gender Manual: A Practical Guide for Development Policy Makers and Practitioners* (London: Social Development Division, DFID).

Desai, V. and Potter, R. B. (2002) *Companion to Development Studies* (London: Arnold).

Due, J. M. and Temu, A. (2002) 'Changes in Employment by Gender and Business Organization in Newly Privatized Companies in Tanzania', *Canadian Journal of Development Studies* 23:2, 317–33.

Elson, D. (ed.) (1995) *Male Bias in the Development Process* (Manchester: Manchester University Press).

Frank, A. G. (1969) *Capitalism and Underdevelopment in Latin America: Historical Studies of Chile and Brazil* (New York: Monthly Review Press).

Geldstein, R. (1997) 'Gender Bias and Family Distress: The Privatization Experience in Argentina', *Journal of International Affairs* 50:2, 544–71.

Hansen, K. T. (1984) 'Negotiating Sex and Gender in Urban Zambia', *Journal of Southern African Studies* 10:2, 219–38.

Haynes, J. (ed.) (2005) *Palgrave Advances in Development Studies* (Basingstoke: Palgrave).

Hill, M. and Hupe, P. (2002) *Implementing Public Policy* (London: Sage).

Hoogevelt, A. (2001) *Globalization and the Postcolonial World* (Basingstoke: Palgrave).

Hulme, D. and Turner, M. (1990) *Sociology and Development: Theories, Policies and Practices* (London: Harvester Wheatsheaf).

Jackson, C. (1998) 'Rescuing Gender from the Poverty Trap', in C. Jackson and R. Pearson (eds), *Feminist Visions of Development: Gender, Analysis and Policy* (London: Routledge), 39–64.

Jackson, C. and Pearson, R. (eds) (1998) *Feminist Visions of Development: Gender, Analysis and Policy* (London: Routledge).

Kerr, J. (1999) 'Responding to Globalization: Can Feminists Transform Development?', in M. Porter and E. Judd (eds), *Feminists Doing Development: A Practical Critique* (London: Zed Books), 190–205.

Kikeri, S. and Kolo, A. F. (2005) *Privatization: Trends and Recent Developments* (Washington D.C.: World Bank Policy Research Working Paper 3765, November).

Lastarria-Cornhiel, S. (1997) 'Impact of Privatization on Gender and Property Rights in Africa', *World Development* 25:8, 1317–33.

Liborakina, M. (2001) 'The Social Consequences of Privatization for Women', *Problems of Economic Transition* 43:9, 34–46.

Martinussen, J. (1997) *Society, State, and Markets: A Guide to Competing Theories of Development* (London: Zed Books).

Mies, M. (1986) *Patriarchy and Accumulation on a World Scale* (London: Zed Books).

Mies, M. (1994) '"Gender"and Global Capitalism', in L. Sklair (ed.), *Capitalism and Development* (London: Routledge), 107–23.

Moser, C. (1993) *Gender Planning and Development: Theory, Practice and Training* (London: Routledge).

Moser, C. and Moser, A. (2005) 'Gender Mainstreaming since Beijing: A Review of Successes and Limitations in International Institutions', *Gender and Development* 13:2, 11–22.

Parker, D. and Saal, D. (eds) (2003) *International Handbook on Privatization* (Cheltenham: Edward Elgar).

Pearson, R. (2000) 'Rethinking Gender Matters in Development', in T. Allen and A. Thomas (eds) *Poverty and Development into the 21st Century* (Oxford: Open University and Oxford University Press), 383–402.

Preston, P. W. (1996) *Development Theory: An Introduction* (Oxford: Blackwell).

Rathgeber, E. M. (1990) 'WID, WAD, GAD: Trends in Research and Practice', *Journal of Developing Areas* 24:4, 489–502.

Rostow, W. W. (1960) *The Stages of Economic Growth: A Non-communist Manifesto* (Cambridge: Cambridge University Press).

Sermelitos, J. and Fusco, H. (2003) *Zambia: Post-Privatization Study* (Washington D.C.: World Bank Evaluation Department, The World Bank).

Simon, D. (ed.) (2005) *Fifty Key Thinkers on Development* (London: Routledge).

Streeton, P. (1995) 'Human Development: The Debate about the Index', *International Social Science Journal* 143, 25–37.

Thomas, A. (2000a) 'Meaning and Views of Development', in T. Allen and A. Thomas *Poverty and Development into the 21st Century* (Oxford: Open University and Oxford University Press), 23–48.

Thomas, A. (2000b) 'Development as Practice in a Liberal Capitalist World', *Journal of International Development* 12:6, 773–87.

United Nations (2005) 'UN Millennium Development Goals', http://www.un.org/millenniumgoals/.

UNDP (2004) *Human Development Report*, http://hdr.undp.org/docs/statistics/indices/technote_1.pdf.

Visvanathan, N., Duggan, L., Nisonoff, L. and Wiegersma, N. (eds) (1997) *The Women, Gender and Development Reader* (London: Zed Books).

Weizsäcker, E. von (ed.) (2005) *Limits To Privatization: How To Avoid Too Much Of A Good Thing* (London: Earthscan).

World Bank (2002a) *Integrating Gender into the World Bank's Work* (Washington D.C.: World Bank), http://siteresources.worldbank.org/INTGENDER/Resources/strategypaper.pdf.

World Bank (2002b) *Evaluation of the Gender Dimensions of Bank Assistance* (Washington D.C.: Operation Evaluations Department, The World Bank), http://www-wds.worldbank.org/servlet/WDSContentServer/WDSP/IB/2002/03/01/000094946_02021604024126/Rendered/PDF/multi0page.pdf.

Young, K. (1997) 'Gender and Development', in N. Visvanathan, L. Duggan, L. Nisonoff and N. Wiegersma (eds), *The Women, Gender and Development Reader* (London: Zed Books), 51–4.

Zollner, A. (2005) 'Women's Rights under Privatisation: The Example of Bulgaria, Poland, Russia and Ukraine', in E. von Weizsäcker (ed.), *Limits To Privatization: How To Avoid Too Much Of A Good Thing* (London: Earthscan), 271–7.

9

Agency

Kalpana Wilson

This chapter traces the notion of 'agency' through a series of transformations: from its roots in the dominant ideology of early European
capitalism and imperialism, through its appropriation by feminists in
countering constructions of gender and race which denied women's ability
to act, to the contemporary re-appropriation of women's 'agency' into neo-
liberal discourses of development.

Agency in the 'malestream'

The notion of agency has historically been rooted in the construction of the
individual in Enlightenment thought, within which agency can be understood
as synonymous with what Ahearn describes as 'socially unfettered' free will
(2001:114). The attribution of agency to an individual in this context is
contingent on his (the individual concerned is inevitably male) ability to
exercise 'rational choice' and act accordingly. Marx exposed this notion of
agency, which ignores both the material constraints of production relations
and the impact of ideology in shaping consciousness, as a specifically
capitalist construction, even while giving a central place to collective human
action in history. 'The social structure and the State are continually evolving
out of the life-process of definite individuals', Marx and Engels wrote, 'but of
individuals, not as they may appear in their own or other people's
imagination, but as they really are; i.e. as they operate, produce materially,
and hence as they work under definite material limits, presuppositions and
conditions independent of their will' (Marx and Engels 1970:46–7).

If the conceptualisation of agency as free will is central to the
philosophical underpinnings of capitalism, it has also been argued that
historically it became an inextricable part of a dominant ideology which
emerged at the specific conjuncture of the rise of European capitalism
fuelled by slavery and colonialism. The 'Protestant work ethic' identified by
Weber glorified 'the accumulation of wealth and the individual's
responsibility for his/her own salvation. Wealth accumulation ... in fact
signified God's approval of an individual, but only when coupled with

appropriate conduct: hard work, strict discipline and a constantly inward-looking concern with improving one's own character' (Fiedrich and Jellema 2003:38). As capitalism matured, this notion of the 'work ethic' and individual responsibility became increasingly dominant, forming part of an armoury deployed to extract ever greater surpluses from the working class and – via missionaries in particular – from Britain's colonial subjects.

Feminist approaches to agency

Feminists have challenged these notions of agency on several levels. Writing of the postwar United States, Gardiner describes how 'whereas men were considered autonomous agents both of their own interests and of the social order as a whole, women were to be responsive to men, waiting to consent to marriage, and responsive to nature, spontaneously caring for children. They were patronised for being unable to act at all and condemned as selfish if they acted independently' (Gardiner 1995:2). This contrast between assumed – or desirable – male 'activity' and female 'passivity' constitutes one of several binary oppositions (for example, public/private, rational/emotional) which structure liberal discourse (see Raia Prokhovnik's chapter in this volume for further discussion of this). Liberal feminists of the first and second wave have countered this by arguing for women's capacity to exercise agency as 'rational individuals'. However, as Jaggar points out, this accepts the 'normative dualism' of liberalism which posits a hierarchical relationship between mental labour and manual labour, mind and body; culture and nature, reason and instinct (Jaggar 1988).

Moving beyond notions of 'equality' with men, socialist feminists sought to understand agency in relation to power and ideology, exploring the nature of the material structures of patriarchy and the construction of masculinity and femininity in the context of a commitment to social transformation. The fact that these debates took place within a collective movement for change meant that they were compelled to transcend the 'structure'/'agency' dichotomy which dominated mainstream social theory. They attempted to address the apparent contradiction that 'to assume that the multiple voices of women are not shaped by domination is to ignore social context and legitimate the status quo. On the other hand, to assume that women have no voice other than an echo of prevailing discourses is to deny them agency and simultaneously, to repudiate the possibility of social change' (Riger 1992, cited in Gardiner 1995:8).

Influenced by Foucault, many feminist writers also explored 'both the pervasiveness and the limits of the exercise of power and the potential for subversion and contestation in the interstices of established orders' (Kandiyoti 1998:141).

Significantly, socialist feminists asserted that agency was not located at the individual level alone and were concerned with its implications for social change, arguing that 'the full theoretical articulation of feminist politics requires that the issue of agency be addressed in relation to the difficult and hazardous issue of collectivity, for feminist politics – like politics in general – is constituted precisely by the interaction, coordination, and mutual implication of individual and collective interests, needs, desires, and perspectives' (Schweickart 1995:230). Despite this, the women's movement in the West continued to ignore, marginalise or exclude Black and Third World women's experiences and individual and collective struggles.

'Race', gender and development

It is easy to draw parallels between the construction of women in Enlightenment discourse as irrational, passive, inferior 'others', who by definition lack agency, and the construction of peoples who were exterminated, enslaved and colonised in similar terms. In both cases what is exposed is the exclusionary nature of Enlightenment 'universalism', what Razack calls 'the paradox of liberalism' where 'all human beings are equal and are entitled to equal treatment; those that are not entitled to equality are simply evicted from the category human' (Razack 2004:40). (For a related discussion of subpersonhood see Laura Brace's chapter in this volume.)

In fact, the 'active/passive' dichotomy was applied to the relationship between colonising and colonised societies as a whole, as an examination of the history of the concept of 'development' makes clear. With capitalism and the possibility of reproduction on an ever-expanding scale had come the idea that there could be constant 'progress'. Development came to be seen as the means through which those 'entrusted' with it would bring 'order' to this progress (Cowen and Shenton 1995:34). However, this notion of constant progress was defined in counterpoint to the non-European societies which were the sources of vast resources for European capitalism through the processes of slavery and colonialism. These societies were assumed to be passive, stagnant and incapable of progress, either lacking history altogether or in permanent 'decline' (see for example Said 1978; Sangari and Vaid 1989). In this context, notions of development and progress in turn became vital in legitimising colonial rule through the notion of 'trusteeship' (later to be immortalised as Kipling's 'white man's burden'). John Stuart Mill, for example, famously argued that India must be governed 'despotically' by 'incorruptible' imperial rulers.

However, the superficial parallel between racialised imperialism and patriarchy does little to challenge the widespread assumption that racism and sexism are 'alternative' forms of oppression. In reality, dominant constructions of both 'race' and gender shape and have shaped the experiences of Black and Third World men as well as women in a variety of ways. Historically, Black and colonised women's experiences of sexual violence, exploitation and dispossession, and the reshaping of the internal relationships within colonised societies in ways which intensified women's subordination, testify to this. But these experiences were made 'invisible' in colonial discourses in which '"women" become dominant-group women', (Pettman 1996:33), in need of white men's protection from 'dangerous' Black men. When colonised women did appear in these discourses, it was frequently in the context of their perceived need to be 'rescued' from 'their' men and/or 'backward' societies (Mani 1987) – in Spivak's memorable phrase 'white men saving brown women from brown men' (Spivak 1988) – a perception which is still prevalent within development discourses and elsewhere. (For a related discussion see Laura Brace's chapter in this volume.)

White women were also implicated in this 'infantilisation' of Black women, for example, in the relationship between missionary women and the women in colonised societies whom they sought to 'help'/'save': 'even where the former saw the latter as sisters, in a precursor to global sisterhood, they retained notions of difference in race and cultural hierarchy that represented "other" women as little sisters or surrogate daughters' (Pettman 1996:29).

It was the continuities with this colonial discourse in 'white feminist' approaches to 'Third World' women in the 1970s and 1980s which led to Black and Third World feminists explicitly raising the question of agency in this context (see for example Carby 1982; Amos and Parmar 1984). These continuities were particularly striking within discourses of 'development' (Mohanty 1991; Bagchi 1999). Socialist feminists from the Third World had put forward cogent critiques of the 'Women in Development' (WID) approach – which was rooted in neoclassical economics and liberal feminism, and this had led to a greater recognition of gender as a social construct and its material basis in patriarchal relations. WID was reconceptualised as GAD – Gender and Development (see Craig, this volume). But power relations inherent within the 'development project' itself, in which Third World people are the 'objects' of development for overwhelmingly white 'experts', continued to shape GAD theory and practice (White 2003).

Mohanty highlighted 'the construction of "third world women" as a homogeneous "powerless" group often located as implicit *victims* of particular socio-economic systems' in Western feminist discourse (Mohanty 1991:57). Focusing on a comparison between 'Western feminist self-presentation and western feminist re-presentation of women in the third world', she argued that 'universal images of "the third world Woman" (the veiled woman, chaste virgin, etc.), images constructed from adding the "third world difference" to "sexual difference", are predicated upon (and hence obviously bring into sharper focus) assumptions about Western women as secular, liberated and having control over their own lives' (Mohanty 1991:74).

These critiques were linked to the rise of broader postmodern ideas about subjectivity and 'difference' and in particular a critique of totalising 'metanarratives' in development which led to the emergence of post-developmentalism (see, for example, Marchand and Parpart 1995). They led to a greater emphasis on the notion of women's 'agency' within mainstream GAD approaches. Women were no longer invariably seen as passive victims; there was an increased focus on women's ability to make decisions and choices under given circumstances. But rather than challenging the power relationship between GAD 'experts' and the women who are the 'objects' of their study and policymaking, this focus on agency, I would argue, has had two interrelated effects which have effectively marginalised feminist approaches within GAD.

Contradictions within 'agency'

Marginalising analysis of power and ideology
Firstly, the concept of 'agency' has worked to invalidate the concept and analysis of women's oppression, which is central to feminism. Describing someone as oppressed and lacking in choices, it is implied, is to portray them as a victim and deny them agency. This not only shifts emphasis away from any systematic analysis of specific oppressive social structures and institutions (particularly material ones), it also – by equating 'oppression' with 'victimhood' – fails to acknowledge the possibility of those who are oppressed themselves engaging in struggle for structural change. The ideas of structural power and the potential for collective struggles for social change, which as we saw earlier are vital to a socialist feminist understanding of agency, are thus ignored and so, inevitably, are historical and contemporary Third World women's movements.

Secondly, the preoccupation with identifying the exercise of agency has shifted the focus away from the study of ideology which socialist feminists had elaborated and developed in the context of patriarchy. Those working within the Gender and Development framework have preferred to emphasise – and often simplify – ideas like the 'patriarchal bargain' (Kandiyoti 1988) in which women within patriarchal households make deliberate compromises in order to protect their own present or future interests. The individual exercising 'free will' thus reappears here, albeit acting within the material constraints imposed by patriarchal power: 'women may sacrifice their immediate welfare for future security; this would be perfectly in keeping with self-interested behaviour, and need not imply a gap between women's "objective" well-being and their perception of their well-being' (Agarwal 1994:434–5). However, as Kandiyoti has subsequently argued in a rethinking of the 'patriarchal bargain', a focus on 'subordinates' rational decisions to conform rather than rebel' can mean 'concealing the evidence of hegemony by relabelling its effects' (Kandiyoti

1998:142). In the process, analysis of the complex effects of ideology often comes to be regarded as 'attributing "false consciousness" to women', and thus ceases to be considered a legitimate avenue for investigation.

Similarly, 'rational choice' rather than the operations of specific patriarchal ideologies are emphasised in discussing women's collusion with or active participation in the oppression of other women – for example in Elson's discussion of son-preference among women in North India (Elson 1991a:8; see also Agarwal 1994; Kabeer 2000). Once again, we are presented with a vision of atomised individuals acting rationally to maximise their self-interest. Some recent writers, for example Kabeer (2000), have argued for a 'middle ground' between individual agency/ rational choice and structure. However, this approach is informed by a view of structure as constituted by socially defined 'values and norms' and 'customs' rather than the Marxist understanding of the material basis of dominant ideologies which informed socialist feminists.

Against this background, the use of the concept of 'agency' has the effect of reassuring us that women do in fact exercise 'choice' in situations where the structural constraints represented by the operation of patriarchal institutions and ideologies mean that women are simply 'choosing' survival. This is the unavoidable implication, for example, of the argument that analysis of systematic gender-bias in nutrition within households in patriarchal societies ignores women's 'agency' by failing to take account of their strategy of tasting the food while preparing it and eating leftovers (Jackson 1998:50).[1] Or (in an otherwise sensitive discussion of militarisation and gender violence which acknowledges that women face 'impossible choices'), the argument that women victims of wartime rape in the former Yugoslavia exercised 'agency' by remaining silent about their experiences because to speak out would have meant risking destitution or forced suicide at the hands of their own families (Kelly 2000:54).

As this suggests, 'agency' is cited in development discourse almost exclusively in the context of strategies for survival rather than trans-formation, and of the individual, rather than the collective.

Agency and resistance

A number of writers have been critical of the use of the concept of agency within feminist scholarship (Abu-Lughod 1990; Jeffery 1998; Ahearn 2001). Ahearn argues that feminists have 'sought to inspire women's activism by rediscovering lost or socially invisible traditions of resistance in the past and present' (2001:115). Parker suggests that in this context, 'the notion of agency has been a convenient rallying-banner, especially for feminist scholars wishing to claim women as the heroic subject of study' (2005a:3).

These writers argue that, influenced by James Scott's 'weapons of the weak' thesis in which he identified what he described as 'everyday forms of peasant resistance' in a Malaysian village (Scott 1985), feminist scholars have tended to 'romanticise' all manifestations of women's 'agency' and equate them with 'resistance', when in reality, 'agency' is frequently exercised in ways which do not challenge, or may even reinforce, patriarchal power. Parker suggests that the term 'resistance' should be limited to 'actions the actors themselves describe as aiming to defy, subvert, undermine, or oppose the power and repression of dominant forces' (2005b:87). Given the fact that gender identities intersect with others (such as class or ethnicity) and women's agency may be exercised within reactionary, essentially patriarchal political movements (such as those of the religious right in South Asia – see for example Sarkar and Butalia 1995; Bacchetta 1996; Jeffery and Basu 1998), she further stresses that 'feminist resistance' should be 'that which is directed against the forces of patriarchy – whether they be individual senior males or an oppressive state' (Parker 2005b:87).

Within the dominant discourses of development, however, it is precisely the manifestations of this type of 'resistance', which by their very nature tend to take a collective, and often an organised and explicitly political form, which are systematically ignored, even as evidence of agency is sought in the most constrained of individual decisions. This is perhaps not surprising, since 'resistance' is frequently to be found in movements which are independent of development initiatives from above. Very often these run counter to the neo-liberal model, demanding the redistribution of resources, challenging the operation of markets or organising against state repression.[2]

Agency and resistance in practice: dalit women labourers in India

A brief discussion of one such movement suggests some possible applications of agency which go beyond the validation of 'impossible choices'. Dalit women agricultural labourers in Bihar in eastern India have been at the forefront of a movement being waged during the last three decades led by a left party, the CPI(ML). The movement is centred around demands for a living wage, land redistribution and an end to caste-based oppression – demands which strike at the roots of agrarian power in the region. Women labourers have played a central role in wage struggles, as the agricultural tasks carried out in the period of peak labour demand when wage demands are put forward are largely those performed by women. It has therefore frequently been women who have initially placed wage demands before employers, and subsequently collectively refused to work. Women have also led marches of thousands to physically occupy land for redistribution, and have been at the forefront of resistance and protest against the repression unleashed by the landowners and the police. It is women who, armed with bricks, small scythes or household utensils, have driven the police out of their villages when they have arrived heavily armed in midnight or dawn raids, or who have surrounded police jeeps and snatched back those arrested, even forcing the police to apologise in some instances (Wilson 1999a).

In a context where larger landowners belonging to upper castes long considered sexual harassment and even rape of dalit women to be their birthright, the movement began in many areas with campaigns to bring local rapists to justice (Wilson 1999a).

For many dalit women, the fact that they are now able to challenge these practices which symbolised and reinforced gender, caste and class power is the most important aspect of the movement. On numerous occasions women told me that the men from the higher caste landowning families who employ them to work in their fields used to sexually harass and abuse them, physically assault them if they missed a day's work, or refused to allow them to take breaks to drink water, telling them to drink the muddy water in the drainage canals, but now they no longer 'dare' to do these things (Wilson 1999a).

These struggles also led women to openly challenge oppressive gender relations within the household. In many cases this has begun with conflict within the home over a woman's participation in the movement, with her husband or in-laws attempting to prevent her from being involved.[3] Women have organised collectively against domestic violence, men abandoning their wives and the increasing incidence of dowry among poor dalit families, although the question of whether tackling gender oppression within the family should be a priority remains a contested one for the movement at a local level (Wilson 1999a). As has been noted in other contexts (see for example Eisen Bergman 1984; Molyneux 1998) a key factor in strengthening such challenges has been the presence of a relatively autonomous women's organisation linked to the CPI(ML).

Initial questions for a feminist consideration of structure and agency to address here might be – did the movement simply allow women to express openly anger which they had already consciously felt? Or alternatively, did the ideas to which they were exposed through the work of the party and specifically the women's organisation lead them to question relations which they had previously considered acceptable (such as men's violence within the home)? Or were there, as I would argue, elements of both of these in a process which, crucially, was catalysed by the experience of collective struggle, and of being able to challenge authority and bring about change?

Examining this process might require for example an exploration of the contested notion of '*izzat*' (honour or respect), which both women and men frequently cite as one of the principles being fought for. Within the dominant upper caste ideology, *izzat* is a feudal patriarchal concept which is closely linked to property ownership. Women can easily damage or destroy it if they do not conform to prescribed behaviour but it is essentially seen as 'belonging' to the patriarchal, property owning family and its male members. However, *izzat* has become a site of struggle on several levels.

On one level, there is an attempt to claim *izzat* in its existing form by sections of the dalit communities – this is reflected in the adoption of upper caste practices associated with women's subordination, such as dowry and (where possible) withdrawal of women from labour outside the home.[4] On another level, the *izzat* fought for by women collectively resisting the sexual violence they face as women workers in the fields is conceptualised differently by them – this gender and class struggle over *izzat* changes its meaning. In fact it runs counter to the dominant discourse of *izzat* which dictates that men must protect women from contact with 'outside' men in order to preserve family honour. These struggles imply that a woman who leaves the 'protection' of the home and moves freely in public spaces has the right to *protect herself*. Thus *izzat* can 'belong' to a woman independently. This change becomes explicit when women demand *izzat* within the family in the context of campaigns against domestic violence (Wilson 1999a).

This very preliminary account suggests a need to go beyond static dichotomies of 'self-interest' vs. 'false consciousness' and 'structure' vs. 'agency' and address the distinct ways in which ideology itself becomes a site of struggle, shaped by, and in turn shaping, changing material relations. The complex interaction between changes in 'ways of thinking' and perceived changes in the balance of social, economic and political power brought about through collective struggle was often expressed by the dalit labourer women I spoke to in terms of 'fear' and the way it had shifted: on the one hand, the landowners, though still powerful, now 'feared' to assault them, on the other, they described themselves as 'no longer afraid' – 'we are even prepared to face bullets'.

But the decline in 'everyday' violence in the fields has been accompanied by the rise of organised terror. Landowner's armies with links with the state and dominant political parties have carried out a series of massacres of agricultural labourers in which women have been targeted for the most brutal violence. Individual women activists have been assassinated. The movement has struck at the roots of feudal and patriarchal power in the region, but clearly the battle is far from over (Wilson 2006).

'Agency' in neo-liberalism

The notion of women's agency, as we have suggested, far from being the preserve of 'feminist scholars', has been appropriated by neo-liberalism. Rather than being used to 'inspire women's activism', it now forms part of a theoretical framework in which feminist analysis is marginalised. This section examines in more detail how this notion of 'agency' has been (re-) incorporated into the mainstream to legitimise and pursue specifically neo-liberal policies.

As we have seen, the concept of 'agency' has been historically associated with the 'free' individual and, more specifically, with the capitalist notion of 'enterprise'. Not surprisingly then, it is in this context of the 'entrepreneurial spirit' that 'agency' is now cited within the discourse of neo-liberal economics which has risen to global predominance since the 1970s. A striking example in the context of 'Third World development' is the work of celebrated Peruvian free market economist Hernando De Soto, who, arguing that the unregulated 'informal' sector is a source of capitalist development which must be legalised, has suggested that state attempts to impose controls on small businesses (such as minimum wage or health and safety regulations) involve treating the poor as 'victims' and denying their ability to exercise agency through entrepreneurship and 'helping themselves'(De Soto 1989).

However, it is in the context of gender that the notion of agency has become central to the neo-liberal discourse – and practice – of development. Postmodern preoccupations with the subject and the recognition of 'difference' – the 'decoupling of the cultural politics of recognition from the social politics of distribution' (Fraser 1997 cited in Beneria 2003:25) – have been incorporated alongside liberal definitions of the 'rational individual exercising free will' to pursue and legitimise neo-liberal economic policies in the name of 'women's empowerment'.

Two interlinked elements of these policies which we will examine in this context are firstly, the promotion of micro-enterprise, and secondly, the withdrawal of the state from social service provision.

Micro-enterprise

Micro-enterprise – the promotion of small-scale income-generating activities through the provision of institutional credit to poor people, and in particular poor women, who have little or no collateral – combines an emphasis on the original 'Women in Development' objectives of widening women's access to the market through education and training, with an explicit focus on the notion of 'entrepreneurial spirit' waiting to be released. It has for more than a decade been regarded by development institutions and aid donors as a key strategy for achieving both poverty reduction and women's empowerment.[5]

However, as a number of writers have argued, a feminist assessment of micro-enterprise would require an examination of the impact of such loans on intra-household gender relations (Kabeer 1995; Mayoux 1995, 2002; Murthy 2004). Clearly, questions such as who actually controls the household's expenditure of the loans, how women's already heavy work burdens are affected by their involvement in micro-enterprise, and how what Mayoux (2002) calls 'feminisation of debt' affects relationships within the household need to be answered before a micro-enterprise project can be considered 'empowering'. But from the perspective of 'agency' – and these development interventions almost invariably claim to discover women's hitherto unrecognised potential for exercising agency (Fjedrich and Jellema

[handwritten note: + 'agency' becomes 'capacity to be active in the market'.]

2003) – what is perhaps most striking is the uncritical assumption that agency operates at the level of individual rather than social change, and must be directed towards 'moving up' existing hierarchies of power, not demolishing them. Micro-enterprise, as Mayoux notes, is 'widely seen as a viable and less socially and politically disruptive alternative to more focused feminist organizational strategies' (Mayoux 1995:66).

The withdrawal of the state

Neo-classical economic theory has always regarded individual freedom as increasing in inverse proportion to the involvement of the state in the economy. Within the neo-liberal discourse of development, the agency and empowerment of poor women have been increasingly conceptualised in terms of the withdrawal of the state from social provision. In the context of the drastic reduction in social service provision as a result of the World Bank – and IMF – directed neo-liberal reforms of the 1980s and 1990s, individual women and women's NGOs in Africa, Asia and Latin America were argued to be freed to exercise their agency as they took over a variety of roles in community service provision in areas like health, education and sanitation; activities which were often reflections and extensions of women's prescribed roles in dominant gender ideologies (Elson 1991b; Bisnath 2001; and Georgina Blakeley in this volume).

Both of these policies – the promotion of micro-enterprise and the shifting of responsibility for service provision from state to 'community' – involve a strategy of intensified exploitation of women's labour to provide a 'safety net' for the effects of neo-liberal economic reforms. As Bisnath points out, 'within mainstream development discourse of the 1990s, (empowerment) was often used by organizations focused on enlarging the choices and productivity levels of individual women, for the most part, in isolation from a feminist agenda; and in the context of a withdrawal of state responsibility for broad-based economic and social support' (Bisnath 2001:11). 'Recognising poor women's agency' can thus be understood here as 'making poor women responsible for development' – without questioning the neo-liberal status quo and its devastating impact on their lives.

[handwritten margin note: ind. + NGOs]

The paradox of 'empowerment'

In fact, it can be argued that there is a basic contradiction in the notions of agency and 'empowerment' as they are applied within the context of development. On the one hand, empowerment is supposed to be achieved by women themselves (in contrast to earlier 'top-down' approaches to development) through the exercise of agency, but in practice it is expected to take place through development interventions which take place within a framework with its own dynamics of power. As Fiedrich and Jellema (2003:60) put it, there is 'an unresolved ambiguity about who is driving the change process and towards what ends'. This contradiction is highlighted by the fact that empowerment has been described by GAD theorists as requiring that women 'should feel that they have been the agents of the transformation' (Young 1997:371). It appears that the power relationships highlighted by Mohanty and other Black and Third World feminists are still in place: the women whom development interventions seek to empower are still implicitly regarded as 'poorer, weaker sisters'.

But the core paradox at the heart of the concept of women's empowerment, and that which differentiates it most clearly from feminist approaches, is that it does not acknowledge that giving more power to women implies taking power away from others (see Meray Ette in this volume).

Interestingly, the far right Hindu nationalist parties who until recently led India's government have their own take on 'women's empowerment' which is illustrative in this respect (see for example Sinha 1993). Within their ideology of *Hindutva*, the promotion of women's militancy on behalf of the 'community' or 'nation' is combined with a deeply patriarchal conceptualisation of woman's role as the centre of the home and guardian of tradition. They have also presided over ongoing neo-liberal economic reforms. For the ideologues of *Hindutva*, *Nari Shakti* (Women's Empowerment) is a concept which is completely acceptable and consistent with their world view. They have identified what many GAD theorists have failed to: the fundamental difference between *Nari Shakti* and the far more subversive and threatening notion of *Nari Mukti* – Women's Liberation.

Agency and 'personhood'

If the incorporation of agency within development discourse and practices relating to gender occurred partly in response to postmodern/postcolonial critiques of the Eurocentric 'meta-narratives' of development, more recently the prescriptive models of women's agency and empowerment being adopted by development institutions and international NGOs have themselves been criticised from this perspective.

The construction of the 'rational self-interested individual' in these models has been questioned, in particular by anthropologists, who cite major cultural specificities in the conception of 'selfhood' or 'personhood' (Apffel-Marglin and Simon 1994; Parker 2005a). They argue that this is 'quite different outside the West', where individuals may be 'defined by their social relationships within family structures' (Parker 2005a:9–10), and notions such as 'self-interest' are not directly translatable. Persons are assumed to have 'more or less open boundaries', and this is especially true of women (Lamb 2000 cited in Fiedrich and Jellema 2003:36).

The problem with this approach however is, firstly that in general it fails to recognise the 'woman as rational agent' model as not simply Western but uniquely capitalist; secondly, it risks falling back into the trap of essentialising 'non-Western' cultures. Thirdly, the latter are portrayed as static and isolated, ignoring the historical and ongoing impact upon them of global capitalism, and once again making invisibile the struggles of indigenous feminist movements.

Thus for example NGOs in Bangladesh have been criticised from this perspective for their stance against dowry giving, when, we are told, these practices are vital to 'poor households' ... ability to participate in the life of the community, their dignity and their sense of identity' (Fiedrich and Jellema 2003:49). This strikingly 'gender-insensitive' statement not only takes no account of the large body of evidence that dowries across classes have been vastly increased by the spread of capitalist relations and by incorporation of local economies into global markets, it also fails to acknowledge the sustained struggles by grassroots women's movements in South Asia against the practice of dowry and the violence associated with it, which have been completely independent of any 'development' initiatives.

'Efficiency' and 'altruism'

Ironically perhaps, the neo-liberal discourse of gender and development can be argued to partially accommodate this view of the less individualised notion of 'personhood' of the essentialised 'Third World woman' in its preoccupation with women's greater efficiency and the 'altruism' which is assumed to be its cause.

The proponents of one of the most frequently cited 'success stories' of micro-credit, the Grameen Bank in Bangladesh, argued early on that firstly women 'have better repayment rates and are therefore better credit risks than men' (Hossain 1987 cited in Agarwal 1994:36) and secondly that the benefits of additional income earned by women are more likely to enhance 'family welfare' and particularly the welfare of children, than that earned by men (Yunus 1994).

This highly 'instrumental' approach has become part of the development orthodoxy. But a feminist analysis would involve questioning the conditions – both material and ideological – which ensure that women take primary responsibility for meeting children's needs,[6] and which rule out the option, presumably available to men, of defaulting on loans, thus making them more 'efficient' and creditworthy as micro-entrepreneurs.[7]

Similarly the World Bank has argued in the context of 'gender empowerment and poverty alleviation' that giving women land rights will increase overall efficiency in agricultural production (see for example King and Mason 2001), notwithstanding the fact that its own policies have severely limited and undermined women's access to and control over land. These arguments once again centre upon two interlinked assumptions. Firstly, there is the idea that women are always 'harder workers' – this once again is linked to women's greater commitment to, and responsibility for, meeting children's needs. Secondly, there is the assumption that women will expend fewer resources (in terms of both leisure time and luxury consumption) on themselves.

Women's greater 'efficiency', whether as farmers, labourers or micro-entrepreneurs, is thus clearly linked to the structures and practices of patriarchy at the level of both economic relations and ideology. Yet despite this, the discourse of 'efficiency' has become so ubiquitous that even writers operating within a broadly socialist feminist framework have tended to treat its underlying assumptions as given.

In fact, the emphasis on women's 'altruism' and commitment to meeting others' needs, especially when contrasted to the absence of these qualities in men, could be argued to undermine demands for gender equality, since in the absence of an analysis of patriarchy it implies that these qualities are uniquely feminine. The moralistic overtones of the development literature's oft-cited contrasts between women's 'good' spending (on food, children's clothes etc.) and men's 'bad' spending (on alcohol, cigarettes, entertainment etc.) (Kabeer 1995:104) are distinct echoes of the Victorian discourse of the 'deserving' and 'undeserving' poor. Such continuities are consistent with the moral framework of neo-liberal economics which ascribes 'duties' to the poor as a condition for the enjoyment of 'rights'.[8]

Most significantly, these arguments about efficiency, like those about empowerment which are framed by the same dominant development discourses, also assume that control over resources such as land or capital will be bestowed upon women by external agents, rather than taken by women themselves. In situations where women have waged struggles themselves, these struggles have frequently been accompanied by a questioning of the precise complex of gender relations which supposedly make women more 'efficient' producers/workers.

This has been the case for the struggles of landless dalit women agricultural labourers in Bihar referred to above. The oppressive domestic relations they began to challenge included the ever-present threat of violence, but also women's primary responsibility for children's welfare and the absence of the 'leisure' time which men can devote to political activity. Savitri Devi, a woman labourer attending the Jehanabad District Kisan Sabha (Peasant Association) conference in 1994, explained how all of these are linked while introducing a song entitled 'Give Women Respect in Society': 'a woman gets up in the morning, she has to wash the utensils, wake the children, take them to the fields to relieve themselves, prepare the meal . . . the man just gets up, goes to relieve himself, comes back, and if the food isn't ready, he'll start hitting her . . .' (Wilson 1999b).

Similarly, the experience of agricultural labourer women in Thanjavur district of Tamil Nadu in India, in a movement demanding that they be paid wages equal to those received by men (Bhuvana 2001), also illustrates the link between involvement in collective struggles and questioning of the notion of the endlessly self-sacrificing 'efficient' woman. In this context, a number of women who were facing violence from family members opposed to their participation in the movement actually left their homes and spent the nights in their union's one-room 'office' at the height of the struggle. While the women labourers were challenging patriarchal relations within the family, their landowner employers were attempting to utilise these relationships to break the strike, urging husbands and parents of the women labourers to put pressure on them to withdraw from the struggle, as otherwise they would be labelled as 'bad' women who neglected their domestic duties and were 'out of control'.

Conclusion

'Agency' has long been a contested concept. The notion of the rational individual who is able to exercise free will has been central to the ideology of capitalism. Marxism provides an analysis in which individual agency is circumscribed by material relations of power and by dominant ideologies but also develops a notion of agency as conscious collective action.

The emphasis upon women's 'agency' initially emerged from feminist analyses of the patriarchal discourse of the Enlightenment in which women were constructed as passive and incapable of rational action. The racialised nature of the agency/passivity dichotomy was highlighted in critiques by Black and Third World feminists of white/Western feminist portrayals of 'other' women as 'victims' needing to be 'saved'.

However, the notion of agency has been incorporated into discourses of gender and development in a way that has marginalised analysis of patriarchal power and ideology. This marginalisation of feminist analysis is reflected in uncritical assumptions about women's efficiency. In the context of the dominance of neo-liberal ideology, the exercise of agency is more often than not sought in women's strategies for survival rather than struggles for transformation, and is once again understood in the framework of individual rational choice. The perceptions of dalit women agricultural labourers engaged in a sustained movement for change in rural Bihar suggest that we need to go beyond the misleading dichotomy of 'rational choice'/'false consciousness' and explore ways in which consciousness is affected by collective action and how certain aspects of ideology can in this context become sites of struggle. The notion of women's 'agency' is currently being deployed by the development establishment – from the World Bank to relatively 'radical' NGOs – to legitimise and promote strategies which compel women like them to pay the price of neo-liberal economic policies. A concept which had been redefined by socialist feminism has now been effectively re-appropriated by global capitalism and is being used to pursue anti-feminist objectives. We need to reclaim it.

Key writers and further reading

The work of Alison Jaggar (1988) is an important starting point for a socialist feminist critique of the concept of individual agency rooted in capitalism, while the collection edited by Gardiner (1995a) brings together some of the debates relating to structure and agency emerging from the feminist movement from the 1970s onwards, although predominantly from a US-centred perspective.

Mohanty's work (1991) along with that of other Black and Third World feminists, was influential in drawing attention to the racialised construction of women's agency, particularly in the context of discourses of development. Kandiyoti's notion of the 'patriarchal bargain' (1988) has been important in foregrounding questions of agency in women's everyday lives, and is particularly interesting read in conjunction with the author's later 'rethinking' of the notion (1998). The concept of agency has also been central to the work of feminist anthropologists: recent overviews of debates over agency and resistance are provided in contributions by Ahearn (2001) and Parker (2005a, b).

As discussed in this chapter, the promotion of the exercise of agency by poor women has become almost ubiquitous as a stated objective of neo-liberal development institutions such as the World Bank. Elson's gendered critique of neo-liberal economic policies (1991) is one of the most widely cited contributions from a rich literature. A recent paper by Fiedrich and Jellema (2003) explores some of the colonial antecedents of the current preoccupation with agency in development.

Notes

1 An interesting discussion of this issue in the context of Haryana in North India can be found in Chowdhry (1999). She suggests that 'women's attempts to eat stealthily are the theme of many jokes and stories ... these jocular tales can be seen as only partial attempts by women to find a clandestine space which may have been foiled by the tight security maintained by the family hierarchy ... they ultimately reinforce the patriarchal order by subtly stereotyping a woman who does not conform' (Chowdhry 1999:279–80).

2 With its roots in colonialism, the discourse of 'development' has a long history of denying or distorting women's organised resistance.

3 As discussed earlier, struggles over gender relations often take place *between* women who are differentially positioned within household hierarchies, particularly in the context of the joint family or 'corporate household' (for example, between mother-in-law and daughter-in-law). In the areas of Bihar referred to here, such households were the norm even among landless dalit families (Wilson 1999b).

4 It is important to note that given their conditions of work and the attacks they face, women may themselves prefer to withdraw from paid labour. A similar point has been made by Black feminist writers critiquing the liberal feminist assumption that waged work is by definition liberating (see for example hooks 1984). At the same time, since it is usually younger women, and in particular young married women, who are withdrawn from this work, this can also be seen as resulting in greater control over them by both men and older women.

5 Jackson has highlighted 'the instrumental interest in women as the means to achieve development objectives such as poverty reduction' and refers to the need for 'rescuing gender from the poverty trap' (Jackson 1998:39).

6 A large body of evidence from different regions suggests that this is overwhelmingly the case: see for example Agarwal (1994).

7 In fact several studies have found that pressure on credit circles to maintain repayments is such that the poorest women are excluded (Mayoux 1995; Rogaly 1996).

8 For example, Fiedrich and Jellema cite a USAID-funded report (Ashe and Parrot 2001) as 'merely making explicit the assumptions buried in other, softer versions' when it lists 'behavioural change', 'hard work' and 'an ethos of self-improvement' as indicators of successful 'empowerment' (2003:45). Dominant discourses on environment and population are also illustrative in this respect.

Bibliography

Abu-Lughod, L. (1990) 'The Romance of Resistance: Tracing Transformations of Power through Bedouin Women', *American Ethnologist* 17:1, 41–55.

Agarwal, B. (1994) *A Field of One's Own: Gender and Land Rights in South Asia* (Cambridge: Cambridge University Press).

Ahearn, L. M. (2001) 'Language and Agency', *Annual Review of Anthropology* 30:1, 109–27.

Amos, V. and Parmar, P. (1984) 'Challenging Imperial Feminism', *Feminist Review* 17 (Autumn), 3–19.

Apffel-Marglin, F. and Simon, S. L. (1994) 'Feminist Orientalism and Development', in W. Harcourt (ed.), *Feminist Perspectives on Sustainable Development* (London: Zed Books), 26–45.

Bacchetta, P. (1996) 'Hindu Nationalist Women as Ideologues: The Sangh, the Samiti and Differential Concepts of the Hindu Nation', in K. Jayawardene and M. De Alwis (eds), *Embodied Violence: Communalising Women's Sexuality in South Asia* (London: Zed Books), 126–7.

Bagchi, J. (1999) 'Women's Empowerment: Paradigms and Paradoxes', in K. Sangari and U. Chakravarti (eds), *From Myths to Markets; Essays on Gender* (Shimla: Indian Institute of Advanced Study), 368–79.

Beneria, L. (2003) *Gender, Development, and Globalization: Economics as if All People Mattered* (New York: Routledge).

Bhuvana (2001) 'Struggle for Equal Wages in Thanjavur', *Women's Voice, Bulletin of the All-India Progressive Women's Association*, January–February, 9–10.

Bisnath, S. (2001) *Globalization, Poverty and Women's Empowerment*, United Nations Division for the Advancement of Women [Online] http://www.un.org/womenwatch/daw/csw/empower/documents/Bisnath-EP3.pdf.

Carby, H. V. (1982) 'White Woman Listen! Black Feminism and the Boundaries of Sisterhood', in Centre for Contemporary Cultural Studies, *The Empire Strikes Back: Race and Racism in 70s Britain* (London: Hutchinson), 212–35.

Chowdhry, P. (1999) 'Ideology, Culture and Hierarchy: Expenditure–Consumption Patterns in Rural Households', in K. Sangari and U. Chakravarti (eds), *From Myths to Markets; Essays on Gender* (Shimla: Indian Institute of Advanced Study), 274–311.

Cowen, M. and Shenton, R. (1995) 'The Invention of Development', in J. Crush (ed.), *Power of Development* (London: Routledge), 27–43.

De Soto, H. (1989) *The Other Path: The Invisible Revolution in the Third World* (New York: Harper and Row).

Eisen Bergman, A. (1984) *Women of Vietnam* (London: Zed Books).

Elson, D. (1991a) 'Male Bias in the Development Process: An Overview', in D. Elson (ed.), *Male Bias in the Development Process* (Manchester: Manchester University Press), 1–28.

Elson, D. (1991b) 'Male Bias in Macro-economics: The Case of Structural Adjustment', in D. Elson (ed.), *Male Bias in the Development Process* (Manchester: Manchester University Press), 164–90.

Fiedrich, M. and Jellema, A. (2003) *Literacy, Gender and Social Agency: Adventures in Empowerment – A Research Report for ActionAid UK* (with N. Haq, J. Nalwoga and F. Nessa), ActionAid, UK.

Gardiner, J. K. (ed.) (1995a) *Provoking Agents: Gender and Agency in Theory and Practice* (Urbana: University of Illinois Press).

Gardiner, J. K. (1995b) 'Introduction', in J. K. Gardiner (ed.), *Provoking Agents: Gender and Agency in Theory and Practice* (Urbana: University of Illinois Press), 1–20.

hooks, b. (1984) *Feminist Theory: From Margin to Center* (Boston: South End Press).

Jackson, C. (1998) 'Rescuing Gender from the Poverty Trap', in C. Jackson and R. Pearson (eds), *Feminist Visions of Development: Gender Analysis and Policy* (London: Routledge), 39–64.

Jackson, C. and Pearson, R. (eds) (1998) *Feminist Visions of Development: Gender Analysis and Policy* (London: Routledge).

Jaggar, A. M. (1988) *Feminist Politics and Human Nature* (Totowa: Rowman and Littlefield).

Jeffery, P. (1998) 'Agency, Activism and Agendas', in P. Jeffery and A. Basu (eds), *Appropriating Gender: Women's Activism and Politicized Religion in South Asia* (New York: Routledge), 226–35.

Jeffery, P. and Basu, A. (eds) (1998) *Appropriating Gender: Women's Activism and Politicized Religion in South Asia* (New York: Routledge).

Kabeer, N. (1995) *Reversed Realities: Gender Hierarchies in Development Thought* (New Delhi: Kali for Women).

Kabeer, N. (2000) *The Power to Choose: Bangladeshi Women and Labour Market Decisions in London and Dhaka* (London: Verso).

Kandiyoti, D. (1988) 'Bargaining with Patriarchy', *Gender and Society* 2:3, 274–90.

Kandiyoti, D. (1998) 'Gender, Power and Contestation: "Rethinking Bargaining with Patriarchy"', in C. Jackson and R. Pearson (eds), *Feminist Visions of Development: Gender Analysis and Policy* (London: Routledge), 135–51.

Kelly, L. (2000) 'Wars against Women: Sexual Violence, Sexual Politics and the Militarised State', in S. Jacobs, R. Jacobson and J. Marchbank (eds), *States of Conflict: Gender, Violence and Resistance* (London: Zed Books), 46–65.

King, E. M. and Mason, A. D. (2001) *Engendering Development – Through Gender Equality in Rights, Resources, and Voice: A World Bank Policy Research Report* (New York: Oxford University Press).

Mani, L. (1987) 'Contentious Traditions: The Debate on Sati in Colonial India', *Cultural Critique* 7, 119–56.

Marchand, M. H. and Parpart, J. L. (eds) (1995) *Feminism/Postmodernism/Development* (London: Routledge).

Marx, K. and Engels, F. (1970) *The German Ideology* (London: Lawrence and Wishart).

Mayoux, L. (1995) 'From Vicious to Virtuous Circles? Gender and Micro-Enterprise Development', *Occasional Paper 3*, United Nations Research Institute for Social Development, United Nations Development Programme.

Mayoux, L. (2002) 'Women's Empowerment or Feminisation of Debt – Towards a New Agenda in African Microfinance', *Report Based on a One World Action Conference*, March 2002.

Mohanty, C. T. (1991) 'Under Western Eyes: Feminist Scholarship and Colonial Discourse', in C. T. Mohanty, A. Russo and L. Torres (eds), *Third World Women and the Politics of Feminism* (Bloomington: Indiana University Press), 51–80.

Molyneux, M. (1998) 'Analysing Women's Movements', in C. Jackson and R. Pearson (eds), *Feminist Visions of Development: Gender Analysis and Policy* (London: Routledge), 65–88.

Murthy, R. K. (2004) 'Organisational Strategy in India and Diverse Identities of Women: Bridging the Gap', in C. Sweetman (ed.), *Gender, Development and Diversity* (Oxford: Oxfam GB), 10–18.

Parker, L. (2005a) 'Introduction', in L. Parker (ed.), *The Agency of Women in Asia* (Singapore: Marshall Cavendish Academic), 1–25.

Parker, L. (2005b) 'Resisting Resistance and Finding Agency: Women and Medicalized Birth in Bali', in L. Parker (ed.), *The Agency of Women in Asia* (Singapore: Marshall Cavendish Academic), 62–97.

Pettman, J. J. (1996) *Worlding Women – A Feminist International Politics* (London: Routledge).

Razack, S. (2004) *Dark Threats and White Knights: The Somalia Affair, Peacekeeping and the New Imperialism* (Toronto: University of Toronto Press).

Rogaly, B. (1996) 'Microfinance Evangelism, "Destitute Women" and the Hard Selling of a New Anti-poverty Formula', *Development in Practice* 6:2, 100–12.

Said, E. W. (1978) *Orientalism* (London: Routledge and Kegan Paul).

Sangari, K. and Chakravarti, U. (eds) (1999) *From Myths to Markets; Essays on Gender* (Shimla: Indian Institute of Advanced Study).

Sangari, K. and Vaid, S. (1989) 'Recasting Women: An Introduction', in K. Sangari and S. Vaid (eds), *Recasting Women: Essays in Colonial History* (New Delhi: Kali for Women), 1–26.

Sarkar, T. and Butalia, U. (eds) (1995) *Women and the Hindu Right* (New Delhi: Kali for Women).

Schweickart, P. P. (1995) 'What Are We Doing? What Do We Want? Who Are We? Comprehending the Subject of Feminism', in J. K. Gardiner (ed.), *Provoking Agents: Gender and Agency in Theory and Practice* (Urbana: University of Illinois Press), 229–48.

Scott, J. (1985) *Weapons of the Weak: Everyday Forms of Peasant Resistance* (New Haven: Yale University Press).

Sinha, M. (1993) Interview with Mridula Sinha, President of the Bharatiya Janata Party Mahila Morcha, *The Telegraph* (India), 7 April.

Spivak, G. C. (1988) 'Can the Subaltern Speak?', in C. Nelson and L. Grossberg (eds), *Marxism and the Interpretation of Culture* (Urbana: University of Illinois Press), 271–313.

White, S. (2003) 'The "Gender Lens": A Racial Blinder?' Paper prepared for the International Workshop 'Feminist Fables and Gender Myths: Repositioning Gender in Development Policy and Practice', Institute of Development Studies, Sussex, 2–4 July. Available at www.siyanda.org/docs/white_genderlens.doc.

Wilson, K. (1999a) 'Patterns of Accumulation and Struggles of Rural Labour: Some Aspects of Agrarian Change in Central Bihar', in T. J. Byres, K. Kapadia and J. Lerche (eds), *Rural Labour Relations in India* (London: Frank Cass), 316–54.

Wilson, K. (1999b) *Production Relations and Patterns of Accumulation in the Context of a Stalled Transition: Agrarian Change in Contemporary Central Bihar*, Unpublished PhD Thesis, SOAS, University of London.

Wilson, K. (2006) 'Who are the "Community"? The World Bank and Agrarian Power in Bihar', *Economic and Political Weekly* 41:1, 23–7.

Young, K. (1997) 'Planning from a Gender Perspective', in N. Visvanathan, L. Duggan, L. Nisonoff and N. Wiegersma (eds), *The Women, Gender and Development Reader* (London: Zed Books), 366–74.

Yunus, M. (1994) *Banking on the Poor* (Dhaka : Grameen Bank).

10

Empowerment

Mercy Ette

Introduction

This chapter examines the concept of empowerment from the conventional 'malestream' conceptualisation to a feminist perspective on the term. Using Nigeria as a case study, it assesses some of the strategies that have been used to empower women. The chapter explores feminist contributions to the empowerment debate and the implementation of associated practices, and argues that the conventional approaches are inadequate because they often are too mechanistic and too focused on goals and not on the dynamics of the process. The chapter takes as its starting point the conceptualisation of empowerment as a process of providing women with the tools and resources needed to live independent, productive and dignified lives. However, it questions the notion of power as something to be given and it argues that the feminist perspective provides a more dynamic and effective approach to the understanding of empowerment.

The chapter's argument is presented in three parts. The first explores the mainstream conceptualisation of empowerment in development/political discourse and practice. The second examines how feminism challenges this understanding and assesses the implications of a feminist perspective on the concept. The third section uses Nigeria as a case study to illustrate how the feminist critique of empowerment has reshaped empowerment strategies in practice.

'Malestream' framework of empowerment

Empowerment is not a new concept but an open-ended and flexible catchword that has gained popularity in a variety of contexts ranging from the social to the political. Despite being a buzzword (Rowlands 1998; Cook 2002), it lacks explicit and conclusive definitions. It is, as Marilee Karl puts it, 'a word widely used, but seldom defined' (1995:14). Flexible and plastic in nature, it takes on a variety of definitions, and is subject to a wide range of explanations and interpretations. Disciplinary differences have also introduced nuances in definitions but even when such differences are taken into account, the term remains implicit and ambiguous. This could be due to the contested terrain of its root word: power. Given this, any discussion on empowerment calls for a clarification of the term to delineate the premise of the analysis. This chapter explores the concept from a political and development perspective and particularly in the context of the empowerment of women.

One mainstream conceptualisation of empowerment is the allocation of power through delegation and authorisation. The World Bank defines it as 'the process of enhancing the capacity of individuals or groups to make choices and to transform those choices into desired actions and outcomes' (World Bank 2001:39). It is generally associated with the 'sense of gaining control, of participation, of decision-making' (Karl 1995:14) and with the process of 'bringing people who are outside the decision-making process into it' (Rowlands 1995:102). Historically traced to the 'dominant culture' of Western capitalism (Cook 2002; Rowlands 1998), as evident in the emphasis on individualism, personal achievement and economic goals, empowerment is traditionally defined in the context of power and its allocation.

Power is a contentious concept, not only in its interpretation but also in how it is experienced by different people. It has been described as 'a social relationship between groups that determines access to, use of, and control over the basic material and ideological resources in society' (Morgen and Bookman 1988:4, as cited by Stacki and Monkman 2003:174). It also refers to the capacity to do something. The literature is replete with several levels of meanings and a variety of definitions. These range from covert to overt power and from the subtle to the forceful. At one end of the scale is the ability of one person to coerce another or group to do something against their will and at the other is the ability to extend power and empower others (Rowlands 1995; Corrin 1999). Conventionally, it is defined in relation to obedience or 'power-over' others (Rowlands 1995).

One dimension of power presents it as 'the capacity not only to impose one's will, if necessary against the will of other parties, but also to set the terms of the argument' (Ward and Mullender 1991:23–4). Dahl offers a simple and useful framework to understand how this works: 'A has power over B to the extent that he can get B to do something B would not otherwise do' (as cited by Lukes 1986:2). This could be summed up as 'power-over' and 'power-to' and it is this dimension that dominates the malestream conceptualisation of empowerment.

Garba (1999:131) has noted that the conceptualisation of empowerment as the allocation of power, particularly in the context of women, suggests being allowed to exercise power. In specific terms, being empowered to 'participate in making decisions that directly or indirectly affects their lives, and to influence those decisions'. Subjected to Dahl's framework, it means those with power-over others could control, influence them and authorise them to exercise power. This speaks of 'power-over' and 'power-to' dominate the disempowered. To become empowered, the disempowered has to submit to the powerful. There is a suggestion of a transition from a position of powerlessness to that where one is endowed with power.

The 'malestream' understanding of empowerment presupposes that powerlessness is a result of a lack of necessary tools and resources for the exercise of power. Empowerment then becomes the process of providing these tools. Wong (2003), in his reflections on the World Bank's conception of power, argues that there is a common assumption that power can be delivered through development projects and that these are seen to be capable of allocating power through the support and benevolence of external interventionists. Empowerment is achieved when set goals and objectives such as economic and political power are met. Missing from this conjecture is the vital issue of the social context of power, such as relationships and setting.

The 'power-to' understanding is reflected in development programmes, which tend to focus on assisting the marginalised to gain control. In the context of the empowerment of women, the assumption is that they 'should somehow be "brought into development" and become "empowered" to participate within the economic and political structures of society. They should be given the chance to occupy positions of "power" in terms of political and economic decision making' (Rowlands 1998:12).

Barry Barnes (1988) was not directly concerned with empowerment but his discussion on power as 'downward' delegation provides a kind of explanation of empowerment. The delegation of power, he argued, entails a 'power-holder delegating some of his capacity for action to a subordinate' while still remaining more powerful than the subordinate and capable of exercising control (Barnes 1988:71). A genuine delegation, he pointed out, empowers and transfers capacity for action to those who otherwise would not be capable.

Two key strands of the malestream conceptualisation of empowerment can be identified as being 'power-over' and 'power-to'. Empowerment entails powerful individuals exercising power over the disempowered by investing in them the ability to exercise power, assigning them a place of power and bestowing and facilitating a change from powerlessness to that of power.

There is no obvious recognition of the limitations of empowerment from this perspective, although the idea of the allocation of power to the disempowered also suggests its denial, for the power to give has a flip side – the power to deprive. Consequently, the process of becoming able or allowed to do something suggests domination of some kind: the recipients of power are often still disadvantaged in power relationships.

It is apparent from the above that the 'malestream' understanding of empowerment underscores the divide between those who wield power and are able to apportion a part to those who have little or none. This endorses a dominant–subordinate relationship and also adopts a top-down view, an approach that has structured development programmes across the world. This approach often entails external assistance, which under close consideration raises a number of questions. Does the mere act of providing the marginalised with resources to access political and economic structures translate into being powerful? When do the disempowered become empowered? How do the powerless evolve into the powerful? Is power a property which can be given away?

Feminising empowerment

Feminists of all strands have for centuries challenged the position of women in society and in doing so have broadened debates on issues that concern women (Corrin 1999). Corrin has noted the incorporation of feminist thinking into most debates on women related issues and the generation of new perspectives as a result of this. This is equally true of the empowerment discourse. Viewing the empowerment debate through the eyes of feminists provides nuances and texture that are absent in the 'malestream' position. Stacki and Monkman (2003) have noted a variety of definitions or dimensions of empowerment that exist for women. These range from psychological to cognitive, from political to economic empowerment. While the association of empowerment with the allocation of power, delegation, domination and, at the end of the spectrum, subordination and subjugation, can be traced to the conventional definition of the concept, feminist explanations are more layered and engage with the distinction between the uses of power either to control or empower.

Although there are several strands of thought within feminist thinking, a common thread of understanding runs through the empowerment debate and that is the emphasis on power as a relational concept. While the 'malestream' understanding emphasises the 'power-over' and 'power-to' dimensions, feminist thinking stresses 'the multi-dimensional nature of power at different levels: personal, group, regional, national and international' (Wong 2003:310). A feminist framework of power takes on different perspectives of power: 'power-from-within', 'power-to', 'power-with' and 'power-over' and is concerned with the social context of power.

It is instructive that feminist thinking does not only challenge the notion of power as something that could be given or bestowed but questions the narrow conceptualisation of empowerment as a top–bottom relationship which is externally driven, and broadens it to make it inclusive. The perspective of 'power-from-within', for example, describes personal power, an idea that sounds strange from the 'malestream' position, despite its association with individualism. Stacki and Monkman describe this as psychological empowerment. This, they explain, 'relates to the development of self-esteem and self-confidence enabling women to recognise their own power and to motivate themselves into action' (2003:181). Wong sums it up as the 'development of trust in terms of self-knowledge. Its main objective is to develop a sense of ability to overcome internalised oppression' (Wong 2003:311).

'Power-with' emphasises the collective forces of people cooperating with each other to solve problems and attain set goals. It celebrates collective action and is concerned with 'capacity building, social networks and organisational strength. It is intended to demonstrate the idea of "I cannot, but we can"' (Wong ibid.). The collective dimension of empowerment becomes a reality when 'individuals work together to achieve a more extensive impact than each could have had alone' (Rowlands 1995:103). Again, this understanding downgrades the notion of power as something to be given and focuses on power as the ability to discover inner strength, collective energy and capacity to take action, not just as a response to external promptings but also in recognition of one's personal and group experience.

While the mainstream notion of empowerment appears mechanistic and instrumental, a feminist position distinguishes it from the simple idea of the allocation of power to a multi-dimensional process that results in increased equity in the exercise of power. Feminist thinking emphasises empowerment as among other things, 'the expansion in people's ability to make strategic life choices in a context where this ability was previously denied to them' (Kabeer 2005 as cited by Santillán et al 2004:535). Margaret Synder and Mary Tasesse expand the scope and argue that empowerment as 'autonomy for women, for the poor, and for nations of the developing world, means that they are able to make their own choices in the realms of politics, economics and society' (1995:15) while Carolyn Baylies, using the experience of women with AIDS in Zambia, contends that empowerment is 'best understood as a process applying in respect of specific context, as contingent upon time, place and sphere of action or thought and as relational in respect of the roles, capacities and resources which may be brought to bear in any particular instance' (Baylies 2002:369). Pulled together, these offer a more layered insight into a complex concept.

Feminists of all leanings critique the conventional or 'malestream' understanding of empowerment for its underestimation of the social context of powerlessness and this has been evident in recent debates. The emerging literature points to a significant shift in the discourse, especially in the context of the empowerment of women (Kabeer 2005; Stacki and Monkman 2003). The World Bank's expanded definition, for example, sees it as 'the expansion of assets and capabilities of poor people to *participate in*, *negotiate with*, *influence*, *control*, and *hold accountable* institutions that affect their lives' (worldbank.org, author's emphasis). In the past the Bank had been more focused on formal systems and structures and had conceptualised empowerment as a means to economic goals. The 'power-over' approach was in operation in its development programmes but that has now been expanded to include the 'power-with' dimension, and though this is still economically oriented, it indicates a major shift in its position (Wong 2003).

The inclusion of power to negotiate with and to influence relevant institutions recognises the right of the marginalised to have a say in what concerns them instead of simple submission to programmes designed and implemented by external agents with the goal of equipping them with skills for set goals, as the 'malestream' understanding of empowerment tends to imply. The broadening of the narrow, instrumental agenda to incorporate collective action, community participation and self-actualisation can be traced to the feminist critique of the conventional approach. Some writers, Santillán and colleagues argue, have even introduced linkages to other related concepts in order to illustrate the complexity of the empowerment of women. Some now associate it with agency and individual self-reliance. Taken to mean 'women's ability to make decisions and affect outcomes of importance to themselves and their families or, put another way, as women's control over their own lives and over resources' (Santillán et al 2004:535), agency is considered to be one of the indicators of empower-ment. Naila Kabeer, writing on gender equality and women's empowerment, identifies agency as one of three closely interrelated perspectives of the concept. She notes that agency 'implies not only actively exercising choice, but also doing this in ways that challenge power relations. Because of the significance of beliefs, values in legitimating inequality, a process of empowerment often begins from within' (2005:14). (For a different perspective on agency see Kalpana Wilson's chapter in this volume.)

The 'malestream' perspective on empowerment pitches its debates mainly at the economic and political level with an emphasis on macro-economic and political restructuring without overt concern with the social context of women's lives (Wong 2003; Sprague and Hayes 2000; Longwe 1998). It overlooks power dynamics, which often deny women access to the resources needed to be empowered. In contrast, feminist writers situate empowerment in a social context and link it to women's struggles to 'create and enact their lives in the context of the social relationships in which they live their daily lives' (Sprague and Hayes 2000:680). They resist the notion that women can be 'added-in' to the sphere of power without a restructuring of the social context where traditional and cultural values and even personal obstacles imposed by relationships undermine women. To them, empowerment for women is impossible without structural transformation, as opposed to the 'malestream' point of view, which seems to ignore structural restrictions in society (Longwe 1998).

Traditionally, empowerment seems to celebrate individualism, self-achievement and economic goals while feminist thinking includes a sense of community. Thus, empowerment can be described as 'a process by which oppressed persons gain control over their lives by taking part with others in development of activities and structures that allow people increased involvement in matters which affect them directly' (Bystydzienski 1992:3). This expanded view incorporates the idea of acting collectively.

Empowerment and the public/private dichotomy

The centrality of economic power in the malestream perspective is not the only problematic issue; political power has also sparked feminist critique. Notwithstanding radical feminists' disdain for participation in practices of formal politics such as elections, voting and political parties, the political empowerment of women has occupied the attention of some commentators (Corrin 1999; Rowlands 1998; Randall 1987). Radical feminists argue that engaging in conventional politics within the existing cultural and ideological context is not a rewarding experience, while the more liberal call for a model of power that incorporates a 'gender analysis of power relations that includes an understanding of how "internalised oppression" places barriers on women's exercise of political power' (Rowlands 1998:14). And given that the arena of politics underlines inequality between men and women because of its male-dominated settings, Bookman and Morgen (1988:14) have pointed out that, 'until we broaden our definition of politics to include the everyday struggle to survive and to change power relations in our society ... women's political action will remain obscured' (cited Bystydzienski 1992). The feminist position seeks to bridge the dichotomy between the public and the private and to offer relevant and meaningful approaches to the political empowerment of women.

The malestream notion of the public and private sphere is premised on the argument that these are separate domains, and are a reflection of the positions and roles of the sexes in society (McDowell and Pringle 1992). (For further discussion of the public/private dichotomy see Georgina Blakeley's and Ruth Lister's chapters in this volume.) Politics as a male-dominated process routinely isolates women and even when they join political parties, they are assigned designated roles and often these are closely linked to their gender. Feminists do not only challenge this entrenched practice but call for a restructuring of the political sphere. They argue that women's efforts to gain control of their lives, participate in decision-making processes and organise themselves to take action at grassroots levels count as political (Karl 1995). Politics is not limited to the allocation of resources and the exercise of power within clearly defined structures and activities, as is the case from a conventional perspective, but it is also about the consideration of power relations (Corrin 1999).

A conventional understanding of politics, Vicky Randall says, is 'the conscious, deliberate participation in the process by which resources are allocated amongst citizens'. She offers an alternative view, which sees politics 'as a process of articulation, a working out of relationships within an already-given power' (as quoted by Corrin 1999:9–10). Others have argued that any activity or relationship based on power being exercised by one group over others is political and some have pushed this notion further to see the personal as political (Eisentein 1983; Wandersee 1988, both cited Bystydzienski 1992). Politicising the personal, Randall (1987) argues, reveals that women have been involved in 'less conventional politics' (Bystydzienski 1992:2). Against this backdrop, a change in the structure and organisation of party politics becomes critical given that political parties and electoral processes often raise barriers against women. As the case study that follows illustrates, the increased participation of women in political activity does not necessarily reflect political empowerment.

Case study: women's empowerment strategies in Nigeria

In principle, the Nigerian state acknowledges the need to empower women. Over the years, different strategies have been implemented to achieve this goal. However, most have been driven by the conventional understanding of the concept. The state and development agencies have attempted to plan for women and have exercised power over them, as evident in the approaches adopted.

Empowerment strategies in Nigeria broadly fall under three headings: political empowerment, economic empowerment and empowerment through integrated rural development (Garba 1999). The economic approach entails 'improving women's economic status by providing them with employment, improving their capacity to be involved in income-generating activities, and in improving their access to credit facilities (Garba 1999:135; Izugbara 2004). The political strategies focus on mobilising women through political education and awareness programmes on their rights and responsibilities to engage in party politics and to seek elective office. This approach is particularly favoured by development agencies. The third strategy, the integrated rural development, is a composite of the first and the second and much more. In addition to the provision of tools and resources to improve women's entrepreneurial capacity and participation in politics, the approach also takes on issues such as literacy, reproductive health, sanitation and environmental protection.

While some women have been 'helped' to gain access to resources for economic activities, political empowerment appears to have been less successful, partly because shackles imposed by tradition and religion remain intact despite institutional and legal reforms. In Nigeria, as is the case in some other places, party politics as an exercise of power in the public sphere is the domain of men. Women's participation remains limited to the fringes and attempts to move from the margin to the centre have been challenged by forces ranging from the traditional to the religious. For example, when

Sarah Jibril declared her intention to run for the presidency of Nigeria in 1992, her political dream was ridiculed and reduced to a joke.

The place of women in Nigeria is culturally determined. In the south, women play key roles in the social and economic sectors and secondary roles in political affairs. However, in the north, which is predominantly Muslim, they are more restricted on religious grounds. Until 1999 Nigeria had successions of military administrations interspaced with short spells of democratic politics. During the country's brief forays into party politics, women played insignificant roles in political parties and were indirectly restricted to their own wings where they were not in any position to wield significant power within the parties. Moreover, there were no women in the upper echelons of the parties to swing support in their favour. Besides, the women did not seem to believe that they could make a difference. As the view of a female politician who criticised Jibril suggested, the women were not prepared to challenge the socio-cultural barriers imposed on them. This is not peculiar to Nigerian women, as surveys of women's wings of political parties in Africa have shown. Many of them are glorified 'housekeeping' sections of the parties (Karl 1995).

Most of the women's wings were made up of elite women and their contributions were limited to glamorising political rallies. Under military rule, women were relegated to the background, in accordance with military traditions where obedience is the rule, but a few were given political positions to silence critics. Under General Ibrahim Babangida, (in power from 1985–93), significant changes took place because his wife Maryam took on a high profile role as first lady. She made herself a champion of women's empowerment and launched a strategy, the Better Life Programme (BLP), in 1987 to mobilise women to play an active role in national development and to raise consciousness about women's rights.

The first lady ran the organisation like a pseudo-charity and conscripted the wives of other military officers to supervise it according to their status. Although a lot of money was pumped into the organisation, it was accountable to no one and was seen more as a pet project of the first lady than a strategic programme for the empowerment of women (Garba 1999). The organisation claimed dramatic results, including the launching of co-operatives, cottage industries, new farms and gardens, new shops and markets, women's centres and social welfare programmes (www.ibrahim-babangida.com).

The outcomes of the BLP were more visible in the media than in reality. Critics insisted that 'what were known were its advertised attributes: glamorous meetings celebrating the elites that made up the national, state and local leadership. But the real benefits in terms of empowerment of rural women whom it was intended to target were never recorded in relation to the level of public funds used to finance it' (Garba 1999:136).

The fact that some of the structures of the programme collapsed long before the Babangida administration ended confirmed its failure to empower rural women. The failure could also be attributed to the implementation approach that was adopted. It was, as Ibrahim puts it, a forum for 'the display of power, influence and prestige by privileged women. Indeed, Maryam Babangida's style of running the BLP was authoritarian and indeed militaristic. She issued orders and expected them to be obeyed without discussion, much less criticism' (Ibrahim 2004).

Beyond the personal style of the founder was the problem of a top-down model of empowerment that attempted to 'add in' women to the programme. Production machines were installed for women although they had no training on how to use or maintain them. Cottage industries and shops were built with little input from the women who were meant to use them and on paper thousands of women were 'empowered' but, in reality, little changed. The highly bureaucratic and authoritarian approach of the BLP only reinforced the division between the powerful and the marginalised.

While one cannot reject the merit of the programme, given its potential to provide initial access to women, it has to be acknowledged that it still smacked of domination. Reducing empowerment to the provision of resources and opportunities to acquire production tools and entrepreneurial skills without any input from the would-be beneficiaries of the programme undermined its success. Studies (Bystydzienski 1992) have shown that the empowerment of women is more likely to be successful when they work together to bring it about.

Empowerment in practice

It is probably in the area of the implementation of empowerment pro-grammes that the impact of the feminist perspective has been most notice-able. Feminist critiques of empowerment have evolved from the theoretical to the practical. In fact, many feminists have raised questions about empowerment programmes based on the top–bottom approach and have advocated strategies that recognise women as agents of change (Afshar 1998). Although perceptions of empowerment are not universal but context dependent, some feminists agree that 'to be considered "empowered", women themselves must be significant actors in the process of change – in other words, they must exercise agency' (Santillán et al 2004:535). Put differently, power cannot be bestowed or allocated because empowerment has to be self-determined. This understanding has re-defined the implementation of empowerment programmes by making women agents of change and not just beneficiaries of power allocation. It has informed a number of development programmes, for example literacy programmes where women have been 'empowered by entering into dialogue with their peers. Through this dialogue they learn to read and write as they experience and speak about their world' (Paulo Freire cited by Bystydzienski 1992:3). In other words, the women learnt to exercise 'power to' change their lives.

In contrast to programmes driven by the conventional perspective, which are often implemented from the top–bottom approach, development programmes based on the feminist position start from local grassroots groups and target particular problems. Implemented alongside efforts to mobilise support at the macro-level, such programmes put women at the centre, not as recipients of power but as sharers of power, and promote awareness building, which Karl describes as 'a basic component of the process of empowerment' (1995:36).

As explained earlier, most empowerment programmes in Nigeria have been driven by the traditional understanding of the concept. But a few organisations have adopted a feminist approach. The Country Women's Association of Nigeria (COWAN) and the Women in Nigeria (WIN) exemplify this. The first was started in 1982 by a woman and, from the beginning, adopted a bottom-up approach. Its main goal was to empower rural women towards self-sufficiency. Although that may sound like the objective of any empowerment programme, COWAN is different because not only do the women have a say in the organisation, but they are also involved in the planning and implementation of programmes. They are agents of change and are empowered to have an effective voice in what concerns them.

Its name may evoke a national and all-encompassing status, but Women in Nigeria is a radical and somewhat confrontational group. Formed in 1983, WIN has worked for the emancipation of women by drawing attention to all forms of oppression and discrimination against women. It has been described as the 'only organisation promoting all women's interests with the potential to mobilise women and men in combining the concern for gender equality with popular democratic struggles' (Corrin 1999:187). However, its approach has been described as having a 'uni-directional goal of struggling for the economic, social, and political conditions for women's autonomy without placing limits on such autonomy' (Garba 1999:137). WIN's successes include the prosecution of incidences of abuse of 'child-wives'; raising awareness about discrimination against women; early marriages and its negative consequences; and rendering financial assistance to indigent female students (ibid.). Although its membership is predominantly made up of the professional class, its focus covers a wide range of issues. However, its feminist identity alienates it from conservative women's groups and gives it an elitist image.

In comparison to the BLP, WIN and COWAN have achieved some degree of success in empowering women, thus confirming that a feminist perspective of empowerment is a more useful way of increasing the capacity of women to make choices and exercise control over their lives.

The Nigerian situation reflects the growing trend in empowerment practices. Majorie Mayo (2004) has explored empowerment in the context of women developing their own agenda to empower themselves in ways that reflect feminist thinking. Community participation in capacity building is emerging as the thrust of empowerment programmes, thus downplaying individualism and self-sufficiency. 'Community participation and empowerment have been increasingly widely advocated, both in the North and the South,' Mayo explains (2004:139). She cites policy change by the World Bank and the IMF as evidence that women are being supported to develop their own agenda for empowerment.

This trend contradicts the 'malestream' notion of 'power-over' and lines up with the feminist position of 'power-from-within' and 'power-with'. The idea of empowerment as gaining power by learning and accepting the rules and conforming has given way to a feminist understanding of active participation in the process of having an effective voice. The United Nations and other major international organisations have declared a commitment to the promotion of the empowerment of women (United Nations 2005). Development programmes now acknowledge and incorporate feminist perspectives (see John Craig in this volume).

The increasing relevance of empowerment in development discourse was highlighted when the World Bank (2001) acknowledged its importance in the fight against poverty. This was seen to demonstrate the Bank's shift from a top–bottom approach, by which power was to be allocated through projects designed and implemented by external agents, to a more inclusive approach that recognises the role of beneficiaries of development programmes. In practical terms intervention strategies to increase women's empowerment have been introduced. These range from those that focus on education to efforts to increase women's representation in formal political structures (Longwe 2000). The role of external agents has also been redefined to move them away from exercising 'power-over' to being facilitators of the empowerment processes (Rowlands 1995). However, it remains to be seen whether this discursive shift represents a genuine attempt to achieve feminist goals or a rhetorical device to legitimise the World Bank's neo-liberal agenda, as Kalpana Wilson argues in this volume with reference to agency.

Conclusion

This chapter has attempted to explore the differences between the conventional and feminist conception of empowerment using Nigeria as a case study. It has argued that the political as well as the economic empowerment of women is best served by a feminist perspective. This conclusion echoes recent changes in the implementation of development programmes by the World Bank and other external organisations. In the past empowerment was conceptualised in the context of investing power in the disempowered by providing them with resources to access the economic and political spheres. Emphasis was often placed on the acquisition of skills and the capacity to participate in development projects without deliberate consideration of possible internalised oppression or social and cultural obstacles that could make such participation unproductive. Recent trends show a shift from a unidirectional and externally driven approach to empowerment as a multi-dimensional, personal and collective process. A focus on access to resources and tools has given way to an understanding of empowerment as a process that must emanate from within disempowered individuals.

As the case study showed, the adoption of an approach that is shaped by a traditional understanding of the concept reduces empowerment to a simple process of the allocation of power through the provision of access to resources to participate in the political or economic spheres. Not only does this approach emphasise the 'power-over' perspective but it also overlooks critical issues such as the social context of women and the realities of their lives.

The chapter has made a case for a feminist perspective both at theoretical and practical levels for, as Haleh Afshar argues, empowerment is a process that cannot be 'done to or for women' (1998:4). It must emerge from women themselves.

Key writers and further reading

Empowerment is a concept that cuts across various disciplines and dominates debates in different contexts. The empowerment of women, in particular, has been explored from many perspectives, particularly in the context of politics and development, but unlike some concepts it is often examined alongside associated practices. Although not clearly situated within the empowerment discourse, Joni Lovenduski and Pippa Norris's (1996) research on women in British politics provides insight into the impact of the political organisation of British politics on women and illustrates power relations and issues of empowerment. Jill Bystydzienski (1992), Vicky Randall (1987) and Judith Astelarra (1992) offer international perspectives on the empowerment of women.

Another important voice in the empowerment debate is that of Haleh Afshar (1998). Her research on the politics of development and women and empowerment makes important contributions to the debate. Chris Corrin (1999) also provides a general feminist perspective on politics, which offers some explanations that are applicable to empowerment.

Bibliography

Afshar, H. (1998) *Women and Empowerment: Illustrations from the Third World* (London: Macmillan).

Astelarra, J. (1992) 'Women, Political Culture, and Empowerment in Spain', in J. Bystydzienski (ed.), *Women Transforming Politics* (Bloomington and Indianapolis: Indiana University Press).

Barnes, B. (1988) *The Nature of Power* (Oxford: Polity Press).

Baylies, C. (2002) 'HIV/AIDS and Older Women in Zambia: Concern for Self, Worry over Daughters, Towers of Strength', *Third World Quarterly* 23:2, 351–75.

Bystydzienski, J. (1992) 'Influence of Women's Culture on Public Politics in Norway', in J. Bystydzienski (ed.), *Women Transforming Politics* (Bloomington and Indianapolis: Indiana University Press), 1–10.

Cook, H. (2002) 'Empowerment', in G. Blakeley and V. Bryson (eds), *Contemporary Political Concepts. A Critical Introduction* (London: Pluto Press, 162–78).

Corrin, C. (1999) *Feminist Perspectives on Politics* (London: Longman).

Garba, P. (1999) 'An Endogenous Empowerment Strategy: A Case-Study of Nigerian Women', *Development in Practice* 9:1 & 2, 130–41.

Ibrahim, J. (2004) 'The First Lady Syndrome and the Marginalisation of Women from Power: Opportunities or Compromises for Gender Equality?', http://www.feministafrica.org/03-2004/jibrin.html.

Izugbara, C. (2004) 'Gendered Micro-lending Schemes and Sustainable Women's Empowerment in Nigeria', *Community Development Journal* 39:1, 72–84.

Kabeer, N. (2005) 'Gender Equality and Women's Empowerment', *Gender and Development* 13:3, 13–24.

Karl, M. (1995) *Women Empowerment: Participation and Decision Making* (London and New Jersey: Zed Books).

Longwe, S. H. (1998) 'Education for Women's Empowerment or Schooling for Women's Subordination?', *Gender and Development* 6:2, 19–26.

Longwe, S. H. (2000) 'Towards Realistic Strategies for Women's Political Empowerment in Africa', *Gender and Development* 8:3, 24–30.

Lovenduski, J. and Norris, P. (1996) *Women in Politics* (Oxford: Oxford University Press).

Lukes, S. (ed.) (1986) *Power* (Oxford: Blackwell).

Mayo, M. (2004) 'Exclusion, Inclusion and Empowerment: Community Empowerment? Reflecting on the Lessons of Strategies to Promote Empowerment', in J. Andersen (ed.), *Politics of Inclusion and Empowerment: Gender, Class and Citizenship* (London: Palgrave Macmillan),139–58.

McDowell, L. and Pringle, R. (eds) (1992) *Defining Women: Social Institutions and Gender Divisions* (Cambridge: Polity Press).

Randall, V. (1987) *Women and Politics: An International Perspective* (Basingstoke: Macmillan).

Riger, S. (1993) 'What's Wrong with Empowerment?', *American Journal of Community Psychology* 21, 279–92.

Rowlands, J. (1995) 'Empowerment Examined', *Development in Practice* 5:2, 101–6.

Rowlands, J. (1998) 'A Word of the Times, But What Does It Mean? Empowerment in the Discourse and Practice of Development', in H. Afshar (ed.), *Women and Empowerment. Illustrations from the Third World* (London: Macmillan), 11–34.

Santillán, D., Schuler, S., Tu Anh, H., Tran Hung Minh, T., Quach Thu Trang, Q. and Minh Duc, N. (2004) 'Developing Indicators to Assess Women's Empowerment in Vietnam', *Development in Practice* 14:4, 534–49.

Sprague, J. and Hayes, J. (2000) 'Self-determination and Empowerment: A Feminist Standpoint Analysis of Talk about Disability', *American Journal of Community Psychology* 28:5, 671–95.

Stacki, S. and Monkman, K. (2003) 'Change through Empowerment Processes: Women's Stories from South Asia and Latin America', *Compare* 33:2, 173–89.

Synder, M. and Tasesse, M. (1995) *African Women and Development: A History* (London: Zed Books).

United Nations (1991) *Women: Challenges to the Year 2000* (New York: UN).

United Nations (2005) 'UN Millennium Development Goals', http://www.un.org/millenniumgoals/.

Ward, D. and Mullender, A. (1991) 'Empowerment and Oppression: An Indissoluble Pairing for Contemporary Social Work', *Critical Social Policy* 11:2, 21–30.

Wong, K. F. (2003) 'Empowerment as a Panacea for Poverty – Old Wine in New Bottles? Reflections on the World Bank's Conception of Power', *Progress in Development Studies* 3:4, 307–22.

World Bank (2001) *World Development Report: The State in a Changing World* (New York: Oxford University Press).

Web pages

www.worldbank.org/empowerment.

www.ibrahim-babangida.com.

11

Time

Valerie Bryson

Introduction

It might seem odd to include a chapter on 'time' in this volume as there is no sustained or readily identifiable tradition of analysing time within mainstream political thought. Although significant work has been done by sociologists, anthropologists and historians on the socially created nature of our sense of time and the power relations that this may involve, few political theorists or scientists have explored these issues. Nor have they explored issues around the use of time and the distribution of disposable time that might be available for political involvement and, although many have seen that economic poverty can exclude or marginalise some groups, the similar effects of 'time poverty' are still not generally recognised.

However, political theorists' lack of interest in time has political implications in itself, concealing certain assumptions about its nature and availability. In this sense time can be seen as a key *latent* concept of political theory – and, like other concepts, its treatment in traditional political theory has reflected the experiences of political theorists themselves – that is, on the whole, the experiences of white, middle-class, western men. In treating time as a given, common-sense fact of life, these men have generally failed to recognise either that many people may experience and understand it in other ways, or that these differences may be politically significant. They have also failed to see that time is often an important but scarce and unevenly distributed political resource which may both reflect and maintain dominant patterns of power and privilege.

Time has been a latent concept for many feminist theorists too (a point made by Christine Hughes 2002:8). However, there is generally a greater awareness of temporal issues amongst feminist writers, and there is a growing body of feminist literature which addresses these directly. Some of this draws on work from elsewhere in the social sciences, which is therefore included in this chapter's initial overview of mainstream approaches. The chapter then discusses recent feminist work on time, and finds that this represents an important contribution to political analysis which has had a significant, although limited, impact on mainstream political theory and practice.

Mainstream approaches

Although self-conscious reflections by mainstream political theorists on the political significance of time have been rare, they have not been unimportant. This work is surveyed briefly below, along with that of some sociologists, anthropologists and historians, and organised under four main headings. Although these draw on quite distinct literatures, the themes and ideas involved are clearly interconnected.

Past, present and future: why time matters

In contrast to the dominant neglect of temporal issues, a few contemporary writers insist that time and history must be included in the understanding of political stability as well as change, and that an awareness of temporal issues should inform all political analysis. Such an approach is exemplified in recent work by the US political scientist Paul Pierson and the UK sociologist Antony Giddens, who both separately argue that a 'moving picture' provides a better basis for political understanding than a 'timeless snapshot'. Although only Giddens makes the link, such understanding was also central to the work of Karl Marx more than a century earlier.

Pierson's analysis builds on the economic concept of 'path dependence', defined by the economist Douglass North as 'a term used to describe the powerful influence of the past on the present and future' (1994:364). Pierson argues that if we are to understand particular political possibilities and outcomes, we need to look beyond the immediate circumstances to slow, long-term processes (such as demographic change) whose effects build up over time, and to the ways in which past choices generate self-reinforcing dynamics that restrict later alternatives (2004). From a very different theoretical starting-point, Giddens' theory of *structuration* claims to 'bring temporality into the heart of social theory' (1995:29) by analysing how social systems and structures of domination are maintained in and across time–space through the repetition of individual acts which accumulate as social practices; he also argues that this need for repeated acts makes them inherently vulnerable to change. Giddens' analysis draws explicitly on Marx's insight that society and its institutions should be seen as a process, rather than a fixed state, and that they should be understood as products of the past that set conditions for the future. Although both he and Pierson reject the primacy of economic development as the driving force in human history, both would probably agree with Marx's famous dictum that 'men make their own history, but they do not make it just as they please; they do not make it under circumstances chosen by themselves, but under circumstances directly encountered, given and transmitted from the past' (1968:97).

This means that all three writers see the importance of temporal locations and processes for political analysis and agree that, although choices and outcomes are inevitably constrained by their context, political actions and decisions are neither predetermined nor pointless. Such temporal awareness could in principle contribute to the development of effective political strategies by those seeking to promote or resist particular changes, by helping them develop a realistic assessment of political possibilities. In addition, a sense of history and existence through time can provide a source of identity and empowerment and a basis for political mobilisation by subordinate groups whose experiences and achievements have been excluded or marginalised in conventional accounts.

Locating temporal ideas in time

The logic of Pierson's, Giddens' and Marx's arguments about the temporal nature of social and political structures and systems suggests that their own ideas should also be understood in the context of their particular circumstances. However, only Marx takes this self-referential step, to argue that his own analysis of the collapse of capitalism and the revolutionary role of the proletariat could not have been produced at an earlier stage of economic development, as the processes which he claimed to identify were not then visible.

Although he did not make the point, Marx's belief in human progress and his confident optimism were also in line with the general spirit and temporal perspectives of the Enlightenment philosophy which dominated western political thought from the mid-eighteenth century (see Bury 1960 and Foley 1994). According to a number of historians of political thought, this was in marked contrast to the idea of cyclical recurrence that characterised pre-Christian thought or the early Christian belief that human history was but a brief interlude between the Creation and the Day of Judgement (see Wolin 1961; Pocock 1973 and, for critical discussion, Lane 2000); Robert Pocock has argued that this view of time and humanity's place within it restricted the imaginative possibilities of political thought well into the seventeenth century.

The Enlightenment focus on secular human time and the potential for progress opened up a new range of political ideas. However, neither its secular assumptions nor its optimism were ever universally held. Today, the increasing political influence of fundamentalist Christianity and Islam means that political debates and actions can still be affected by temporal assumptions that lie outside the framework of human, earthly time: for example, significant numbers of US citizens hold a belief in the imminence of the Day of Judgement which may affect their attitude to global warming or conflict in the Middle East. Belief in the progressive nature of human history is also perhaps harder for secular thinkers to sustain today, for recent western thought has inevitably been shaped by the horrendous political experiences of the twentieth century, and by the possibility that scientific knowledge will lead, not to human progress, but to environmental or military catastrophe on an unprecedented scale. Uncertainty about the future has been reinforced by developments in natural science which appear to show that time itself is relative, and has found philosophical expression in post-structuralist and postmodernist critiques of the idea of progress, certainty and objective knowledge.

Time culture(s)

Although political theorists have not generally drawn on the literature, the idea that human conceptions of time have themselves changed over time is supported by some sociologists, anthropologists and historians, who have built on the pioneering work of Durkheim and Evans-Pritchard in the early and mid-twentieth century to see time as a variable social construct, a 'social institution' which links the individual to the collective and meets a given society's need for social collaboration (for overviews, see Hassard 1990; Gell 1992). It is also in line with the work of a number of recent historians who have identified a significant change in human relationships with time in western societies between the fifteenth and nineteenth centuries, coinciding with the advent of capitalism and factory production. This has often been described as a shift from a traditional to a modern time culture: that is, from the natural, seasonal, local, task-oriented time of traditional, pre-industrial and pre-capitalist society to the commodified, linear, clock time of modern capitalist, industrial societies, in which time does not simply pass, but is measured, controlled, spent, invested, wasted or saved (see in particular, Thompson 1999 and Thrift 1990). Some see this as having since given way to the fragmented, incoherent time of postmodern society, in which time is simultaneously compressed and expanded; so that our lives are bound up both with the unimaginably fast speed of digital technology and the unimaginably, glacially slow pace of evolutionary change; and in which time is relative rather than objectively observable or measurable (for overviews and critical discussion, see Adam 1990, 1995, 2004; Nowotny 1994; Macnaghten and Urry 1998).

Writers have linked these changes to a range of intellectual, scientific and cultural developments, often interlinked with technological developments such as the invention of mechanical clocks in the late thirteenth/early fourteenth century and the digital technology of the late twentieth century, and some follow Marx in identifying the changing needs of capitalist accumulation as the driving force behind changes in the social nature of time. Here the work of the historian E. P. Thompson has been particularly influential. In a famous essay, first published in 1967, he linked the shift from natural to clock time to Marx's analysis of capitalism's need for synchronised, commodified labour, and argued that the disputes over working hours which Marx had identified had been preceded by what

Thompson called a struggle *against* time – that is, against the whole idea that activities must be dictated by the clock, and that employees should work day in day out, selling their time rather than completing a task, and turning up regardless of the weather or the season, or the traditional demands of 'St Monday' (dedicated to drink and relaxation) (Thompson 1999).

Some later writers have questioned the whole distinction between natural and clock time, arguing that it disguises the extent to which we all inhabit natural as well as social time (see in particular Adam 1990, 1995). Some have also argued that the distinction implies the superiority of western or male time cultures (see Greenhouse 1996). However, as with Thompson's analysis of the imposition of time discipline on an initially resistant workforce, the recognition of competing time cultures may help us understand wider issues of power and control. It can involve a forceful reminder that 'Not all time is money. Not all human relations are exclusively governed by the rationalized time of the clock. Not all times are equal' (Adam 1995:94), and that the time needed to respond to human needs, whether this involves performing particular tasks however long they take, or caring for and communicating with others, or building relationships, should not be subordinated to the rigid dictates of clock time. Such considerations have complex implications for gendered roles and responsibilities and for the notion of time as a scarce, measurable resource, discussed in the following section.

Time as a scarce resource

The idea that time is a scarce and objectively measurable resource is inherent in Marx's analysis of exploitation in capitalist class society, in which the worker sells his *time* rather than the product of his labour: indeed he said that 'In the final analysis, all forms of economics can be reduced to the economics of time' (in McLellan 1973:88). This in turn means that time is central to the politics of class struggle, a point recently reaffirmed by Pietro Basso (1998).

Although only a few political theorists have explored the implications, time can also be seen as a scarce *political* resource, whose uneven distribution has implications for the development of social capital and for citizenship, particularly the model of active citizenship that has been advocated by recent UK governments, and which stresses citizens' involvement in the provision of public services, as well as community involvement, responsible parenting and paid employment (see Barnett 2002). Here, a number of writers have expressed concern that long-hours working, particularly in the US and UK, is having detrimental effects on civic involvement and the quality of life, leading towards 'not only the parent-free home, but also the participation-free civic society and the citizen-free democracy' (Hochschild 1997:243; see also Schor 1991 and Bunting 2004).

Others, however, dispute the claim that there has been a decline in leisure (for an overview of debates on this see Jacobs and Gerson 2004). Although Robert Putman has famously identified a decline in social capital in the United States, and says that 'Participation in politics is increasingly based on the cheque book, as money replaces time', he blames this on watching television ('the one activity most lethal to community involvement') rather than long-hours working and a lack of time (2000:40, 92).

Although again few political theorists have addressed the issue, 'free' time can also be seen as a primary good whose distribution should be governed by principles of social justice. This point was discussed briefly by the political philosopher John Rawls in his later work, where he argued that if someone chooses to go surfing rather than work a standard day (which he suggested might be eight hours), they cannot expect to have their needs met by other members of society (Rawls 2001:60, 179). This position has been developed by Tony Fitzpatrick (2004) to argue that a just allocation of 'meaningful time', which he sees as a basic human right, would require a radical challenge to the temporal imperative of market capitalism.

The rapidly expanding field of quantitative time-use research claims to provide the kind of empirical evidence on which discussion of such issues could be grounded. In particular, diary-based studies, in which respondents record their activities (and sometimes additional contextual information) at fixed times throughout the day and night, are now available for more than twenty countries since the 1960s and are now being conducted in many more. Although this work has not been explored in detail by political theorists or scientists, its proponents elsewhere in the social sciences see it as 'an important scientific innovation, something akin to a social microscope', a source of 'hard, replicable data' that enables us to identify long-term patterns of social change and to put together 'a comprehensive account that covers all daily activities, paid work, unpaid work, leisure or consumption time, and sleep' (Harvey and Pentland 1999:8; Robinson 1999:47; Gershuny 2002:25). If so, time-use studies should shed light on changing patterns of political participation and the distribution of leisure, paid work and domestic responsibilities, including differences between women and men.

Feminist critiques and contributions

With the exception of work on time use, the mainstream work discussed so far is effectively 'malestream' in its neglect of gender issues and its unreflecting assumption that male-based experiences and perceptions can provide a comprehensive view of the world. It does, however, have interesting implications for feminist theory and practice, and some feminist writers have extended and critiqued existing work in important ways. In terms of the headings used so far, feminist ideas on the relevance of history and temporal location are discussed briefly together below. However, most feminist contributions are concerned with time cultures and the distribution of work and leisure time; the chapter therefore considers these in more detail.

Feminism, history and time

There is a sense in which any feminist challenge to existing gender arrangements involves a particular notion of temporality, as it assumes that these are historically produced rather than 'natural' or eternally given, so that the future need not be simply a continuation of the past.

Many feminists have long seen the political significance of accounts of the past in sustaining or contesting subordination, and they have attempted to re-write history in a number of ways (for a good recent overview, see Cowman and Jackson 2003). At the most straightforward level, this has involved recalling the lives of illustrious foremothers whose achievements have been written out of the history books, and who can provide both an inspiration and a reminder that women have not simply been passive victims. Some feminists have also revisited the past to support a sense of collective identity by women as a whole and, increasingly, by particular groups of women (Weston 2002).

In contrast to the male writers discussed earlier, most feminists are interested in gender inequalities in the private as well as the public sphere, so that the subject matter of history should include domestic and sexual relationships and procreation. From this perspective, the Marxist theory of history needs to be re-written to include conditions of (re)production as part of the material economic basis of society which may both have their own dynamic and generate widespread social and political effects (see Bryson 2004). Such a perspective in turn suggests that if, as some writers discussed in the following section suggest, women have a distinct sense of temporality linked to their reproductive role, then this too may change over time, along with material conditions of (re)production (such as the development of reliable contraception or fertility treatment for older women).

Other feminists have applied Giddens's claims that social systems and structures are only maintained over time through the cumulative effect of repeated acts to the idea of gender as 'performance'. Here it is claimed that gender has no stable or natural base, that it is therefore not something that one *is* but something that one *does*, and that while it can be maintained by acts that conform to gender norms, it can also be disrupted by transgressive behaviour (see in particular Butler 1990, 1993 and, for the link with Giddens, Weston 2002). Normatively prescribed behaviour which maintains gender over time is in turn bound up with the *use* of time; indeed Cynthia Epstein has argued that time norms are central to the maintenance of gender boundaries, as 'professional women with heavy workloads and men oriented to sharing childcare in the home each face social disapproval for spending "too much" time at activities not regarded as their primary obligation' (Epstein and Kalleberg 2004:17–18).

While anthropologists and historians have generally focused on differences in time culture between societies or over time, some feminist writers have suggested that there may also be important gender differences, reflecting the different experiences of women and men. This view has produced a body of work contrasting the linear, clock time of modern capitalist employment with the more natural, cyclical time culture of domestic and caring activities; this has led some to talk about 'women's time' and 'men's time' (see in particular Davies 1989; Forman with Sowton 1989; Nowotny 1994; the critical discussion in Adam 1990, 1995, 2004, and the overview in Hughes 2002).

Some of this feminist analysis builds on a point made, but not developed, by the historian E. P. Thompson, who noted in the course of his discussion of a general movement from natural to clock time that the mothers of young children still live partly in the former, and have 'not yet altogether moved out of the conventions of "pre-industrial" society' (Thompson 1999:382). Many feminist writers have argued that this is true of caring activities more generally, including the care of elderly or disabled people and the provision of emotional support, and applies whether the activity takes the form of paid employment or unpaid responsibilities in the home or community. Such activities cannot be fully automated, they are highly resistant to attempts at 'time management', and their temporal rhythms are often necessarily slow and in the present, with the processes of feeding, cleaning, dressing and reassurance repeated over and over again, and the timing of activities determined at least partly by need rather than the clock (you change the nappy because it is dirty, not because it is four o'clock). Karen Davies has introduced the concept of 'process time' to describe the kind of temporal consciousness that such activities often require. Process time emphasises that *'time is enmeshed in social relations'* (Davies' italics), and she distinguishes it from both task-oriented time, which 'tends to stress the task per se and risks separating the activity, at least conceptually, from its context', and 'the dominant temporal consciousness in our society: the linear hand of the clock' (1994:280, 278).

Although most writers are clear that they are referring to gendered activities rather than innate qualities, some have argued that the temporal perspectives of men and women may also be rooted in biology, particularly women's ability to give birth. Some eco-feminists have argued that this gives women a longer temporal perspective, a concern for the future and the care of the planet (discussed in Macnaghten and Urry 1998:155–7). Other writers have suggested that women's life-creating powers may give them an existential sense of being that has not been recognised by male philosophers:

in particular, Heidegger's influential vision of life lived in the knowledge of death excludes women's experience of *giving* time: women 'do not only live in time (from birth to death), they also give time and that act makes a radical difference to Being-in-the-World' (Forman 1989:7). The French feminist Julie Kristeva's influential *Women's Time*, first published in 1979, makes related points about the centrality of reproduction and motherhood to female subjectivity, which she links to monumental time (eternity) and cyclical time (repetition), and contrasts to the linear time of history, politics and language (Kristeva 1986). However, Kristeva also argues that women can and should now move beyond either seeking to join linear time (by claiming a career and political rights) or celebrating their right to remain outside it; rather, they should reject the dichotomy between masculine and feminine and the fixed nature of female subjectivity and experience that this assumes.

While the 'French feminism' with which Kristeva is associated remains highly controversial, many feminist writers agree with her rejection of dichotomy: indeed, the critique of the binary either/or thought which under-lies western political thought is a recurrent theme within contemporary feminism (as discussed in several chapters in this volume). These feminist critiques have exposed the artificial and hierarchical nature of dichotomies such as the public and the private or reason and emotion, and the male/female dichotomy that underlies and sustains them. They suggest that while men and women are likely to have relationships with time that are identifiably distinct, these are also fluid and open to change; they also alert us to the likelihood that any differences will work to the disadvantage of women. Such thinking supports the kind of conceptual distinction between 'male time' and 'female time' advocated by Davies, who does not claim either that all women share female time or that all men benefit from the privileged position of male time, but who uses the term 'male time' as

> shorthand for the dominant temporal consciousness and structuring which have historically developed out of certain power interests. By inserting the adjective male, [the term] stresses and draws attention to the patriarchal character of the groups and classes that have been able to influence this concept and measurement of time. (1989:17)

This kind of analysis enables us to see that the temporal rhythms arising from the caring responsibilities that are primarily held by women are forced into the 'shadow' of linear and clock time and that 'male time' has priority if time cultures clash: for example, the naturally slow processes of getting a child out of bed, dressed and fed have to be rushed through to get her to the childminder in time for her mother to catch the train which will get her to work no later than her colleagues (on this kind of clash, see for example Benn 1998 and Buxton 1998). It also helps us see that 'male time' is extending into areas of life for which it is particularly inappropriate.

Some writers have described the extension of 'male time' into the home and intimate relationships as the 'Taylorisation' of the home, as long hours in paid employment have led to an extension of notions of time management, efficiency and 'quality time' into personal life, so that the emotional as well as the physical relationships and needs of partners, family and friends are reduced to a tick list of tasks to be performed in pre-allocated slots of 'quality time'. The well-documented result is stress, for the personal needs of children and adults do not conform to the demands of the clock: dropping a child off at nursery is not the same as dropping the car off at a garage, while adult relationships too have their own, frequently unpredictable, rhythms. As Arlie Hochschild has said, there is a danger that time pressure in the home can make this seem like a place of work, and one which becomes less attractive than the paid workplace, as 'the tired parent flees a world of unresolved quarrels and unwashed laundry for the reliable orderliness, harmony and managed cheer of work' (Hochschild 1997:44). The clash of time cultures is particularly and dramatically clear in modern obstetrical practices, which often impose clock time on the processes of childbirth, treating this as a form of 'assembly line manufacture' which has to be 'actively managed', rather than as a natural and creative process with its own temporal requirements (Fox 1989:128).

Similar stresses are encountered for caring work that is done in the workplace, when it is expected to be slotted into a rigid time framework that is frequently inappropriate and counter-productive: for example, policies which assume that students go into crisis only during designated 'office hours' are likely to increase drop-out rates compared with an apparently time-consuming open-door approach, while patients are likely to get well quicker if the nurse who is changing their sheets 'wastes' a few minutes chatting to them. The stress experienced in working environments which do not acknowledge the need for such 'process time' may be partly a straightforward consequence of staff shortages, but they are also a consequence of inappropriate temporal values which in turn reflect patriarchal power structures. While recent moves in many western societies towards more flexible and 'family-friendly' employment policies may represent a partial acknowledgement of the needs of a subordinate time culture and a response to feminist campaigns, they do not really address these underlying issues. Moreover, as discussed in the previous section, the dominant time culture is not just male, it is also capitalist, and further changes in this direction are likely to be halted if they appear to threaten the imperatives of profit maximisation.

Women, men and time as a scarce resource

The above arguments assume that women and men typically spend their time in different ways. Here it is important to recognise the diversity of women's experiences, and the extent to which some are able to act like men by buying the labour of other women. Nevertheless, the available evidence from empirical research supports the 'commonsense' expectation that, despite recent changes in some areas, there are still significant general differences in time use between women and men in every social group and in every country of the world. These differences seem to be lowest in the Scandinavian nations, where there has been some convergence in recent years, but even here the general pattern remains. Two clear and important aspects of this general pattern are firstly, that women and girls spend more time than men and boys on housework and caring activities (and this includes not only physical work, but also the provision of emotional support and advice for friends, family members and work colleagues). Secondly, women do not lose their primary responsibility for domestic and caring work when they get involved in work outside the home. (For overviews and discussion, see Gershuny 2000; Folbre and Bittman 2004; Michelson 2005. For current research see the papers from the annual conferences of the International Association of Time Use Research at www.iatur.org.)

Such patterns have clear political implications, affecting women's ability to participate in political activities both directly and indirectly. As discussed above, malestream political theorists have generally ignored the importance of time as a political resource. In contrast, feminists have long pointed out that women's domestic responsibilities can result in a lack of disposable time that restricts their opportunities for political participation: as the suffrage campaigner and socialist Hannah Mitchell famously said nearly 100 years ago, 'No cause can be won between dinner and tea, and most of us who were married had to fight with one hand tied behind us, so to speak' (Mitchell 1977:130). Women's domestic responsibilities also clearly restrict their employment opportunities and are a key factor behind their lower earnings; this in turn means that they generally have less access than men to the financial resources and the well-placed contacts that often facilitate effective political activism. Many feminists therefore agree with Ruth Lister that women's work privileges men 'in a way that gives them a head-start over women in the public sphere and that enables them to maintain their power over women inside and outside the home' (Lister 2003:133). From this perspective, if women are to exercise political equality with men in 'any more substantial form than the equal right to vote' (Phillips 1991:101), there will have to be a more equal division of responsibilities within the home.

Malestream writers' failure to 'see' women's domestic labour produces a skewed perspective which can produce such absurdities as Giddens's assumption (echoing Marx) that time left over from paid employment is available for workers to spend as they please: 'The converse of the "public time" introduced by the rule of the clock is the "private time" that is freely disposable by the individual' (Giddens 1995:153). This view fails to analyse the nature of temporal rhythms outside the workplace, and fails to see the necessary and constrained nature of many of the activities that take place within the home and their social and economic importance. Giddens shows no sign of having read any Marxist feminist analysis of domestic labour (or indeed any feminist work since the mid-1970s); and he is apparently oblivious to the extent to which the non-work time of women is likely to be significantly less 'free' than that of men. Marx's own neglect of domestic work creates problems for his vision of a just, fully communist society, in which technology would liberate people from unnecessary toil, as it fails to take into account the time-consuming nature of caring work, which cannot be automated but is dependent upon social interaction (see Bubeck 1995). In his brief discussion of a just distribution of time, Rawls too ignored the private sphere. Although his later work acknowledges the work of feminist writers such as Susan Okin in extending his principles of justice to gender, he did not seem to appreciate the radical implications of this, and did not discuss her argument that the distribution of time spent on unpaid labour within the family is a central issue of justice, both in itself and because of its consequences (Okin 1990:4).

As discussed in Ruth Lister's chapter in this volume, some feminists have argued that women's traditional caring responsibilities are not simply constraints, but also a source of citizenship-enhancing values or even a form of citizenship activity in their own right. Some have also demanded that the economic value of the unpaid domestic and caring work for which women are disproportionately responsible (and which includes agricultural work in subsistence economies) should be recognised. They have also demanded that this value should be measured in terms of the time it takes. This demand had significant success at the 1995 UN World Conference on Women in Beijing, and the resulting *Platform for Action* required signatories to conduct regular time-use studies to quantify such work and assess its value.

This means that there has been a feminist impetus behind the recent growth of time-use studies, which at first sight seem an exception to the general neglect of gender issues in academic work on time. Nevertheless, the research has not been utilised much by non-feminist political analysts, as opposed to sociologists and economists, and it has often been framed by male assumptions which make it difficult to conceptualise the nature of women's caring responsibilities or the effects of these on women's time use. In particular, because many studies have asked individuals to record only one activity in any time slot, they have lost sight of the childcare that is often undertaken as a secondary activity and the ways in which women's 'free' time, including time available for political activity, is affected by childcare responsibilities. (A time-use diary would record a woman watching television as engaged in a leisure activity, but if there were a child asleep in the house and no adult present, she would not be free to leave the house. When canvassing during one election campaign, I met several women in this situation who were unable to go to the polling station.)

The studies have also been used by Jonathan Gershuny, a leading time-use researcher, to claim that women's lack of free time in western society is a myth which 'the facts' disprove (2000:8–9). Later studies suggest that men do have around thirty minutes a day more free time in much of Europe and the US (Aliaga and Winqvist 2003; Sayer 2005). While this may not be politically significant, a focus on total time ignores the extent to which women's 'free' time is not only more often constrained, but also much more fragmented and therefore less 'usable' than men's. These issues have been highlighted in other recent work which takes women's experiences as much more central, and in this sense time-use studies are increasingly feminist-influenced (see for example Bittman and Wajcman 2000; Craig 2002; Mattingly and Bianchi 2003; Folbre and Bittman 2004).

Nevertheless, time-use studies remain based on the assumption that time unfolds as a series of discrete, measurable activities which can be assigned a monetary value. In this sense, they endorse what was identified above as 'male time', that is, the linear, commodified time of the clock. As such, they cannot capture the qualitative, 'being there' nature of mothering and other forms of care. This means that although time-use studies can be an important resource for feminists, they should be handled with care and their limitations recognised.

Conclusion

What feminism can bring to the concept of time is the double insistence that it is a central political concept and that its analysis has particular relevance for women. Endorsing those writers who argue for the importance of historical context and development for political understanding, feminism extends such analysis to argue that gender relations too have a history, and that understanding the process through which they are created and sustained can help in the development of realistic political strategies for change.

Feminism sees that time is politically important as a scarce resource alongside and interacting with status, money and power (although this occurs in complex rather than straightforward ways). It also exposes the particular nature of clock time and challenges the hegemony of male time culture, showing that time is central to the maintenance of male privilege, not just at the level of who does what and who has spare time (although this is important), but at the more basic level of identifying and thereby offering the possibility of resistance to the commodified clock time of patriarchy and capitalism.

All this means that campaigns around time are becoming increasingly central to feminist politics indeed it is now almost a feminist platitude to say that the key to greater equality between the sexes is greater equality in time use within the home. This of course requires significant changes in male behaviour; as such it rejects the 'normality' of current male models and requires public policies to enable men as well as women to fulfil their domestic and caring responsibilities. Such analysis is absent from most malestream political theory. Nevertheless, it is having some impact on public policy in the UK, where men now have limited rights to paternity and family leave, and has gone further in many other European nations. However, as with the class struggles around time which Thompson identified during the industrial revolution, the issue is not simply one of hours, but involves a struggle *against* commodified clock time, or at least against its ubiquity – and that struggle is one which, I would suggest, it is both much more difficult and much more important to win. These issues are not just 'something for the girls', let alone a problem that only affects career women with children. Rather, they go to the heart of both empirical and normative questions about the kind of society we live in and the kind of society we want.

Key writers and further reading

As discussed in this chapter, time has received little explicit attention from mainstream political theorists and scientists. Key exceptions which treat time as central to social and political analysis are Marx (whose ideas on time are scattered throughout his work), Pierson (2004) and Giddens (1995). Important work on the relationship between beliefs about the nature of time and the development of political thought is provided by Wolin (1961) and Pocock (1973). E. P. Thompson's (1999) essay, first published in 1967, remains highly influential. Key recent overviews of time-use studies and their findings are provided by Gershuny (2000) and Michelson (2005).

In recent years, Adam's work on our human relationship with time has been particularly innovative and influential (1990, 1995) and, although on the whole her work is not overtly feminist, it does reflect some feminist concerns. Of explicitly feminist work on time, Kristeva's (1986) essay, first published in 1979, is now almost a classic text; Forman with Sowton's (1989) edited collection makes an important contribution; Davies' (1989) work on 'women's time' is widely cited, and the collection edited by Folbre and Bittman (2004) reflects the impact of feminist concerns on time-use studies.

Bibliography

Adam, B. (1990) *Time and Social Theory* (Cambridge: Polity Press).
Adam, B. (1995) *The Social Analysis of Time* (Cambridge: Polity Press).
Adam, B. (2004) *Time* (Cambridge: Polity Press).
Aliaga, C. and Winqvist, K. (2003) *How Women and Men Spend their Time: Results from 13 European Countries* (Luxembourg: Eurostat).

Barnett, N. (2002) 'Including Ourselves: New Labour and Engagement with Public Services', *Management Decision* 40:4, 310–17.

Basso, P. (1998) *Modern Times, Ancient Hours. Working Lives in the Twenty-first Century* (London and New York: Verso).

Benn, M. (1998) *Madonna and Child: Towards a New Politics of Motherhood* (London: Jonathan Cape).

Bittman, M. and Wajcman, J. (2000) 'The Rush Hour: The Character of Leisure Time and Gender Equity', *Social Forces* 79:1, 165–95.

Bryson, V. (2004) 'Marxism and Feminism: Can the "Unhappy Marriage" be Saved?', *Journal of Political Ideologies* 9:1, 13–30.

Bubeck, D. (1995) *Care, Gender and Justice* (Oxford: Clarendon Press).

Bunting, M. (2004) *Willing Slaves: How the Overwork Culture is Ruling our Lives* (London: HarperCollins).

Bury, J. (1960) *The Idea of Progress: An Inquiry into its Growth and Origin* (New York: Dover Publications Inc.).

Butler, J. (1990) *Gender Trouble: Feminism and the Subversion of Identity* (London: Routledge).

Butler, J. (1993) *Bodies that Matter: On the Discursive Limits of 'Sex'* (London: Routledge).

Buxton, J. (1998) *Ending the Mother War: Starting the Workplace Revolution* (London and Basingstoke: Macmillan).

Cowman, K. and Jackson, L. (2003) 'Time', in M. Eagleton (ed.), *A Concise Companion to Feminist Theory* (Oxford: Blackwell Publishing), 32–52.

Craig, L. (2002) *The Time Costs of Parenthood: An Analysis of Daily Workload* (Sydney: Social Policy Research Centre, University of New South Wales).

Davies, K. (1989) *Women and Time: Weaving the Strands of Everyday Life* (Sweden: University of Lund).

Davies, K. (1994) 'The Tensions between Process Time and Clock Time in Care-Work: The Example of Day Nurseries', *Time and Society* 3:3, 277–303.

Epstein, C. and Kalleberg, A. (2004) 'Time and Work: Changes and Challenges', in C. Epstein and A. Kalleberg (eds), *Fighting for Time: Shifting Boundaries of Work and Social Life* (New York: Russell Sage Foundation), 1–21.

Fitzpatrick, T. (2004) 'Social Policy and Time', *Time and Society* 13:2/3, 197–219.

Folbre, N. and Bittman, M. (eds) (2004) *Family Time: The Social Organisation of Care* (London and New York: Routledge).

Foley, M. (1994) 'Progress', in M. Foley (ed.), *Ideas that Shape Politics* (Manchester: Manchester University Press), 208–24.

Forman, F. (1989) 'Feminizing Time: An Introduction', in F. Forman with C. Sowton (eds), *Taking Our Time: Feminist Perspectives on Temporality* (Oxford: Pergamon Press), 1–9.

Forman, F. with Sowton, C. (eds) (1989) *Taking Our Time: Feminist Perspectives on Temporality* (Oxford: Pergamon Press).

Fox, M. (1989) 'Unreliable Allies: Subjective and Objective Time in Childbirth', in F. Forman with C. Sowton (eds), 123–34.

Gell, A. (1992) *The Anthropology of Time* (Oxford: Berg Publications Ltd).

Gershuny, J. (2000) *Changing Times: Work and Leisure in Postindustrial Society* (Oxford: Oxford University Press).

Gershuny, J. (2002) 'Service Regimes and the Political Economy of Time', in G. Crow and S. Heath (eds), *Social Conceptions of Time: Structure and Process in Work and Everyday Life* (Basingstoke: Palgrave), 24–37.

Giddens, A. (1995) *A Contemporary Critique of Historical Materialism* (Basingstoke: Macmillan).

Greenhouse, C. (1996) *A Moment's Notice: Time Politics Across Cultures* (Ithaca and London: Cornell University Press).

Harvey, A. and Pentland, W. (1999) 'Time Use Research', in W. Pentland, A. Harvey, M. Lawton and M. McColl (eds), *Time Use Research in the Social Sciences* (London and New York: Kluwer Academic/Plenum Publishers), 3–17.

Hassard, J. (ed.) (1990) *The Sociology of Time* (New York: St Martin's Press).

Hochschild, A. (1997) *The Time Bind: When Work Becomes Home and Home Becomes Work* (New York: Metropolitan Books).

Hughes, C. (2002) *Key Concepts in Feminist Theory and Research* (London: Sage).

Jacobs, J. and Gerson, K. (2004) *The Time Divide: Work, Family and Gender Inequality* (Cambridge, Mass.: Harvard University Press).

Kristeva, J. (1986) 'Woman's Time', in T. Moi (ed.), *The Kristeva Reader* (Oxford: Blackwell), 187–213.

Lane, M. (2000) 'Political Theory and Time', in P. Baert (ed.), *Time in Contemporary Intellectual Thought* (Amsterdam: Elsevier), 233–50.

Lister, R. (2003) *Citizenship: Feminist Perspectives* (Basingstoke: Palgrave Macmillan).

Macnaghten, P. and Urry, J. (1998) *Contested Natures* (London: Sage).

Marx, K. (1968) 'The Eighteenth Brumaire of Louis Bonaparte', in K. Marx and F. Engels *Selected Works* (London: Lawrence and Wishart).

Mattingly, M. and Bianchi, S. (2003) 'Gender Differences in the Quantity and Quality of Free Time: The U.S. Experience', *Social Forces* 81:3, 999–1030.

McLellan, D. (1973) *Marx's Gundrisse* (St Albans: Paladin).

Michelson, W. (2005) *Time Use: Expanding Explanation in the Social Sciences* (Boulder and London: Paradigm Publishers).

Mitchell, H. (1977) *The Hard Way Up* (London: Virago).

North, D. (1994) 'Economic Performance Through Time', *American Economic Review* 84:3, 359–68.

Nowotny, H. (1994) *Time: The Modern and Postmodern Experience* (Cambridge: Polity Press).

Okin, S. (1990) *Justice, Gender and the Family* (New York: Basic Books).

Phillips, A. (1991) *Engendering Democracy* (Cambridge: Polity Press).

Pierson, P. (2004) *Politics in Time: History, Institutions and Social Analysis* (Princeton: Princeton University Press).

Pocock, J. (1973) *Politics, Language and Time: Essays on Political Thought and History* (London: Methuen and Co. Ltd).

Putman, R. (2000) *Bowling Alone: The Collapse and Revival of American Community* (New York: Simon and Schuster).

Rawls, J. (2001) *Justice as Fairness* (Cambridge, Mass: Harvard University Press).

Robinson, J. (1999) 'The Time-Diary Method', in W. Pentland, A. Harvey, M. Lawton and M. McColl (eds), *Time Use Research in the Social Sciences* (London and New York: Kluwer Academic/Plenum Publishers), 47–89.

Sayer, L. (2005) 'Gender, Time and Inequality: Trends in Women's and Men's Paid Work, Unpaid Work and Free Time', *Social Forces* 84:1, 285–303.

Schor, J. (1991) *The Overworked American. The Unexpected Decline of Leisure* (New York: Basic Books).

Thompson, E. P. (1999) 'Time, Work-Discipline and Industrial Capital', in E. P. Thompson (ed.), *Customs in Common* (London: Penguin Books), 352–403.

Thrift, N. (1990) 'The Making of a Capitalist Time Consciousness', in J. Hassard (ed.), *The Sociology of Time* (New York: St Martin's Press), 105–29.

Weston, K. (2002) *Gender in Real Time. Power and Transience in a Visual Age* (New York and London: Routledge).

Wolin, S. (1961) *Politics and Vision. Continuity and Innovation in Western Political Thought* (London: George Allen and Unwin Ltd).

Index